Sailor

IN THE

White House

Sailor
IN THE
White House
THE SEAFARING LIFE OF FDR

Robert F. Cross

NAVAL INSTITUTE PRESS
ANNAPOLIS, MARYLAND

Naval Institute Press
291 Wood Road
Annapolis, MD 21402

Library of Congress Cataloging-in-Publication Data
Cross, Robert F., 1950–
Sailor in the White House: the seafaring life of FDR /
Robert F. Cross.
p. cm.
ISBN 1-55750-318-4 (alk. paper)
1. Roosevelt, Franklin D. (Franklin Delano), 1882–1945.
2. Presidents—United States—Biography.
3. Sailors—United States—Biography.
4. Seafaring life—United States—History—20th century.
5. Sailing—United States—History—20th century.
I. Title.
E807 .C76 2003
973.917'092—dc21
2003009159

Printed in the United States of America
on acid-free paper ∞

10 09 08 07 06 05 04 03   9 8 7 6 5 4 3 2
First printing

For Sheila,
with love and appreciation

That's the fun of sailing.
If you're headed for somewhere
and the wind changes,
you just change your mind
and go somewhere else.

FRANKLIN D. ROOSEVELT,

13 JULY 1932

CONTENTS

FOREWORD

Every land-bound sailor will tell you that being on a boat (preferably a sailboat, but almost any "boat" will do) at sea, even for a short sail, provides a perspective and stimulus to a passion largely unobtainable anywhere else on earth. Being at sea also reduces almost everything else to its essentials, to a more manageable scale, and helps the sailor cut through distracting chaff to the core of problems, challenges, and issues.

I am no historian—amateur, academic, or professional. I have spent much of my adult life choosing to avoid the lore and luster of my more famous ancestors. Although others in my generation are far more qualified to write a foreword to this wonderful and special book, I am honored and pleased that Robert Cross and our mutual friend Wint Aldrich asked me. Perhaps it was because I can bring a fresh perspective to reading about my grandfather, Franklin D. Roosevelt the sailor, and his relationship with the sea. More likely it was because my last name is Roosevelt.

Like my grandfather, I have an overwhelming, lifelong love of the sea and sailing. And much of my adult life has been devoted to protecting the oceans, coastal waters, and the marine environment. I learned at a relatively early age that water and the sea are precious to life in general. My own life and psyche are inextricably intertwined with them. Perhaps in that respect I reflect a heritage that came down genetically and socially through my father from my grandfather and ancestors farther back.

Life is replete with evidence that history repeats itself. This is also true within generations of the same family where both good and bad patterns repeat. I know my own father relished happy experiences when he, often along with his siblings, was on a boat with his father. He spoke frequently of these warm memories. Picturing my father—and my grandfather—on a boat, I smile as the famous "Happy Warrior" cliche comes to mind: They always were joyful, enthusiastic, and vigorous sailors who respected the adversary—the overwhelmingly powerful and sometimes fickle sea—and sublimely enjoyed and were refreshed by every second of the experience.

FDR was known for his insurmountable, indomitable confidence. Certainly some of this came from his status as an only child and the support and encouragement he received from his doting parents. Until his mother Sara's death in 1941, FDR knew that she always stood behind him; her wealth would provide for any necessities or unexpected circumstances. FDR's father personally taught him to ride horses, to understand farming and agriculture, and, most important, to sail and appreciate being on the water. So much of FDR's confidence came from his relationship with the sea and sailing.

I have sailed many of the very same New England waters as FDR, first with my own father, FDR Jr., and later with my wife and children. I gladly admit that my strong personal links to FDR affect my objectivity regarding this book. Grandfather, son, and now grandson have all loved the same renowned New England coastal waters. An appreciation for sailing and seamanship, as well as a knowledge and appreciation of naval history, has been passed down through the generations. Our lives have been impacted by our seagoing experiences. As a sailor and grandson, I applaud Cross's superb effort documenting FDR's sailing life. Cross shows how a sailor can also be a leader of men, a man of courage, a man of versatility, a juggler of options and alternatives during a challenging and turbulent time, and how this particular sailor became larger than life for so many.

My family's sailing traditions go back much farther than three generations. Both sides of FDR's heritage, the Roosevelts and the Delanos, were seafaring people, explorers and adventurers. The first known Roosevelt in the New World was Claes Martenszen van Rosenvelt. Known as "Little Claes" for his exceptional height, he sailed on Henry Hudson's Half Moon into the Hudson River estuary. He supposedly jumped ship somewhere just south of where Albany is today. Claes returned months later to

Nieuw Amsterdam with maps that he had made of the entire area east of the Hudson and west of what is now Long Island Sound. Another Roosevelt later was said to have been involved in the infamous "triangle" trade between the New World, Africa, and the Caribbean. Ancestors on the Delano side were involved in the China tea trade, whaling, and other seaborne commerce.

Given the myriad histories, biographies, and analyses written about FDR, his life, and his presidency, it is surprisingly refreshing that Cross, a talented historian and writer, elected to help us better understand FDR through his greatest passions: sailing and the sea. A sailor who loves being on the water, I can easily see and understand the connections Cross draws between the skills, temperament, and passions that make a person a great sailor, and those same elements that make a person a great politician and world leader.

Cross documents qualities desirable at sea: the necessity to learn how to "change tack" and be versatile in the face of changing weather, the need to understand the tradeoffs and consequences of compromise, the requirement for an explicit chain of command and leadership when aboard any vessel at sea, the desirability of confidence in choices and decisions made at sea, the influence good cheer can have on team work, and the ability to withstand and endure bad weather, storms, and discomfort—sometimes outright pain. Cross ably demonstrates that these are the same qualities consistently required of a leader on land, whether a politician, a wartime commander in chief, a pied piper leading a country out of a depression, or a skilled negotiator among the world's powers. The same confidence and inspirational qualities that FDR learned and practiced as a young sailor and "Skipper" at sea were his strength in overcoming polio. His almost superhuman effort to overcome polio, in turn, gave him complementary qualities. FDR learned to endure frustration and pain; he acquired courage, patience, empathy for others similarly afflicted by pain or misfortune, and the determination to succeed and make progress against insurmountable odds.

Sailing and the sea were always a huge source of enjoyment and fun for FDR. Not only were his water trips a way to escape and relax, they were also a fount of refreshment and rejuvenation for both body and spirit. It is hard to properly describe to a landlubber the clearing of the mind that occurs when sailing or at sea. Worldly cares and worries brought aboard melt away and vanish. The brain becomes comfortably occupied with the complexities of sailing, properly planning for time at sea, navigation, choosing safe harbors and anchorages, taking care of the ship, and managing the crew. Similarly, one becomes freed of concerns and focuses on the pleasures of being on the water. Nature's beautiful miracles are appreciated as the trim and able ship moves through the water, guided by a gentle yet firm hand on the tiller, sensing every nuance of the boat's motion, responsiveness, and direction.

For me, something I did not expect to get from Robert Cross's book and greatly appreciate is an understanding of the immense dimensions of the challenges facing the country and the world at that time. FDR not only had a handle on the seriousness of the situation, but he had the ability to mold responses appropriate to the problems and bring the rest of the country and the world along with him. His versatility and openness to change, alternate solutions, and compromises were, in so many ways, hallmarks of his presidency.

As I write today, the free world is again in turmoil. Serious disarray stems from terrorist troubles and potentially dangerous despots, each with varying degrees of reach and ripples. There lingers in me a yearning that all leaders could gain perspective on these challenges by comparing yesterday to today. Superimposing an appreciation of the world's history of war, particularly naval history, and the experience of being a sailor and being at sea might possibly result in better judgment. Possibly a better sense of proportionality could be achieved? Possibly more alternatives might present themselves? The comparison of yesterday to today may seem unfair to some, but it should not be avoided. Perspectives on who our government serves and who the government responds to are remarkable when comparing the two time periods. The difference between the flexibility and adroitness (yes, the ability to "tack") of yesterday and today's often dogmatic zealotry and artificially forced solutions is striking. As I'm sure Robert Cross would agree, give me a dynamic and resourceful sailor as my leader any day and the world will be a better place for us all. In another time and for another day, FDR was that sailor, on the water, at sea, and on land.

Christopher du P. Roosevelt

PREFACE

The genesis of this book began with a visit to a former fishing shanty on Nantucket Island's Old North Wharf. On a crisp fall morning in 1990 I first had an inkling of the extraordinary untold story of Franklin D. Roosevelt's lifelong love affair with the sea. I began to recognize how his time on the water helped define the character of our wheelchair-bound president, the man who became an inspirational force for millions of Americans during one of the darkest periods in our nation's history.

"Franklin Roosevelt was an honorary member," noted Charles Sayle Sr. as he proudly lifted one of the large, dusty old journals from the shelf in the one-room waterfront shack that today serves as a clubhouse for the venerable and unique Nantucket Wharf Rat Club. Sayle, who was commodore of the club during my 1990 visit, remembered the day Roosevelt sailed into Nantucket Harbor. Commodore Sayle recalled watching President Roosevelt, at the helm of a twin-masted schooner, sail around Brant Point in June 1933 on the second day of his four-hundred-mile New England cruise. Sayle slowly turned the pages of the old book. Handwritten entries, carefully made by a previous club commodore, Herb Coffin, brought to life that June day when the president of the United States sailed into Nantucket Harbor and stayed overnight.

Commo. Herb Coffin, his thirteen-year-old son, and summer residents Joseph and Miriam Price, who knew Roosevelt from their days in

New York, rowed out to greet the country's thirty-second president to induct him into the Wharf Rat Club, give him a club flag and a booklet describing the organization, and deliver a bowl of hot quahog chowder, an island favorite. "On arriving alongside, we found the president asleep," Coffin wrote in the club journal. "But we left the chowder and flag and Mr. Price wrote on the booklet 'please read this booklet.'"

As the sun began to set early that evening, the group rowed out again and, to their surprise, the Wharf Rat flag was flying on the president's schooner. They had a pleasant chat with Roosevelt before rowing ashore to tell their friends of their visit with the chief executive of the United States.

After reading several of Commodore Coffin's entries on the FDR visit, I decided to further explore the 1933 cruise. What I discovered along the way was quite astounding. Not only had President Roosevelt piloted his small sailboat from Marion, Massachusetts, to his summer home on Campobello Island, New Brunswick, but such trips were quite common for this president despite the fact that polio had left him unable to walk, or even stand, on his own in 1921. On trips, the president and his amateur crew often were alone on the water, sometimes completely out of touch with the security guards and U.S. Navy personnel who were trying to keep up with the sailor-president.

At the helm of a sailboat, FDR's disability was irrelevant. When sailing, he was the master of his environment, his movements, and his destination. He could free his mind from the burdens of the world's problems.

It quickly became clear to me that Roosevelt had a special relationship with the sea, a connection that has never been explored in any significant detail. I set out to fill in this missing chapter in his extraordinary life, a chapter integral to his entire makeup as well as to the accomplishments of his twelve-year presidency.

Franklin Roosevelt loved the sea. A natural blue-water sailor, he could read the water, wind, and tides. He could navigate a vessel through thick fogs and shoal-ridden waters using nothing more than a compass, chart, and his keen knowledge of the sea. Roosevelt spent more days at sea than any American president, before or since, and still holds the record for being the country's greatest seafaring president, logging hundreds of thousands of miles afloat.

Beginning at the age of three, Franklin Roosevelt started sailing the world's oceans, first with his parents as a passenger aboard luxury transatlantic liners, making nine Atlantic Ocean crossings by the age of fourteen. He was aboard at least 110 named vessels, ranging from tiny sailboats to 45,000-ton warships, as well as countless other motor launches and sailing vessels whose specific identities have escaped mention in historical records. As president, he frequently was afloat for weeks at a time. He officially logged more than 110,000 miles on the water plus scores of cruises on various presidential yachts and fishing trips in small boats launched from navy warships in the Atlantic and Pacific Oceans and the Caribbean Sea.

As my research continued, I had the great good fortune to meet and interview a number of FDR's younger contemporaries. Some had traveled with the president on his cruises and, for the first time, told their stories of the days afloat with Roosevelt. Secret Service agents and others accompanying Roosevelt as he sailed the oceans of the world also shared their recollections in never-before-told stories. In addition, a number of photographs—some published here for the first time—help to illustrate the days at sea that Roosevelt so enjoyed. A never before published 1935 photograph—depicting FDR in a wheelchair aboard the luxury yacht *Nourmahal*—is only the third photograph known to exist in which the president is shown seated in his wheelchair.

FDR spent so much time sailing the world's oceans that some of the most important decisions and significant milestones in his life occurred while afloat, including his decision to use his life savings to purchase a run-down Georgia resort for use as a polio treatment facility. His strenuous 1932 New England trip in a tiny, leaking yawl helped convince the public that Governor Roosevelt was capable of assuming the presidency; he was not a helpless cripple, as some had argued. During a 1939 cruise near Newfoundland, FDR received word that Germany and Russian had signed a nonaggression economic assistance pact, signaling Adolf Hitler's intention to go to war. In 1940, after receiving a letter from Winston Churchill while at sea in the Caribbean, Roosevelt conceived the Lend-Lease program, a creative way to provide an urgently needed boost to Great Britain's naval forces. Then, in 1941, Roosevelt and Churchill had a secret meeting at sea in which they drafted the Atlantic Charter, outlining their principles for war and peace. Roosevelt also received plenty of sad news while at sea, including news of the deaths of President William McKinley in 1901, former president Theodore Roosevelt in 1919, former personal secretary Marguerite LeHand in 1944, Theodore's youngest son

Quentin Roosevelt in 1918, presidential secretary Marvin McIntyre in 1943, and Gen. "Pa" Watson, a military aide who suffered a cerebral hemorrhage aboard USS *Quincy* while returning with FDR from the 1944 Yalta Conference.

Focusing on Roosevelt's seafaring activities brings to light fascinating and important aspects of the life and character of our country's thirty-second president. I invite FDR enthusiasts, sailors, and all readers to join me in exploring Franklin Roosevelt's seagoing adventures. The appendix at the end of this book chronologically lists many of the named vessels FDR was aboard. The glossary lists common nautical terms.

ACKNOWLEDGMENTS

I must first thank my loving parents, Francis and Rita Cross, who gave me every opportunity to explore and to learn. They helped lay the foundation for all that I have accomplished. Appreciation also goes to my two sisters, Janet Dobbs and Linda DiPanni, for their unending devotion and encouragement.

My dear wife, Sheila, has been of extraordinary assistance to me, offering encouragement, praise, incisive criticism, and a sharp red pencil when warranted. She is my most loving and constructive reviewer, carefully identifying—with the patient precision of a surgeon—those aspects of the book that needed clarification, and helping me flesh out the details and thus allowing me to better tell the tale of our country's greatest seafaring president.

My good friend, mentor, and general expert on a host of FDR-related matters is J. Winthrop Aldrich, who also was the first person to suggest I write this book. Wint's hours of meticulous research and his wealth of contacts, advice, guidance, and friendship are more than any author ever could expect. He never seemed to tire of my project—even, at times, when my own enthusiasm waned. Wint's friendship, encouragement, and perseverance make this book as much his as it is mine.

Many people generously gave me their time and tolerated my persistent questioning while I probed their memories of events and people long since passed. Remarkably, their memories of the people and incidents were as fresh as though they took place last month, rather than six decades ago. To all with whom I spoke or corresponded over the course of this project, I owe a special debt of gratitude. I hope—for those who still are with us—that they are pleased with the final product. I give my special thanks to Amyas Ames, A. J. Drexel Paul, Curtis Roosevelt, Eleanor Roosevelt Seagraves, Paul Drummond Rust III, Sarah Powell Huntington, Edmund Tripp, Seward E. Beacom, Lewis Haskell, Robert Hopkins, Dr. Howard Bruenn, Linnea Calder, James Griffith, Helen Baxter, Ann Easter, Charles Sayle Sr., Philip C. Murray, and Abe Barron for taking time to patiently answer all of my questions. Anthony W. Lobb, my cousin as well as a Secret Service agent in 1941–1942, provided important insight into the Roosevelt White House. His remarkably clear recollections of guarding the president were greatly appreciated.

My good friend, Diane Lobb Boyce, a National Park ranger at Springwood, the National Historic site in Hyde Park, has been a tremendous help in searching out missing facts and retrieving information for me from the archives of the Franklin D. Roosevelt Library. Diane, sometimes assisted by her ever-patient husband Roy, spent countless hours sifting through boxes and boxes of files for some obscure fact I needed to fill in a blank space in the manuscript. She never complained or seemed to tire when I called with "just one more question," and always seemed to know right where to look for the answer.

I would be remiss without applauding the excellent staff of the Franklin D. Roosevelt Library. Led by Director Cynthia M. Koch, the archivists are true professionals who are second to none in dedication and talent. I especially want to thank Mark Renovitch, Raymond Teichman, Virginia Lewick, Karen Anson, and Robert Clark for their assistance. President Roosevelt would be very proud of the professional and able staff assembled by Dr. Koch.

Writing a book while also trying to carry out the responsibilities of an unrelated full-time job can be a challenging undertaking. The primary requirement for success is having an understanding boss. And, I have been fortunate that my boss—and friend—is Gerald D. Jennings, mayor of the city of Albany, New York. Mayor Jennings supported me as I feverishly tried to meet my publisher's deadline, even at one point offering, "Let me know if I give you too much work." A boss like that doesn't come along very often! Also, I must mention Mayor Jennings's farsighted vision for New York's capital city. Thanks to him the only World War II destroyer escort still afloat in the United States found a permanent home. Moored in the Hudson River at Albany, USS *Slater* has been faithfully restored by scores of World War II–era volunteers, along with assistance from the Jennings administration. This "trim but deadly" warship, which proudly served our nation in the past, plays a pivotal role in the renaissance under way along Albany's historic Hudson River waterfront today. Upon seeing this national treasure, one cannot help but feel a great sense of pride in the generation of Americans who fought for our freedom so many years ago. They are, without a doubt, "the greatest generation."

Research and writing would not amount to much, however, unless a publisher can be found. Thanks to my friend, naval historian Dr. Martin Davis, I was able to have my work considered—and accepted—by one of the oldest and most-respected publishing houses in the country. I also am indebted to Fred L. Schultz, editor-in-chief of *Naval History,* and Fred H. Rainbow, managing editor of *Proceedings,* for taking a keen interest. Tom Cutler, senior acquisitions editor for Naval Institute Press, has been supportive and helpful. As I worked day and night to finish the manuscript, Tom offered good cheer and sage advice to a sometimes-weary writer— advice only a seasoned author like Tom could provide. "Even a labor of love is still labor," Tom said. After taking some time to relax and recharge, I came back to the project with renewed determination and energy.

I also owe a great debt to the long list of Franklin Roosevelt biographers. So much of what I have learned about this man was gleaned from the pages of the scores and scores of excellent books written over the last six decades, many of which are mentioned in the bibliography.

Gratitude also goes to my uncle, Robert Dorflinger Beilman, who first introduced me to Nantucket Island and to the wonderful old Wharf Rat Club. My good friend, William Fitzgerald, offered daily support, good cheer, and prayers when they were needed throughout the writing process. I also thank Christopher Roosevelt for his insightful foreword; Brooke Astor; Katharine Aldrich; Gerald Morgan Jr.; Geraldine Gardiner Salisbury; Frank J. Lasch and Tim Rizzuto of USS *Slater;* Joe Elario, Albany's premier photographer; Joseph A. Jackson of the New York Yacht Club; Eleanor P. Fischer of the U.S. Coast Guard; Henry W. Stevens and Paul B. Cole III of the Roosevelt Campobello International Park Commission; and P. Hamilton Brown of the Association of Former Agents of the U.S. Secret Service, who helped me track down the agents who protected FDR. Copy editor Barbara Johnson contributed significantly to the clarification and polish of the manuscript, for which I thank her.

I know that I have left out people who assisted me in so many differ-ent ways. I apologize for my inability to remember all the wonderful and generous people who helped and inspired me throughout this fascinating journey of discovery. I can only say "thank you" with the deepest sincerity to all who helped me tell FDR's remarkable "untold story."

Sailor

IN THE

White House

CHAPTER 1

He Always Had His Eyes on the Sails

It was a glorious day, clear and sunny with a slight southwest breeze. Linnea Calder was washing dishes at the kitchen sink when she heard a tapping on the cottage windowpane. "There comes his yacht around the head," the Royal Canadian mounted policeman said, his scarlet uniform glistening in the bright afternoon sun. Mr. Roosevelt was coming home.

Things were different since he last visited his boyhood summer home. When Franklin Roosevelt left his Campobello, New Brunswick, cottage twelve years ago, he was carried out on a canvas stretcher, his legs limp and useless from polio. Clutching Duffy, a Scottish terrier purchased by Franklin and Eleanor on their 1905 honeymoon, Roosevelt was lifted through the window of a waiting train and spirited to a polio treatment hospital in New York City. His once-promising political career appeared over; he was facing the prospect of life as an invalid.

But Roosevelt's fortunes had changed. On 29 June 1933, he was returning to the place he loved so much, the place where he first learned to sail, and the place where his parents brought him when he was just a teething baby. He was returning not as an invalid or a failed politician but as the most powerful man in the world. Franklin D. Roosevelt, the new U.S. president, was coming home to Campobello.

As he sailed into Friar's Bay, the blue presidential flag was hoisted and flapped in the breeze for the first time since Marion, Massachusetts, when he began his four-hundred-mile vacation cruise along the New England coast. "Skipper" Roosevelt, who skillfully navigated his tiny schooner over dangerously rough seas and through pea-soup fog and heavy squalls, and averting at least one life-threatening disaster, was again "Mr. President."

Linnea Calder, the daughter of Campobello's caretaker, was busy seeing to preparations for the president's visit to his seaside cottage. Although the twenty-two-year-old woman, whose mother was a lifelong Roosevelt family servant, was excited at the prospect of seeing Mr. Roosevelt, she recalls that her main concern was to make sure everything was ready for his visit and for the great picnic that was planned.[1]

With a stiff following wind, Franklin Roosevelt sailed around Friar's Head, a large rock reportedly used for target practice by the British in the War of 1812, and received a gala presidential welcome. The harbor was filled with all types of craft, pennants and buntings blowing in the wind. Two destroyers, USS *Ellis* and USS *Bernadou;* coast guard cutters; and other boats accompanied FDR's forty-five-foot schooner *Amberjack II* on its eleven day cruise. In addition, Linnea Calder recalls Connors Brothers' fleet of sardine carriers and boats from American factories, along with dozens of private fishing vessels, including a tug boat carrying Scottish pipers, all brightly decorated and parading in formation to honor their distinguished visitor.

The U.S. Navy's new heavy cruiser USS *Indianapolis,* on one of its first voyages, gave the president a traditional twenty-one gun salute as *Amberjack II* crossed its bow. The *Indianapolis's* band played "The Star Spangled Banner" as the ship's entire crew manned the rail. Thousands of excited residents on shore strained to get a glimpse of the new U.S. president. A day of pageantry, excitement, and good will, Campobello welcomed the first American president to visit its shores.

A few hours earlier, *Amberjack II* had stopped briefly at West Quoddy Bay so the president and his crew could have lunch and change from the rumpled clothes of yachtsmen into more appropriate attire for a presidential ceremony. They then set sail for Lubec Narrows, heading for Friar's Bay. "Promptly at four o'clock, as he had promised, our skipper took the *Amberjack* alongside the dock at Welchpool on Campobello Island and disembarked," wrote James Roosevelt, the president's oldest son and first mate for the entire cruise.[2]

When President Roosevelt was assisted from *Amberjack II* onto the Campobello dock, it marked the first time that he had left the schooner since his trip began in Marion on 18 June. Along the way, hundreds of well-wishers coaxed and pleaded with him to come ashore, but the president had vowed not to leave his boat. Beginning his vacation cruise at the conclusion of the president's "First Hundred Days" in office, Roosevelt pledged that he would not step foot on dry land the entire two weeks—and he kept that promise.

During the second day's overnight stop on Nantucket Island, thirty miles off the Massachusetts coast, Roosevelt politely—yet firmly—declined invitations from Selectman William Holland, chairman of the town's Democratic Committee, to come ashore. "I am having a bang-up good time enjoying this cruise immensely, and I do not intend to go ashore anywhere along the coast," Roosevelt was quoted as saying in a newspaper account. "This is my vacation and I am going to stay aboard this boat the whole two weeks."[3]

Ten days later, a tanned and invigorated Franklin Roosevelt came ashore at Campobello, his final destination, and was driven to the local yacht club where thousands of people waited to see and hear him. Welcomed by a host of dignitaries, Roosevelt, from the back seat of his car, spoke: "I think that I can only address you as my old friends of Campobello—old and new. I was figuring this morning on the passage of time and I remembered that I was brought here because I was teething forty nine years ago. I have been coming for many months almost every year until about twelve years ago, when there was a gap."

Although the president did not explain the "gap," friends and neighbors on Campobello knew that the hiatus from 1921 until this day was the period that Roosevelt was waging a fierce comeback battle since being diagnosed with polio while vacationing here. According to one anecdote that found its way into local lore, a handful of old island friends came to say goodbye back in 1921. Roosevelt, lying in bed and smiling grimly, had replied: "I won't see you again until I am president of the United States."

Back among his friends, Roosevelt continued his coming home speech:

It seems to me that memory is a very wonderful thing, because this morning when we were beginning to come out of the fog off Quoddy Head, the boys on the lookout in the bow called out "land ahead." Nevertheless, memory kept me going full speed ahead because I knew the place was Lubec Narrows. . . . I was thinking also, as I came through the Narrows and saw the line of fishing boats and the people on the wharves, both here at Welch Pool and also in Eastport, that this reception here is probably the finest example of friendship between Nations—permanent friendship between Nations—that we can possibly have. . . . I hope and am very confident that if peace continues in this world and that if the other Nations of the world follow the very good example of the United States and Canada, I shall be able to come back here for a holiday during the next three years.[4]

Unfortunately, presidential duties and the war would only allow Roosevelt to return to his "beloved island" two more times in his life.

Campobello is a picturesque and historic place, filled with friendly residents who value independence and courage, qualities displayed proudly at Franklin Roosevelt's triumphant return. It was an emotional day not only for FDR but for his friends, neighbors, and sailing pals who hadn't seen him since he left on a stretcher twelve years ago. The outpouring of friendship and excitement was partly due to the high public office Roosevelt now held, but a large part of this emotion was due to the warm feeling the community had for their old friend.

A. J. Drexel Paul, whose father canoed with FDR when the two were attending Groton, was an eighteen-year-old friend of FDR's son, Franklin Jr. Accompanying Roosevelt on the final leg of the vacation cruise, Paul remembered the Campobello welcome they received and how pleased the president was by the warmth with which he was greeted by his Canadian neighbors. Paul readily understands these warm feelings for Roosevelt; he felt the same warmth after spending six days with him at sea. Paul later served aboard minesweepers and destroyer escorts during the war. "He was a delightful person to be with," Paul recalled. "He was an expert sailor and felt completely at home, thoroughly enjoying everything." Paul said Roosevelt was in total command of *Amberjack II* except when forces beyond his control intervened.

Paul recalled vividly the three days immediately prior to their arrival at Campobello, during which even the president of the United States was powerless. Skipper Roosevelt and his crew were held at bay in Lakeman Bay, Roque Island, which was shrouded in a blanket of fog described in newspaper accounts as being "as thick as sour cream." The fog cut off *Amberjack II* from its navy escort and Secret Service guards for several hours. Wireless radios were available, but they were too bulky for small vessels such as *Amberjack II*. The president and his amateur crew were alone. Anchored, the tiny schooner and its flotilla of destroyers, cutters, and press boats could only wait and hope that the fog would lift soon. Unfortunately, the hope was in vain.

Paul said the president stayed aboard *Amberjack II* and did a lot of paperwork during those three days, while the rest of the crew were entertained by a "very attractive young naval officer," Lt. John Stuart Blue, who showed them movies. Blue, assigned to command the presidential yacht *Sequoia* in March 1933, was a direct descendant of Capt. James Lawrence who had immortalized the phrase "Don't Give Up the Ship" during the War of 1812. Lieutenant Blue later died when his cruiser, USS *Juneau,* was torpedoed in the Battle of Guadalcanal in 1942.[5]

Although newspaper accounts reported that the president was in no danger, Col. Edmund D. Starling, chief of the Secret Service White House detail, later would write about his concern for Roosevelt's safety. Starling became alarmed when he received wireless reports from the destroyers accompanying the chief executive that they had lost touch with *Amberjack II*. Fearing the nation's new president could become the target of kidnappers or gangsters who were plying their bootlegging trade along the coast, the agent took action. Starling, who was following Roosevelt's course in a car along the coast, asked local villagers if they knew of anyone who would be willing to pilot a boat in an attempt to penetrate the heavy fog in search of the president.

Henry Wallace, a local fisherman, agreed to take on the mission in his flimsy, homemade boat, powered by a Ford engine that sounded "tubercular" according to the Secret Service agent. "Henry stood erect, one hand on the hand-whittled tiller, the other on a stick which controlled the speed of the engine," Starling wrote. "Between his feet he held an old brass compass. From time to time he glanced down at it. He seemed to know exactly what he was doing, and we rolled through the fog as nonchalantly as if we had broad daylight to guide us. After what seemed like a long run, Henry shut off the motor and said, 'Here's one of your Navy boats.'"

The navy men told Starling that *Amberjack II* was "just over those rocks, in a cove." When Wallace navigated his boat around a jagged rock, the tiny white schooner came into view. Starling said Roosevelt was loafing on deck, smoking a cigarette. "Hello, Ed," said the president, clad in an old gray sweater and flannel trousers. "Where did you come from? I thought we'd lost you."

Roosevelt, sporting three days' growth of beard, threw his head back, flashed his dazzling smile, and told Starling that he was "having a wonderful time. I don't care how long this fog lasts." By then, however, other members of the crew were not as content—they were running out of cigarettes and fresh meat. Starling and Wallace made several additional trips to *Amberjack II* over the next couple of days, bringing food, mail, and cigarettes.

Starling later wrote that, although Roosevelt had no objection to Secret Service surveillance, "his absolute lack of fear made it difficult at times for him to understand the safeguards with which we surrounded him." While Roosevelt may have understood the need for security, he never missed an opportunity to try to evade or play tricks on his protectors. FDR's sense of humor in this regard was legendary. Agent Starling said Roosevelt led the rest of the fleet on a "merry chase" over the course of the eleven day New England cruise. Starling wrote that the president "knew the coast thoroughly, and he put his small, fast craft into places where bigger boats could not follow. Thus, he maintained the privacy he desired; the photographers seldom got within shooting distance."[6]

Throughout his presidency, Roosevelt always made time for the sea. He was unquestionably the greatest seafaring U.S. president, a record that continues to this day. Even as the Seventy-third Congress was gaveled to a close on 16 June 1933, Roosevelt's bags already were packed for the trip to Marion, where *Amberjack II* was waiting in a quiet cove, guarded by Secret Service agents in patrol boats. Roosevelt's First Hundred Days, a period that would serve as a standard of productivity for all future presidents, resulted in historic achievements and the enactment of a remarkable number of sweeping new laws to help guide the nation from the depths of the Great Depression.

Roosevelt's bold and vigorous leadership convinced a desperate Congress to enact most of his New Deal programs during the First Hundred Days period, including the Emergency Banking Act, giving Roosevelt broad new powers over the nation's banks; the Civilian Conservation Corps, providing immediate jobs for a quarter million Americans; the Federal Emergency Relief Act, authorizing cash grants to states with relief programs; the Agriculture Adjustment Act, providing instant relief to U.S. farmers; and the Federal Securities Act, giving Washington broad new controls over the sale of stocks and bonds.

In addition, Congress quickly approved Roosevelt's National Employment Systems Act, to provide Federal assistance and money to states with programs to help the out-of-work; the Home Owners Refinancing Act, to provide American homeowners with cash to pay mortgages, taxes, and repairs; the National Industrial Recovery Act, which created the Public Works Administration to supervise construction of roads, bridges, and public buildings throughout the country; and the National Recovery Administration, to help stimulate competition and establish fair trade.

With many of his immediate goals behind him, it was time for the triumphant but tired president to take a break. Plans for this vacation cruise had been in the works for months, even before Roosevelt took the oath of office on 4 March 1933. In a 30 December 1932 letter to George Briggs, an officer in the U.S. Naval Reserve and an old sailing buddy of Roosevelt who would accompany him on the trip, Roosevelt acknowledged that his son Jimmy was searching for a boat to charter for a summer cruise. "I am reasonably certain," wrote the president-elect, "we can get a craft as there will be few additional millionaires by that time."[7]

Arrangements were finalized in April, a little more than a month after Inauguration Day, to charter *Amberjack II*. The schooner's owner, Paul Drummond Rust Jr. of Marblehead, Massachusetts, was a friend of Jimmy Roosevelt, and was more than willing to make his craft available to the president. Paul D. Rust III described his father as a "millionaire playboy" who inherited a fortune from his lumber baron grandfather in 1929 and enjoyed spending every last penny.[8]

Rust Jr. had commissioned the construction of *Amberjack II* in 1931 after his first black-hulled schooner, *Amberjack I,* was wrecked near Gloucester. His new white-hulled, twin-masted forty-five-foot vessel was built by George Lawley and Son of Neponset, Massachusetts, and had a forty horsepower Scripps gasoline engine as an auxiliary. Despite its modest size, *Amberjack II* was seaworthy and easy to handle. It finished third in Fastnet, the 1931 transatlantic race to England, but was later moved to fifth because of a technicality. Rust had piloted *Amberjack II,* which was the smallest craft to participate in the grueling three thousand mile race.[9]

During the New England cruise, Roosevelt's crew consisted of some of the same individuals who accompanied him when he interrupted his campaign for president in 1932 to sail a tiny, leaking yawl from Long Island to New Hampshire. His sons Jimmy, John, and Franklin Jr. along with George Briggs, John Cutter, Amyas Ames, Drexel Paul, and Rust would also come along.

Despite the furious executive and legislative activity going on in Washington during his first few weeks in office, the president paid close attention to the details for his vacation cruise. In a 24 April 1933, letter to Roosevelt, George Briggs described *Amberjack II* and included his crude sketch that showed accommodations.

In a tongue-in-cheek reply dated 11 May 1933, President Roosevelt wrote:

> It was grand to hear from you and to have that excellent architect's drawing of a vessel that must look like the one Robinson Crusoe built. The end where the wheel ought to be is, I think, a parrot and the extension bunk seems to be supported by a large marrow bone, but perhaps it is really a center board well. I see two double berths, a berth and a quarter berth! Who uses the latter? I hope she is not too much down by the bows but most of the space forward of the foremast seems to be taken by a large area marked "ice." What kind of a party do you think this is going to be anyway? I see no place marked "motor" so I take it that this is towed astern![10]

As Congress began to wind down, plans for the trip were finalized. The White House prepared an official schedule indicating that the president would begin his cruise in Marion, and conclude eleven days later at Campobello. George Briggs sailed the schooner to Marion, where it was anchored at Dr. William McDonald's dock, awaiting the president's arrival. McDonald, a prominent neurologist specializing in polio treatment, attended Roosevelt for two summers after the onset of polio in 1921. Roosevelt swam often in Buzzards Bay and performed hours of exercises using a "walking board" device in a futile attempt to regain the use of his legs. One of Dr. McDonald's treatments consisted of lowering patients from a floating position into warm salt water for group exercises, a treatment that Roosevelt later would use at his own polio rehabilitation facility in Warm Springs, Georgia.

After taking a dip in the newly constructed White House pool and leaving instructions for his staff, the country's thirty-second president boarded his private railroad car at Washington's Union Station late in the evening of 16 June to head to Boston. At Boston, he visited his sons Franklin Jr. and John at Groton School, located northwest of the city. Roosevelt had missed Frankie's graduation a day earlier because he was unable to leave Washington until Congress departed. On 17 June, he motored from Groton to Marion, where *Amberjack II* rocked at anchor, awaiting its skipper. Dr. McDonald had rigged Roosevelt's old "walking board" as a ramp so the president could walk directly from the wharf to the schooner.[11] Provisions such as corned beef hash, peas, and stewed corn already were stowed aboard for the eleven day cruise.

H. Edmund Tripp, a Marion resident whose grandfather was a whaler there in the 1860s, remembers the day the president came to town. Tripp, a school teacher when the president visited, was struck especially by the massive amount of security just prior to and during the visit. "There was unusual activity on the part of the Secret Service as just previous to this time Mayor Cermak had been killed in Florida while with Roosevelt," Tripp said. "Guards were everywhere." He continued:

> I can remember what an impressive affair when the procession arrived in Marion Center and proceeded to the doctor's home. It was late in the afternoon and a threatening storm started to make it dark. The group was lead by about twenty Massachusetts State police and motorcycles roaring. They were followed by three cars full of presidential guards. Then came the president and his family with a dozen guards running along side the car as it entered the town center. I certainly was impressed with the condition of these men as they ran along for a couple of miles looking the crowd over for any assassins.[12]

This high level of security would stand in stark contrast to the alarming lack of security—by today's standards—surrounding Roosevelt during the next eleven days while the president was at sea. The Secret Service, however, had devised an emergency plan to rescue the president in the event of illness or a threat to his safety. The destroyers accompanying the flotilla had been rigged with special slings to hoist FDR off *Amberjack II* in the event of an emergency.[13]

Helen Baxter, another Marion resident, also remembers the day Roosevelt arrived in town. She and her husband, Dr. Raymond Baxter, a colleague of Dr. McDonald, were invited to dine with the president aboard

Amberjack II. She remembers going aboard the schooner with Dr. and Mrs. McDonald for a dinner of Beef Wellington, which was cooked on the coal stove on board. There was no talk of politics that night, no talk of Roosevelt's extraordinary accomplishments during his First Hundred Days. Instead, they had cocktails, followed by dinner, and an enjoyable evening of small talk. Relaxing small talk was standard fare at many of FDR's informal—as well as formal—gatherings. After eating, the guests left Roosevelt and retired to the Baxter home, where they sang and Helen Baxter, a concert pianist, played the piano until midnight. Meanwhile, aboard *Amberjack II,* the president retired for the evening with plans for an early start on his vacation cruise the next morning.[14]

A clear, crisp northwest wind greeted the president the next morning. After a hearty breakfast of scrambled eggs, bacon, and coffee, Roosevelt was at the helm as *Amberjack II.* With the presidential flag flapping above, the schooner made its way from Marion to its first port of call—Hadley's Harbor, Naushon Island. Roosevelt dined aboard ship on hash, tomato soup, peas, and bread with W. Cameron Forbes, the former governor general of the Philippines and former ambassador to Japan, who had brought the basket lunch. The rest of Roosevelt's crew left the schooner for a horseback ride around the island. Later that afternoon, Roosevelt set sail for Nantucket Island but was forced into nearby Martha's Vineyard by a severe squall. Capt. Irwin Hall, skipper of one of the press boats trailing the president, praised Roosevelt for altering his plans, because he said Nantucket was a bad place to hit after dark, especially with a following wind. Roosevelt and his crew spent the night in Edgartown Harbor after a dinner on sea bass, caught and grilled by John Cutter, *Amberjack's* unofficial cook.[15]

To stay on schedule, the president decided to skip the Nantucket stop, heading directly for Provincetown after he left Martha's Vineyard on 19 June. Again the weather intervened and, after eight foot seas around Handkerchief Shoal tossed his schooner around for five hours, Roosevelt, using signal flags, wigwagged to his escorts a change in plans. FDR changed course and made for Nantucket because he felt the trip around Cape Cod would be "decidedly unpleasant, especially for landlubbers aboard the press boat, who were already showing unmistakable signs of seasickness."[16] With President Roosevelt at the helm, *Amberjack II* led a convoy of destroyers, coast guard cutters, scout boats, and press boats

through heavy seas and stiff northwest winds to the relative safety of Nantucket Harbor.

Four press association reporters and four staff correspondents trailed
the president in two vessels. *New York Times* White House Correspondent Charles Hurd said that when the eight newsmen originally boarded
the boat Roosevelt's advance people had hired for them, they discovered
that it was designed to sleep only eight, including a single crew member,
and no luggage. Three crew members already were on board and had
taken the best three cabins. The reporters arrived, toting their luggage,
typewriters, and other baggage. This would never do, so the newsmen set
out to find another boat to rent. After looking through the local telephone
directory for boats to rent, the skipper of *Mary Alice* met with the
reporters and agreed to charter his craft, which Hurd described as quite
luxurious. In these bleak economic times, it wasn't difficult to find a skipper willing to rent his vessel. The thirty-eight foot vessel was powered by
an engine capable of delivering an easy ten miles per hour. It had a roomy
cockpit, a generous main cabin, and other features that made it a very
comfortable craft in which to be at sea over the next two weeks.

Correspondent Hurd later wrote that he thought Roosevelt envied the
press boat. "[W]e had the impression that the president never quite felt
the same about his own boat after seeing *Mary Alice*." Hurd said it had a
more powerful motor as well as other nice features, such as canvas cur-
tains to protect the cockpit during stormy weather. Hurd also noted that
the yacht's owner sent a case of "reliable Bourbon whisky" as provisions
were being loaded on board.[17]

On the president's Nantucket stop, the whole town greeted his arrival.
Hundreds of cheering residents packed the wharves and piers; bells,
horns, and whistles sounded in honor of his visit. A contingent of local
officials filled Capt. Ed Burchell's forty-foot fishing sloop *Beatrice B* when
it went out to greet the president. Charles Sayle Sr., a well-known Nantucket ivory carver and expert ship model builder, recalls passing Roosevelt's schooner as he was rowing his fourteen-foot skiff into the harbor
for a little quahogging. Years later Sayle would carve the ivory whale for
the first, now-famous Nantucket basket handbag designed by Jose Formosa Reyes. According to Sayle, a few days after *Beatrice B* was tied up
next to *Amberjack II* with its contingent of "official Nantucket" on board,
the boat exploded and sank off Great Point, killing a crew member. A

gasoline leak was blamed for the tragedy; a tragedy that would have taken on worldwide proportions had the explosion occurred while the vessel was tied up alongside *Amberjack II*.[18]

Roosevelt's visit to Nantucket fostered plenty of island lore. While in Nantucket Harbor, Roosevelt was made an honorary member of the Nantucket Wharf Rat Club, an exclusive and—even to this day—closely-knit organization first established around 1915, whose members are mostly fishermen, sailors, native residents, and a sprinkling of summer visitors. Later its membership was expanded to include a variety of others, including such notable off-islanders as explorer Adm. Richard E. Byrd and U.S. Supreme Court Justice William J. Brennan Jr. Roosevelt was pleased to be inducted, and was presented with a club flag and a bowl of quahog chowder by Herbert H. Coffin, the club's commodore.

Amyas Ames recalls everyone laughing at the Wharf Rat Club flag as the president held it up for all to see. The triangular blue flag, depicting a dapper-looking white rat holding a cane and smoking a churchwarden pipe, was designed for the club by member Tony Sarg, an illustrator for the *Saturday Evening Post*. Sarg, who had a studio on the island, also was the designer of the first helium balloons for the Macy's Thanksgiving Day Parade in New York City.

Although the president stayed aboard *Amberjack II*, the rest of his crew toured the quaint little island, once the whaling capital of the world, with its cobblestone streets and gray-shingled houses. During the afternoon, enterprising Nantucketers rowed townfolk out, for a quarter a head, so they could get a closer look at the new president. The next morning the sun was shining brightly over the hills of Shimmo as Roosevelt gave the order to weigh anchor. At 5:45 A.M., with the president at the helm and his new Wharf Rat Club flag hoisted on the foremast, *Amberjack II* set sail for its next destination—Provincetown.

As *Amberjack* made its way out of the harbor, however, Roosevelt's peace was disrupted by the destroyer USS *Bernadou* moving toward him at a high rate of speed. "The president sighed and ordered Frankie and Johnnie to get ready to anchor. He roared 'Ha-a-ard alee!' in his best boatswain's voice and brought *Amberjack* smartly up into the wind. The hook splashed overboard and the jib came down on the run," according to an account of the incident. Assistant Secretary of State Raymond F. Moley was ferried from the destroyer to confer with the president, who had brought his schooner to rest near Pollock's Rip.[19]

After receiving orders from the chief executive, Moley departed Nantucket Harbor bound for London where he would represent the United States at the World Economic Conference. Ferried to a waiting navy seaplane, Moley was lifted skyward near Pilgrim's Tower at the tip of Cape Cod, the site of the Pilgrims' first landing. After bidding farewell to Moley, Roosevelt decided that the weather was so good he would skip Provincetown and head straight for Gloucester, a run of more than fifteen hours. Roosevelt skillfully navigated some of the most treacherous waters on the New England coast, arriving in Gloucester around midnight. Since the seaport's founding in 1623, some ten thousand fishermen have died in that area's foggy, shoal-ridden waters. According to one press report, the accompanying destroyers and power boats plowed cautiously along behind the rugged sailor-president, trusting the navigational judgment and sailing skill of their commander in chief.[20]

The next morning, 21 June, was filled with ceremonies, gift presentations, and visitors greeting the president and his party as they rocked at anchor in Gloucester Harbor. Capt. Ben Pine visited and presented Roosevelt with an oil painting of his fishing schooner, *Gertrude L. Thebaud*. Roosevelt admired the vessel but doubted whether he was skillful enough to take it out to the Banks. Pine replied, "I'd trust you with her anywhere," which was high praise indeed from such an experienced old sailor.[21] Around noon, Roosevelt gave the order to weigh anchor and set sail for Ipswich Bay.

Amyas Ames, next door neighbor and Harvard classmate of Jimmy Roosevelt, was another member of the president's *Amberjack II* crew. He recalled the trick Roosevelt played on his navy and coast guard convoy that day. As they departed Gloucester, the president appeared to be steering his schooner to round Cape Ann when, suddenly, he decided to take a shortcut through the narrow and crooked Annisquam Canal instead of sailing around the cape.

"Ames, will you take us through?" the president asked.

"Through what?" the young crew member replied.

"Through the canal," Roosevelt said.

Ames hesitated, "Well, I've done it," his voice trailing off nervously. It was the last thing in the world he wanted to do at that moment.

"She's yours," President Roosevelt said, handing the wheel to Ames, who had navigated the canal only a few times previously while summering in the area.

Ames describes the trip as the most tense one he ever had taken through the canal, owing in no small part to the fact that he had the president of the United States on board. But he successfully navigated the sandbars and other obstacles and completed the six mile journey safely. "I know what he [the president] was doing. He wanted to play a joke on the destroyer captain and the Coast Guard boat, who were all ready to go with us around Cape Ann," Ames said. Of course, those large vessels could not navigate the narrow canal, and were forced to take the longer journey around the cape to Ipswich Bay, leaving *Amberjack II,* with the president of the United States aboard, to make its way through the canal. Ames was with the president at the start of the cruise at Marion and stayed aboard until Southwest Harbor, on the seventh day, when he left to return to work in Boston.

"He always had his eyes on the sails," Ames recalled, describing Roosevelt as a "natural sailor" who ran a tight ship. Roosevelt felt completely at ease at sea. His expertise as a sailor was second to none, and his sailing ability won high praise from professional sailor and crusty old salt alike.[22]

In a 28 June 1933 confidential memorandum to the president, Lt. H. C. Pound, USN, sailing aboard USS *Ellis,* commented on Roosevelt's ability on the water: "I have watched with deep interest the navigation of your ship. You have done splendidly. If you were a private citizen, I would commission you in the Naval Reserve for your exploits."[23]

Roosevelt, indeed, had a keen sense of the sea, with a great skill at reading charts and the water, and an uncanny ability to know where sandbars and shoals lurked. He used dead reckoning to steer and plot courses while on his vessels. A navigational method that uses courses steered and distances run to give the theoretical position of a ship after making necessary allowances for tides and currents, dead reckoning was done without the use of land, sights, astronomical observations, or the high-tech electronic navigational aids well-known today.

The skills required to be a good sailor have much in common with those required by a good politician. Both are subject to much that is beyond their control, and Roosevelt used the same skills that made him the country's greatest seafaring president to navigate the equally treacherous political waters over the course of his entire career in public service. He refused to get "locked in" on a single course in case there was a shift in the political landscape. Instead, he remained ready to alter courses, make compromises, and shift positions as situations required. In other words, he was a master at dealing with the unexpected. He excelled in the statehouse and the White House, and on the open sea.

Skipper Roosevelt's next stop was Little Harbor, New Hampshire, a thirty-five mile run from Gloucester and the final destination of a 1932 cruise he took with three of his sons at the start of his first presidential campaign. As was the case at most of the stops, excited residents anxiously waited as their new president skillfully piloted his small schooner inside the Isles of Shoals. After a restful night's sleep, the president welcomed aboard Marguerite "Missy" LeHand, his personal secretary, who was vacationing at her home in Somerville, Massachusetts. He next was greeted by Jimmy's wife, Betsey Cushing Roosevelt. The daughter of famed surgeon Harvey Cushing, Betsey brought aboard the president's fifteen-month-old granddaughter, Sara Delano Roosevelt. "It was with great difficulty that she was induced to go ashore," Jimmy said, "and we all hope she'll be as good a sailor as her grandfather."[24]

Just before noon on 22 June, *Amberjack II* weighed anchor and set out for Chandler's Cove near Portland, a fifty mile trip, where the schooner would take on two additional crew members. Roosevelt's first vacation since being inaugurated president was nearly half over.

CHAPTER 2

Flames Licking
out of the Bilge

In what was described as "lazy sailing weather," the president and his crew passed the midway point of the four hundred mile cruise, and pulled into Chandler's Cove, about ten miles northeast of Portland, Maine, on 22 June 1933. Roosevelt was looking forward to the arrival of his sons Franklin Jr. and John from Groton. Frankie's friend, A. J. Drexel Paul, would also be joining the crew. Along with his son Jimmy, Cutter, Briggs, Rust, and Ames, Roosevelt had a crew of eight to assist him. *Amberjack II* had more hands on board than needed and more crew members than there were bunks. The president, therefore, divided the crew into three shifts, and ordered bunk space be provided aboard one of the accompanying destroyers for the crew members on the off-watch.

The hardest and most exciting day's sail followed, according to the recollections of First Mate Jimmy Roosevelt. "It was blowing a fresh breeze out of the northwest and, with full sail, plus the fisherman staysail, we logged nearly eight knots all the way to Pulpit harbor," he wrote. "The trip around North Haven, through Deer Island Thoroughfare to Southwest Harbor, was magnificent. The skipper appeared to have enjoyed that day more than any other on the cruise, for East Penobscot, Blue Hill and Frenchman's Bays all lie in the most beautiful part of the Maine coast. It was well after dark before we came to anchor at Southwest Harbor."[1]

With a stiff breeze sweeping down the craggy coast, the president led his flotilla of guardians on a merry chase, in and out of the islands dotting the rugged Maine coast. Although the destroyers tried to follow Roosevelt, they were too large and had to retreat to the deeper waters away from the coast. Roosevelt was having a grand time. The destroyer USS *Ellis,* assuming FDR would stop at Tenants Harbor, anchored there. Much to the *Ellis* captain's surprise, Roosevelt sailed right by that port and headed to Pulpit Harbor, a cove on the northwest side of the island of North Haven. It gets its name from a pulpit-shaped rock guarding the entrance to the harbor and serving as a nesting area where fish hawks raise their young.

When the destroyer finally caught up with *Amberjack II,* Roosevelt wigwagged a message: "Glad to see you back." *Ellis* replied, "Thank you, *Amberjack.*" Roosevelt signaled back: "We will anchor in Pulpit Harbor." The now-wary destroyer replied: "We'll believe it when the anchor is overboard." First Mate Jimmy Roosevelt observed: "Evidently, they won't be fooled twice in a row."[2] Before modern radio communication between ships, the wigwag system was used to convey messages. A hand flag or light was used to send messages, using the dot-and-dash language of Morse code. The sender, facing the receiver, makes a motion from the vertical ninety degrees to the sender's right. This is a dot. A similar motion to the left is a dash.[3]

At Pulpit Harbor *Amberjack II* crew's quick action averted what could easily have been a disaster. On 23 June, in the tiny, nearly landlocked area, Roosevelt came face-to-face with the one fear that haunted him his entire adult life—fire. Jimmy said that fire was the only thing that he ever heard his father confess to fearing physically after he contracted polio. Having seen the destruction caused both to property and people, FDR frequently lectured his children on the dangers of carelessness with fire. He feared that he would be unable to help himself if he was caught in a fire. As a result, he had taught himself to crawl, propelling himself across the floor with his powerful arms. "If I ever get caught in a fire, I might be able to save myself by crawling," FDR reportedly told his son.[4]

Amyas Ames recalls vividly an incident that happened on that clear June morning in Pulpit Harbor, an incident that escaped notice both in Jimmy Roosevelt's account of the trip and the daily press accounts. It certainly would strike fear in the heart of any Secret Service agent assigned to protect a president, especially one who was unable to walk on his own. Normally, security men were aboard FDR's vessel only when it was anchored for the night, and the president and his crew were asleep. The rest of the time, the president and his amateur crew were on their own.

The president was in his cabin and Ames was on deck. Ames recalls hearing a great commotion down below and then suddenly seeing "the president's head come flying up out of the hatchway." Flames were licking out of the bilge, Ames recalls, and Jimmy and Paul Rust, both below deck, grabbed the president and threw him up the hatchway. Ames and others on deck "caught him as he came and sat him aft by the wheel." Ames recalls that "there was considerable speed" on the part of the crew to remove Roosevelt from the fire danger.[5]

Press accounts mentioned that *Amberjack II* did experience a "balky motor" at Pulpit Harbor, but they failed to report the fire or the fear for the president's safety. Although it may seem amazing by today's standards, no security agents were aboard the schooner when the fire broke out. Ames said he believes the U.S. Coast Guard and Secret Service were notified about the fire after Jimmy put it out with a fire extinguisher. He said a mechanic from a coast guard cutter or one of the destroyers then came aboard to inspect and repair the motor.

The *New York Times* reported that the engine trouble was "comparatively trivial" and that mechanics from the destroyer *Ellis* determined that the problem was a defective valve spring. Because *Amberjack II* had no spare parts on board, a new valve spring had to be obtained from a boatyard in nearby Camden.[6] The *Boston Daily Globe* noted that "the only report of trouble from the *Amberjack* is that her stove isn't so hot."[7] Roosevelt and his crew may have done a superb job of keeping the fire incident from the reporters aboard *Mary Alice* and *Old Glory,* both of which were trailing the president. Even if the correspondents had learned of the potentially serious incident, it's possible they would have refrained from reporting it. Reporters operated under an injunction that dictated that the president was quoted only with his approval. This is quite an amazing contrast to the reporting of today.

Once the immediate danger to the president had passed, Roosevelt used the down time to catch up on paperwork that had been accumulating over the past several days. Completed paperwork was placed in a mail pouch and ferried by the U.S. Coast Guard to the mainland to be taken by train to Washington.

As Roosevelt did paperwork, area residents sailed and rowed their craft around his schooner to get a look at the country's new president.

Anchored near Minister's Creek, it was difficult for visiting boats to come near, but one eighty-seven-year-old lobsterman, "Uncle" Solomon H. Parsons, rowed his dory out to *Amberjack II* and presented two large lobsters to the president according to a newspaper account. Local lore had it that Solomon was the oldest living Democratic voter in Maine. Upon shaking FDR's hand, Solomon reportedly said: "I never thought I'd shake hands with a damned good old Democratic president."[8]

The president and his party enjoyed the lobsters for lunch, along with strawberries and cream that had also been delivered to him by local residents. They were a welcome change from the standard fare of corned beef hash, peas, stewed corn, tomatoes, and fruit. North Haven summer residents Miner Patton and Eliot Beveridge had picked several baskets of strawberries the morning of the president's arrival, but were uncertain as to how they would deliver them to the chief executive. Patton recalls: "Then Eliot spotted Foster Snow, who somehow had a rowboat nearby, and soon he was persuaded to take us aboard and we were on our way. The first stop, of course, was at the beck of the guard boat. We explained our purpose, and assuredly it was clear that we posed no threat to anyone, and on we went. Then we were at the side of *Amberjack II* and handing the boxes of strawberries to the security men on deck," Patton said. Jimmy came up top to thank them and invited them to come aboard and meet the president. "We were quickly on board and followed James across the deck and down the companionway. The president was sitting up in a bunk on the port side of the cabin, a blanket across his lap, and a huge smile on a happy face," Patton recalled. After a pleasant chat, the men excused themselves and returned to their rowboat.[9]

Another visitor to *Amberjack II* was Herman Crockett, the local postmaster and proprietor of the Haven Inn. He brought the inn's guest register for the president to sign. Some sixty years earlier, another president—Ulysses S. Grant—had stayed at the inn (known at that time as the Mullen House) for a night and signed the register. Grant had been delayed en route to Bar Harbor because of heavy fog, and reportedly came ashore and sat in the hotel lobby, smoking his cigar and telling stories about the Civil War. President Roosevelt signed and dated the register twenty-six lines below President Grant's signature. According to Eleanor S. Beverage of the North Haven Historical Society, Crockett, being a true Democrat, wanted to make sure he had a Democrat president's signature in the register, as well as one from a Republican.[10]

After engine repairs were made in Pulpit Harbor, Roosevelt gave the order to weigh anchor on 24 June and *Amberjack II* set sail at 4 P.M., a few hours later than desired. However, Roosevelt intended to get as far as possible by sundown.

Ames, who would leave *Amberjack II* at its next stop, recalls his last night with Roosevelt. As the president sailed into Blue Hill Bay near Southwest Harbor, where they would spend the night, he called to Jimmy: "The sun is over the yardarm." Jimmy immediately went below and got a well-filled silver cocktail shaker, Ames recalled. Jimmy brought the shaker up and gave it to the president, who was sitting by the wheel. "The president took the cocktail shaker and held it up over his head and shook it, laughing, fit to kill," Ames said. The big cocktail shaker, gleaming in the late afternoon sun, was in full view of the two destroyers and coast guard boats. "It got a great laugh—on our boat, anyway."[11]

Of course, Prohibition was still the law of the land, although the repeal amendment had been proposed four months earlier. In March Congress had passed an amendment to the Volstead Act of 1919 that permitted the sale of beer and wine with an alcohol content of 3.2 percent. Recognizing a good potential source of revenue, Roosevelt quickly had added a federal tax on such sales. Prohibition was not officially repealed throughout the country until 3 December 1933. Jimmy Roosevelt left *Amberjack II* the next day aboard the destroyer *Bernadou* to attend a Prohibition Repeal Convention in Boston where, as a delegate, he cast his vote in favor of repeal.

Times White House Correspondent Charles Hurd, who was assigned to follow Roosevelt during the cruise, recalls another incident that reveals the president's penchant for good-natured fun. Roosevelt invited some of the reporters aboard *Amberjack II* for a brief visit. Hurd described a conversation: "He (Roosevelt) asked us what we had established as routine aboard *Mary Alice* where, in his eyes, to be a passenger must be a monotonous life. We replied that we wrote, ate, slept and caught up on our reading, and then relaxed with cocktails after we had anchored for the night and sent off our dispatches." Hurd reported the following exchange:

The President: Drinking? Have you got liquor on board?
Reporter: We have a few medicinal supplies, Mr. President.
The President: Well, that's all right—especially since you're not
   accustomed to the cold and wet. You have enough?

> *Reporter:* We are husbanding it carefully, sir. You're very thoughtful. How about yourself?
>
> *The President (speaking firmly):* Of course, we've no liquor. For the time being this boat is a commissioned Navy craft. The Navy is dry.
>
> *Reporter:* We had thought . . . it's too bad you can't join us, sir.
>
> *The President (impatiently):* But we have ice and glasses and water, and if someone would occasionally bring along. . . .
>
> *Reporter (reaching for a bottle rolled in his rain coat):* Mr. President, we'd be honored.
>
> *The President:* You'll find the ice chest in the galley forward. And the glasses are on a shelf just above it.[12]

Roosevelt's sense of humor and wit were legendary, as evidenced by many similar incidents. For example, when confronted by the Women's Christian Temperance Union, which was criticizing the use of champagne to christen ships, Roosevelt replied, "Madam, remember: After a ship has tried alcohol once, it takes to water the rest of its life."[13]

Ames agrees that the cocktail shaker incident was typical of Roosevelt's knack for having fun and playing tricks on what the president described as "our wagging tail"—the contingent of destroyers, coast guard cutters, and press boats that followed along on the cruise. "The president loved doing it," Ames recalled. "He was sort of kidding the officers of the United States Navy."[14]

First Lady Eleanor Roosevelt, who was motoring to Campobello to supervise preparations for the president's arrival, stopped by the next morning, 25 June, to visit with FDR and her sons. Along with her friends, Mary E. Dreier, Nancy Cook, and Marion Dickerman, Mrs. Roosevelt went aboard *Amberjack II* and visited with the skipper and his crew for about two hours. Mrs. Roosevelt next went aboard one of the vessels carrying the press to visit with reporters traveling with the president.

Meanwhile, Roosevelt had one of the destroyers take Jimmy to Boston for the Prohibition Repeal Convention. In addition, crew members Ames and John Cutter also left schooner. Ames had to attend the wedding of his sister, Evelyn, who was marrying Haskell Davis, son of Ambassador-at-Large Norman E. Davis. He also had to get back to his job at Kidder Peabody and Company in Boston. Three decades later, after a career in investment banking, Ames became the chairman of Lincoln Center and the New York Philharmonic Orchestra. Cutter, an FDR cousin and cook on the cruise, was scheduled to return to *Amberjack II* within the next day or two after picking up supplies for the remaining days at sea.

President Roosevelt, minus three of his crew members, departed from the peaceful waters of Southwest Harbor at Mount Desert Island, and set sail for Roque Island, about forty miles away, where he would drop anchor for what he thought would be an overnight stay. However, thick fog would strand the president and his flotilla in Lakeman Bay for three days.

Before departing Southwest Harbor, Roosevelt sent word that he would like Ambassador Davis to brief him on the Geneva Disarmament Conference. Once *Bernadou* dropped off Jimmy, Ames, and Cutter, Roosevelt ordered it to return with Davis. In addition, the destroyer would bring Marvin H. McIntyre, a presidential assistant. He would replace Stephen T. Early, who had accompanied FDR since Marion, because he was scheduled to return to Washington. Louis McHenry Howe, the president's trusted secretary, also would join Davis in his trip to see the president.

Unfortunately, the heavy fog shrouding *Amberjack II* and its flotilla would prevent Davis and the others from reaching Roosevelt until the third day of the president's forced captivity. Meanwhile, Davis visited with reporters aboard *Mary Alice,* moored some distance from FDR, and provided them with some background on the conference. Finally, Davis, McIntyre, Howe, and returning crewmen Jimmy and Cutter were able to navigate the fog. Davis, McIntyre, and Howe conferred with the president aboard *Amberjack II* for about two hours. Reporters then were invited aboard. Everyone crowded into Roosevelt's tiny cabin and queried Davis and the president on the disarmament conference.

Concluding what was the president's second "seagoing" conference on international affairs (the first was with Assistant Secretary of State Raymond Moley in Nantucket Harbor on 20 June) since he first sailed from Marion, Massachusetts, ten days earlier, Roosevelt seemed satisfied with the "excellent progress" reported by Davis. The ambassador would be returning to Geneva the following week. Ultimately, however, no arms limitation treaty would emerge from the conference. *Times* correspondent Hurd later wrote that it was evident that no great power really planned on disarming. In fact, within months of the conference, large amounts of funds were found to speed up U.S. building of so-called "treaty warships." This greatly helped restore jobs in the country's shipyards and stimulated employment among subcontractors.[15]

Although Roosevelt obviously was pleased to receive the firsthand report of the conference, he was most likely equally as pleased at being released from the steady diet of canned beans, hash, brown bread, and fresh lobster while idled along Roque Island's rocky coast. Later that afternoon, Cutter surprised the president with a meal of broiled steaks and fresh vegetables that he had brought from Boston, thus providing somewhat of a delicacy for FDR and his crew. Jimmy reported that the president and his crew patiently passed the time while fogbound, playing cards, reading, fishing, and, for a few adventuresome souls, rowing along the island's shores, where they found lots of trees and rocks, but little more.

One foggy morning, six lobsters were brought to *Amberjack II* by a local fisherman. Jimmy wrote of his younger brother's unpleasant experience: "Franklin, being interested, picked up one and made the mistake of putting his nose a little too close to one of the claws. With astonishing speed, the lobster let go a straight left to the jaw and Franklin let go of the lobster just in time to save himself, but lost that lobster overboard. Hence, one lobster is free and one member of the crew ate lightly for lunch."[16]

The president also took advantage of the forced isolation as a time to catch up on thank you notes for the dozens of gifts given to him at various stops along the way. Paintings, ship models, an ivory carving of a whale, a silver cigar case, books, local seafood, and home-baked delicacies were only a few of the items area residents proudly presented to their new president. In a letter to F. W. Hartford, editor and publisher of the *Portsmouth Herald,* Roosevelt thanked him for his "thoughtfulness in putting aboard a number of Portsmouth books during our brief stay. They were a very welcome addition to our ship's library, especially during those fog-bound days off Roque Island, when they helped to widen the horizon from a bare visibility to one which was ocean-wide."

The Franklin D. Roosevelt Library in Hyde Park, New York, is filled with copies of similar letters. Those were the days before presidents had automatic signature machines and a staff of hundreds to respond to letters and gifts such as these. Dictated personally and then later signed, Roosevelt thanked average American citizens who took the time to send him a gift as a memento of his visit. Even the gift of a few fresh lobsters merited a presidential thank you note. In a brief note to George O. Beal of Jonesport, Maine, the president observes that "it was very good of you to send those delicious lobsters. All of us greatly appreciated them. I am delighted to be back in these waters again."[17] Today, it is unlikely that security personnel would allow a president to enjoy the home-baked goods and hot quahog chowder that were delivered to FDR by admiring citizens. Sara Roosevelt, the president's devoted mother, recognized FDR's enthusiasm for writing letters at an early age. She recalled, "They say that few public men conduct anything like the personal correspondence which Franklin has enjoyed almost since he has held office, and no amount of persuasion has ever succeeded in making him abandon his custom of attending to his own mail even in the face of the most exacting duties."[18]

After three full days of captivity at Roque Island, the president decided the time had come for executive action. As crew member Drexel Paul recalls, Roosevelt said enough was enough, and he gave the order to start sailing: "One morning, the president got sort of itchy and we quietly pulled up anchor and snuck out on the fleet," Paul remembers. "Nobody knew we'd gone, and the president was sort of like a naughty little boy." Roosevelt's guardians soon learned that *Amberjack II* was missing, however. "This Coast Guard boat came roaring up behind us as we were on our way to Campobello. They were as mad as the devil!"[19]

Roosevelt, well versed in the area's topography and an expert sailor to boot, released himself from his fogbound trap and sailed the final leg of his long journey. Foghorns sounding, Roosevelt led the ghost-like procession along the treacherous New England coastline into the open water. The fog was so thick that the boats were unable to see each other most of the way.

The president arrived at Campobello, bathed in bright sunlight, to the cheering of thousands who anxiously were waiting for him to complete his first vacation since his inauguration only three short months ago. "Skipper" Roosevelt, captain of *Amberjack II,* old friend to hundreds of Campobello natives, was now commander in chief of the United States. Franklin Roosevelt, sailor, neighbor, and now America's thirty-second president, had come home to see his friends.

CHAPTER 3

He Must Have His
Relatives with Him

"That's not yachting," an old sea captain declared after watching President Franklin Roosevelt deftly navigate some of New England's most treacherous waters during his 1933 vacation cruise. "That's Gloucester fishing sailing, by all that's holy. He must have his relatives with him."[1]

The old captain was right. Roosevelt's ancestors were inextricably linked to the sea. He was related to whalers, shipbuilders, and sea captains engaged in the China Trade. Their life was the sea. They knew how to sail—and so did Franklin. It was in his blood.

FDR's distant cousin, Amasa Delano, at age twenty-six, undertook a voyage of commerce and discovery in 1789 aboard *Massachusetts,* a nine-hundred-ton merchant ship, the largest vessel of its kind in the United States at that time. Although having no previous experience as a sailor, Amasa Delano was conditioned to the sea very early in his father Samuel's shipbuilding business. Both Amasa and his brother Samuel served in the French and Indian Wars.[2] Warren Delano II, FDR's grandfather, operated a fleet of ships in the China Trade during the great age of clipper ships. FDR's great-grandfather, Warren Delano, was a swashbuckling ship captain engaged in trade with the Orient. Ephraim Delano, FDR's great-great-grandfather, had sailed from New Bedford in search of whales.

In 1843, thirty-four-year-old Warren II married eighteen-year-old Catherine Robbins Lyman, who later would give birth to Sara, FDR's mother. Immediately following the wedding, the newlyweds boarded one of his clipper ships for a 104 day voyage to Macao, off the coast of China, where he owned a magnificent estate. During his time in China, he became quite wealthy in the tea trade, and returned to the United States a few years later to live in another spectacular mansion, Algonac, on the Hudson River near Newburgh, New York.

During the depression of 1857, the financial resources of Warren II began to decline so he decided to lease, after unsuccessfully attempting to sell, his Hudson River mansion. He returned to China in an effort to rebuild his fortune. He went alone, calling for his wife and family to join him a few years later. In June 1862 Catherine, her seven children including Sara, a nurse, maid, and nanny all set sail for Hong Kong where Warren II now lived. He chartered the clipper ship *Surprise* for their trip. Young Sara celebrated her eighth birthday aboard *Surprise* during its four month voyage around the Cape of Good Hope, into the Indian Ocean, and on to the China Sea.

During the American Civil War, Warren Delano II continued to live in Hong Kong, where Russell and Company's clipper ships were used to ship opium to the United States. Delano was a partner in the firm and later served as its president. President Abraham Lincoln's medical corps used opium as an analgesic; it was taken in pill form or sprinkled by the surgeon on a wound. Warren II's business was profitable and he quickly rebuilt his fortune.[3] President Lincoln appointed Delano as special agent in China during the war years, and he was able to establish pioneering trade agreements with the Chinese empire.

Franklin Roosevelt's ancestors on his father's side also had a strong connection to the sea. John Aspinwall, FDR's great-grandfather, was the son of Capt. John Aspinwall, an influential New York City merchant and privateer. John Jr.'s son, George, was the owner of the first iron steamer in the United States to engage in open ocean coastal trade. Two other sons, William Henry and John Lloyd Aspinwall, owned the firm that launched *Sea Witch* and *Rainbow;* they also loaned money to President Lincoln to help finance the Civil War. The Aspinwall brothers would later found the Pacific Mail Steamship and Panama Railroad Companies.[4]

FDR's passion for the sea loomed large in his life. He enjoyed reading, writing, and talking about it. He sketched pictures of sailing vessels and painstakingly built miniature ship models. At age twenty-two, he was elected as a member of the New York Yacht Club, the venerable New York

City institution where his friend, Vincent Astor, later would serve as commodore. He was the first member to become president of the United States.

While a law school student at Columbia University, FDR worked successfully to amalgamate the Naval History Society and its distinguished collection of prints, maps, manuscripts, and artifacts, with the New York Historical Society. Roosevelt was a member of both organizations. Alfred Thayer Mahan's *The Influence of Sea Power upon History* became a bible to young Franklin. Mahan, a renowned naval strategist and historian, argued that a large and strong navy was key to a nation's supremacy. Roosevelt remembered the lesson and strove for a strong navy as assistant secretary of the U.S. Navy in 1913 and, two decades later, as commander in chief.

Roosevelt loved to sail. His skill—whether sailing on the ocean or gliding across the ice-covered Hudson River—was second to none, and he sought out the sea as a means of relaxation and therapy his entire life. "Even as a little mite, he declared himself a seafaring man, and a lively imagination took him off on journeys without end," recalled his mother Sara, whose father, grandfather, and great-grandfather all were sea captains. "I shall never forget the sailboat—so-called by Franklin and Edmund Rogers, who built it on the top of a hemlock tree. In it they sat for hours while we wondered at what moment they would come hurtling down from their self-styled hurricane deck, bringing to an abrupt end their jaunt to Borneo or Cathay."[5] Rogers was a childhood friend and neighbor of Franklin; he accompanied the Roosevelt family when they attended the 1893 World's Fair in Chicago.

At the age of three, young Franklin and his parents, returning from a European trip, embarked from Liverpool aboard the British steamer RMS *Germania* for a transatlantic crossing, a trip that nearly ended in disaster. The family was only two days at sea when, on Easter Sunday, a fierce North Atlantic storm battered the ocean liner, injuring several crew members, including the captain. Although water poured into the cabins, the steamer did not sink, but was forced to turn around and return to Liverpool. This was only the first of a number of such transatlantic voyages young Franklin would take with his parents aboard luxury liners. By age fourteen, Franklin Roosevelt had made nine transatlantic crossings with Sara and James.

In 1889, Sara and James decided to take a trip to Europe. Despite Franklin being "very feverish" and diagnosed with malaria, Dr. Edward H.

Parker advised the Roosevelts that a sea voyage would be the right medicine for the seven year old. As the White Star steamer RMS *Adriatic* departed New York Harbor in the early morning hours of 31 July, Franklin and his parents were on board. Franklin's condition worsened, and his temperature reached 103 degrees. The ship's doctor was summoned. The doctor gave his young patient a dose of medicine, which his mother said made him "much worse and blotches came out."[6] The following day, Franklin's high fever continued and he was "suffering pain all over" according to a diary kept by his mother. She had stayed by his bed throughout the night. Franklin showed little improvement over the next few days, and the ship's doctor concluded that he was suffering from typhoid.

After arriving in Liverpool, Franklin was moved on his mattress to a waiting ambulance that transported him to the home of a local doctor, Dr. Gemmell, who was a cousin of *Adriatic*'s captain. Franklin began to show some improvement as the doctor administered daily doses of cold, boiled, fresh milk and a "tiny dose of brandy," a treatment that had been initiated at sea. As he continued to recover, his daily regimen included milk, soda water, and beef jelly. Later, he was given bread and a milk and arrowroot drink that contained port wine, which was judged by Franklin as "so fruitful."[7]

Two years later, Franklin and his parents were aboard the White Star liner RMS *Teutonic*, bound for England and Europe. Sara and James took Franklin to a naval exposition and, later, ordered a boat their nine-year old son admired in Cologne. Franklin took swimming lessons at a bath in Friedberg. In 1914, the Royal Navy requisitioned *Teutonic*, which became Britain's first armed merchant vessel. Over the next five years, Franklin traveled with his parents aboard floating palaces during four more European crossings. The budding sailor began to feel at ease sailing the world's oceans.

Ocean liners patronized by the Roosevelts during the early twentieth century were a study in sophisticated elegance. For example, the opulent RMS *Mauretania*, the largest and fastest ocean liner of its day, boasted an elegant and richly decorated interior including a sweeping staircase and a two-story dining room. Mahogany paneling and gilt carvings were seen throughout the first-class section, which accommodated 563 passengers. The Roosevelts always traveled first class.

Franklin Roosevelt discusses *Mauretania* in recollections dictated years later. "I well remember that the woodwork of her public rooms and corridors was unusually elaborate. Nothing like it will ever (again) be built into an Atlantic liner," President Roosevelt recalled. "The Latvian oak panels of her dining saloon, as I remember, were hand-carved, every one being 'individually different.'"[8]

Roosevelt further stated that "the fame of *Mauretania* does not live in the clothes she wore, but in what she stood for and the work she did." *Mauretania*, like sister ships RMS *Lusitania* and RMS *Aquitania*, represented an earlier age of grace, elegance, and sophistication, something Franklin Roosevelt became accustomed to as he sailed aboard these luxury liners during the years of his youth and young manhood. "Every ship has a soul," Roosevelt dictated, "but the *Mauretania* had one you could talk to . . . as Capt. Rostron once said to me, she had the manners and deportment of a great lady, and behaved herself as such."[9]

Roosevelt said *Mauretania* "always fascinated me with her graceful, yachtlike lines, her four enormous black-topped funnels, and her appearance of power and good breeding." Later, Roosevelt lamented, great cruise ships such as this would be replaced by newer liners that boasted "needless swimming pools and private baths, which passengers rarely used the whole trip (other than the toilet) after they'd payed heavily for the foolish honor." Roosevelt continued, "For some of us, myself included, the sea persists in remaining romance, vaguely enticing, dimly alluring, always maintaining its distance."[10]

In 1887, at age five, young Franklin wrote his first letter. Addressed to his mother, it included two detailed pen-and-ink drawings of sailboats. One of these remarkably detailed drawings shows a boat under steam and full sail, and the other depicts three sailboats on the ocean.[11] That same year James Roosevelt took his young sailor-suited son to the White House to meet President Grover Cleveland. During the visit, President Cleveland told the five year old: "I am making a strange wish for you, little man, a wish that I suppose no one else would make—but I wish for you that you may never be president of the United States."[12] As Franklin grew older, he wanted to attend the U.S. Naval Academy at Annapolis, a wish that was vetoed by his father.

Sara Delano Roosevelt was proud of her sea heritage. A Delano had a hand in building the first ironclad war ship, the *Merrimack*. The Delanos also were involved in building the frigate *Constitution* and Farragut's *Hartford*. Sara's grandfather, Warren, built a house in nearby Fairhaven, Massachusetts, where young Franklin and his mother would visit frequently.

At the "Homestead," as it was called, Roosevelt would hear tales of sea-faring adventures from his sea captain grandfather, Warren II, and look through musty old trunks for remnants of those early years. His grandfather gave him a battered old sea chest, which he cherished. In it he carefully maintained a collection of the family's nautical memorabilia.[13]

Years later, while serving as New York's governor, FDR would recall those summers in Fairhaven and the tales of the glorious days of whaling. In an introduction to a book, *Whale Ships of New Bedford,* Governor Roosevelt wrote:

> Forty years ago, a little boy sat on the old string-piece of his grand-father's stone wharf at Fairhaven. Close by lay a whale ship, out in the stream another rode at anchor, and over on the New Bedford shore near the old winding wooden bridge a dozen tall spars over-topped the granite warehouses. Even then, he felt that these great ships were but the survivors of a mightier age, that in some way they were no longer the focal point of the busy community, that the cotton-mills with their tall stacks had superseded the whaling industry. In the library of his grandfather's homestead, bound volumes of the pictorial reviews of the fifties showed the woodcuts of the Whaling Fleet—ships by the score, sailing for the South Atlantic, for the Indian Ocean, for the North Pacific.[14]

At the age of nine, young Franklin was thrilled when his father, James, purchased the fifty-one foot auxiliary yacht *Half-Moon* and began schooling the boy in the art of sailing. They sailed on the Hudson River, just out the back door of their Hyde Park home. They sailed along the New England coastline and, north, to the rugged and icy Bay of Fundy, where James built a summer house on Campobello Island, in the Canadian province of New Brunswick off the coast of Maine.

Campobello—only nine miles long and three miles wide—was remote, and much less civilized than the precincts to which the Roosevelts were accustomed in New York City and Hyde Park. The only way to get there, short of sailing, would be a long train ride to Eastport, Maine, and then a boat ride to Welshpool on Campobello. Today, the island is linked to Lubec, Maine, by the Franklin D. Roosevelt Memorial Bridge, which was dedicated in 1962. Even in the summer, temperatures are chilly and heavy fogs and torrential rains are commonplace. The ocean water always is cold, although this never stopped young Franklin from taking a dip. The tides, said to be among the highest in the world, made sailing exhilarating—one of the main attractions that led James Roosevelt to purchase four acres on this remote island.[15]

Beginning when he was only one-year-old, Franklin Roosevelt spent almost every summer at Campobello until 1921, when he was stricken by polio at the youthful age of thirty-nine. The Roosevelts spent July, August, and part of September there every year. At Campobello Roosevelt learned to sail through swirling ocean currents and the rough and treacherous reaches of the area. He learned to "read" the water, in the days before the existence of sophisticated electronic navigational devices. Roosevelt became a master sailor and, years later, he would make sure his children also learned the art of sailing the waters that he loved so much.

Jimmy Roosevelt, the president's oldest son, remembers spending a good portion of his childhood at Campobello, as well as the difficulty each year in reaching the tiny spit of land. The family first would take a long train ride from New York to Boston, and then travel to Eastport, Maine, by steamer or sleeper train. When the tides, which he recalled rose by more than thirty feet at the Bay of Fundy, were right, they would cross by motor launch from Eastport to Campobello. He also recalls toting all of the family's belongings—some forty or fifty trunks, suitcases, boxes, and barrels. They would be pushed in wheelbarrows by servants up the hill to their house.

The Roosevelt "cottage" was actually a thirty-four room, gambrel-style house with eighteen bedrooms. There was no electricity and the house was heated by a coal heater and fireplace. Dinner was cooked on a coal stove; kerosene lamps were used for reading. There was no telephone or radio. Mail came by boat one day late, and newspapers arrived about one week late. After FDR became president, arrangements were made to telephone urgent messages to Eastport; they were relayed to him immediately by boat.

Jimmy Roosevelt recalls:

We played in the woods, picked berries and walked the beaches. There was a kind of clay court where we could play tennis. We might take a dip in the icy ocean, but seldom really swam. He [FDR] did teach us to sail, maybe because this was one activity he loved above all others and wanted us to love. He was a superb sailor. The straits and narrows around Campobello and the nearby

islands are treacherous, the tides strong and tricky, but he knew
them well. While he would not tolerate our fooling around on
board a boat, he delighted in demonstrating his own ability with a
near-reckless handling of his ship through rocky passages, so close
to jagged reefs as to scare the wits out of us.[16]

Although she did not share FDR's love of the water, Eleanor Roosevelt
loved Campobello nonetheless. Here she finally could be in charge of a
household, instead of living in her mother-in-law's Hyde Park home. Their
own New York City apartment was chosen and furnished by Sara Roosevelt, who maintained an adjoining townhouse with connecting doors.
The endless Campobello fogs and howling winds comforted Eleanor and
made her feel serene.[17]

When FDR turned sixteen, his parents presented him with his very
own boat—a twenty-one foot, two-masted knockabout. Called *New Moon,*
formerly named *Bauble,* it arrived at Campobello on a schooner from New
York on 8 July 1898. Roosevelt had chosen the design of the boat himself
while studying at Groton, and sent the plans to his parents so it could be
built to his specifications. He sailed *New Moon* almost every summer at
Campobello, further honing his skills at learning how to read the tides,
currents, and fickle weather of the often-unpredictable area.[18]

Sara Roosevelt remembers one Campobello adventure of Franklin and
Lathrop Brown, his Groton School pal and, later, Harvard roommate. One
summer Roosevelt and Brown set sail in *New Moon,* heading for Grand
Manan Island, following a rumor that the hidden treasure of the famous
pirate, Captain Kidd, was buried in a cave there. When they located the
cave, they began digging. They struck a plank on which were carved the
initials W.K. They spent the entire afternoon tunneling through layer after
layer of soil, only finally to realize that the board must have been inscribed
by some practical joker. "On the way home a fog set in," Sara Roosevelt
recalled, "and it got to be dinner time with nothing in sight but some eggs,
a chafing dish, and no spirits with which to ignite the wick. Gloom was dis-
pelled, though, when they discovered a flask of rum which had been hidden away against an emergency, and with it they refueled the chafing dish
and cooked what must have tasted like a veritable feast."[19]

On another summer day at Campobello, Roosevelt, now a student at
Harvard, set off on his own for a day or two of sailing. In the night, a small
schooner sailed into the harbor where Roosevelt had anchored *New Moon.*

When Roosevelt awakened the next morning and saw the schooner, he went over to investigate and went aboard. He asked the captain, described later by Sara as a "rather reprehensible character," what cargo he was carrying; the captain replied, "potatoes."

"Potatoes from Grand Manan Island to Maine," Roosevelt quizzed the captain. "Isn't that the reverse of the usual procedure?"

"Yes," the captain replied, "but this year it is the other way around."

"Where do you keep those potatoes?" Roosevelt asked.

The captain replied, "Down here in the hold," pointing to a trap door held down with a small stick of wood.

"My mother spent much of her life in China, and something tells me that cargo of yours is Chinese potatoes," Roosevelt said.

"You're too smart for your own good, young fellow," the captain said.

But Roosevelt persisted, "How many potatoes have you?"

"Eighteen," the captain said.

"And what do Chinese potatoes fetch this year?"

"A hundred dollars a piece."[20]

Roosevelt made his way back to *New Moon*, leaving the captain to his business of smuggling Chinese citizens to the United States. Of course, this was in violation of the Chinese Exclusion Act, a law passed in 1882 during a wave of anti-immigrant sentiment against Chinese laborers coming to the United States.

In 1908, Hall Roosevelt, Eleanor Roosevelt's brother, recalls a cruise he and two other classmates took at Campobello with Roosevelt at the helm of *Half Moon*. Hall was seventeen and FDR was twenty-six. Hall remembered that the group had hoped to do no cooking and packed the boat with plenty of food. Within a short time, heavy fog had set in and the group was in desperate need of a safe harbor and a doctor. They had packed a nicely cooked ham in the same locker with a "grand big cheese" and, although they could not tell when they were eating it, the cheese had "a most unmistakable influence on the ham."

Hall Roosevelt recalled: "We were in a terrible rush to get to a drugstore, because there wasn't even bicarbonate of soda on board, but in the fog it took Franklin some time to feel his way through the mist into Yarmouth Harbor and find a mooring. We promptly trooped to the drugstore and drank innumerable glasses of water and bicarbonate of soda, to the consternation of the drug clerk." After recovering, the group was again on its way to its next port of call, the house of one of their Nova Scotian crew members. Roosevelt wanted his friends to see a typical fishing village. Navigating the heavy fog, the sailors finally dropped anchor in the channel near the house. After a sumptuous meal at the Nova Scotian's dinner table, Roosevelt and his crew would soon discover that they had anchored in shallow water.

As they were returning to *Half Moon*, they saw it was capsizing because the turn of the tide had swung the vessel around so the keel was over the mud flats and, as the tide receded, the boat was listing toward the channel. Hall Roosevelt recalled that night: "For the next half hour we worked frantically in that dense fog to save the *Half Moon*. Under Franklin's orders, we broke out all rope and anchors aboard. We tied ends of ropes to the mast tops and the other ends to anchors which we carried out in the dinghies as far as possible in the direction opposite the list. All this was done gropingly in a black fog, so that we in the small boats were guided only by shouts from on board." They were successful and, after a tension-filled night in which no one slept, the vessel and its crew weighed anchor the next morning.

The next challenge came from a fierce storm that tossed the tiny vessel around for hours. FDR was at the wheel and he successfully navigated his craft through the heavy winds, huge swells, and tumultuous seas. "He [FDR] relished such a challenge as this, and as far as I ever saw was absolutely without a single fiber of physical fear in his entire make-up," Hall wrote years later.

The next stop, Gull Island, was one of the few areas known at that time as a gull breeding ground. After exploring the barren island, described by Hall as a virtual gull hatchery, the group set sail again. Within a short time, they spotted a school of sperm whales. Hall recalled that he and the other crew members attempted to shoot the whales, but were unsuccessful in their efforts. Franklin explained that the trick was to wait for a whale to blow, then shoot at a spot on the nose just behind the first spout of water. All they got for their effort, however, were sore shoulders from the rifle's kick. FDR's whale-hunting ancestors would have been proud of their descendant if he had succeeded.[21]

Whether he was negotiating dangerous tides and rocky shoals in the icy waters of the Bay of Fundy, or traveling at extraordinary speeds over the frozen Hudson River, Roosevelt felt at home aboard sailing craft and excelled as both a navigator and a skipper. Roosevelt's uncle, John Aspinwall Roosevelt, owned the fastest and largest U.S. iceboat, which he sailed over the frozen Hudson. *Icicle,* built in the prosperous post–Civil War era, was more than 68 feet long, had 1,070 square feet of sail, and weighed more than a ton. Young Franklin was impressed and excited, and became quite adept as a "hard water" sailor.

The earliest records of iceboating came from Holland in the eighteenth century, and it is thought that the Dutch brought the technique to America. Although there are records of early iceboats in New Jersey, the Hudson River saw its first craft around the time of the Civil War. The first iceboat club was supposedly founded in 1861 in Poughkeepsie. Over the years, sleek ice sailing craft, which were lighter than the original Dutch boats, became more common, particularly among wealthy families living along the Hudson. When a competing boat defeated John Roosevelt's heavy *Icicle* in a Hudson River race, he immediately ordered construction of another yacht. The second *Icicle* was smaller and lighter and eventually captured the interstate Ice Yacht Challenge Pennant four times between 1888 and 1899.[22]

Great skill and daring are two ingredients necessary for successful navigation over frozen waters. Speeds upwards of 100 miles per hour have been achieved in brief spurts by iceboaters, with a 144 mile per hour speed clocked in 1907 by the iceboat *Clarel* at Long Branch, New Jersey, recorded as the fastest man had ever traveled in an engineless vehicle. The great speeds attained by iceboats, often several times the speed of the wind, are reached by sailing across the wind.[23]

Young Franklin Roosevelt was thrilled when his mother presented him with his own iceboat, *Hawk,* while still a student at Harvard. He enjoyed the challenge and excitement of iceboating, and hoped that one day his grandchildren would experience the same enjoyment on the Hudson's frozen waters. Roosevelt even served as vice commodore of the Hyde Park Ice Boat club in those years when he enjoyed hard-water sailing.

Curtis Roosevelt, Anna's son who was nicknamed "Buzzie" when he lived in the White House, recalls how much his grandfather loved iceboating, although he said his mother, Anna, was "scared stiff" of the sport. Curtis, along with his sister, Eleanor, lived with FDR at the White House from 1933 to 1937 and again from 1943 to 1945. He remembers FDR's excitement when he spoke of sailing the frozen Hudson. "They spoke of it as a scary sport, but thrilling," Curtis said. Neither he nor his sister ever

had a chance to board one of the boats, however, as FDR never participated in the sport again after being stricken by polio in 1921. "It was not
the sort of thing you would take children on anyway," Curtis noted.[24]

Erastus Corning II, who had served more than four decades as mayor
of Albany, New York's capital city, found out just how important iceboating was to FDR when then–State Senator Corning paid a visit to President Roosevelt at Springwood, his Hyde Park home, in the late 1930s.
Officials from the newly constructed Port of Albany had requested that
Senator Corning ask the president to override a U.S. Coast Guard decision to abandon the use of icebreaker boats to keep the Hudson open for
commerce during the winter months.

Corning met privately with Roosevelt and presented the case that
Roosevelt should order the U.S. Coast Guard to keep the river open,
thereby helping the economy of a Democratic city still in the throes of the
Depression. As the meeting drew to a close, Corning recalled that the
president seemed somewhat bemused. He asked Corning to step over to
the French windows looking out to the southwest, and tell him what he
saw. Corning said he saw the Hudson River.

"That's right," President Roosevelt said.

> This is the Crum Elbow reach, where I learned to use a kayak and
> to sail as a boy, and to iceboat at the helm of my own *Hawk*, and
> with my uncle on his bigger iceboats. My iceboating days are
> behind me, but I look forward to seeing my sons take their sons
> out on the family's boats on winter days in the future. The problem
> is, Erastus, the channel here is nearer my shore than the other
> and, if kept open, would leave too little ice for good sailing. So, my
> answer to the good people of the Port of Albany is a regretful "no",
> but the reason is strictly off the record.[25]

Pressures from commercial interests and the war would finally pre-
vail, and icebreakers eventually would maintain the navigation channel
despite FDR's avowed opposition. Today, although iceboats can still occasionally be seen gliding over the icy reaches of the Hudson and its tidal
coves, their numbers are fewer than in those early days when at least fifty
boats sailed the frozen waters for sport every winter.

While FDR's iceboating days may have been over, his sailing days certainly were not. A vigorous and daring sailor, FDR continued to sail both
small and larger craft throughout his two terms as New York governor and

four terms as president. It was one of the few sports he could continue to pursue even though polio had left his legs limp and useless. In fact, it was the last vigorous sport he had engaged in on the very day the polio virus appeared. "He loved to get out on the water," recalled his grandson Curtis Roosevelt. "He was somebody who liked adventure, somebody who was innovative, somebody who could cope with bad weather conditions—he could cope and he did it well."[26]

In 1913, Roosevelt was just beginning his second term in the New York State Senate, when Josephus Daniels, President Woodrow Wilson's new secretary of the navy, tapped him to be his new assistant secretary. He was the youngest ever to hold that position; his cousin, Theodore, had been nearly forty when he was appointed to the same post. The thirty-one-year-old Roosevelt accepted the offer immediately and without hesitation. On St. Patrick's Day 1913, Roosevelt was sworn in to his new post, and quickly penned a note to his mother. "I am baptized, confirmed, sworn in, vaccinated—and somewhat at sea."[27]

When Daniels decided to appoint Roosevelt as his assistant, he was warned by a Republican senator from New York: "You know the Roosevelts don't you?" he asked. "Whenever a Roosevelt rides, he wishes to ride in the front," an obvious reference to the senator's view that Roosevelt would not be satisfied as Daniels's assistant.[28] Daniels, however, appointed him anyway, believing that Roosevelt was a "singularly attractive and honorable courageous young Democratic leader."[29]

Roosevelt took his new responsibilities seriously, and relished the fact that career naval officers were bypassing the secretary and coming directly to him for advice and guidance. The naval officers considered him one of their own. On 29 July 1914, Assistant Secretary Roosevelt was among a number of dignitaries aboard the newly commissioned destroyer USS *McDougal* at the opening of the Cape Cod Canal. The man-made waterway connected Buzzards Bay with Cape Cod Bay, thus reducing the distance boats traveled between New York and Boston by some seventy-five miles. The destroyer led a procession of private yachts through the eight-mile-long canal.

Roosevelt enjoyed the visibility and pomp and circumstance that went along with the job. While attending the Panama Pacific Exposition in San Francisco in 1915, he received word that one of the navy's submarines, the F-4 (SS-23), had submerged off Honolulu, Hawaii, and had not resurfaced. All twenty-one men died on board. The American public was deeply distressed over the loss of life, as was Roosevelt. But he said that this is "only one of the sad things that must be expected in a great Navy." To help calm the nation—and also to garner a bit of publicity that had escaped him so far on the West Coast trip—Roosevelt boarded a K-7 submarine, SS-38, a 154-foot submarine that was conducting shakedown and training along the California coast before departing for experimental duty at Pearl Harbor.

Roosevelt ordered the captain to dive in the rough waters off San Pedro. Roosevelt and his friends Livingston Davis of Boston and Owen Winston of New York explored the harbor bottom sixty feet down for about a half hour. Resurfacing, Roosevelt remarked to a waiting press: "It was fine and for the first time since we left Washington, we felt perfectly at home." The party then boarded the destroyer USS *Paul Jones,* which took them to San Diego.[30]

In January 1917, the assistant navy secretary decided to take a trip to Haiti and Santo Domingo to inspect American troops stationed there. Departing Washington in a driving snowstorm were Roosevelt, his friend Livingston Davis, Gen. George Barrett and his aide, John A. McIlhenny, and Capt. Ralph S. Keyser.[31] After arriving at the Key West railroad yard, the party boarded USS *Macdonough,* bound for warmer climes. As the sun set on 23 January, Roosevelt and his party arrived in Havana harbor. That night, after several rounds of "delicious daiquiris," they dined on the roof of the Plaza Hotel; later they were entertained by a troupe of Spanish dancers. Next, it was off to the theater.

The following morning, Roosevelt and his traveling companions donned frock coats and silk hats for an audience with President Mario Garcia Menocal at the president's palace. After lunch, Roosevelt, Davis, and George Marvin, an old friend of FDR's, boarded a car driven by a marine colonel in what later was described by Davis as "a vain attempt to visit Madam Abrea, the lady of monkeys, ourangoutangs and elephants."

"After killing a goat in the road, and narrowly missing many natives, the ride came to a sudden end by the blowing out of a tire six miles from Havana and forty minutes to train time," Davis wrote in the trip log.[32] Commandeering a passing automobile, they broke all speed records in order to get to the hotel, gathered their belongings, and raced to the train station. The Cuban railroad took them to Santiago, where they boarded USS *Wainwright* for the next leg of their journey.

Steaming past the Island of Gonares, the entire seventy-two-vessel

Atlantic fleet came into view in the Bay of Port au Prince, silhouetted by the bowl-shaped mountains rising in the distance. They were in formation for inspection by Assistant Secretary Roosevelt. Roosevelt and his party, again dressed in full regalia despite the intense heat, went ashore in the admiral's barge. They were met at the end of the pier by "half the population of the town," Davis recalled. Roosevelt, meanwhile, mistook a number of men in long frock coats and silk hats, carrying a scroll, as the mayor of Port au Prince, and representatives of President Philippe Sudre D'Artiguenave. Top hat in hand, Roosevelt bowed and proceeded to deliver, in French, a speech he translated "with a good deal of difficulty." Departing the pier by car, the group was met at the shore end of the wharf by another official-looking delegation. This time it *was* the mayor, so Roosevelt, having prepared only one speech, delivered it again, in French. After arriving at the president's palace, Roosevelt gave the speech a third time to the president and his cabinet.

On one of the days during their Haitian visit, Roosevelt and his party decided to visit the tiny Island of Gonare. Traveling by tug to the island, Roosevelt said the government sent a detachment of gendarmes to protect the visitors, as the island was populated "almost exclusively by convicts or runaways who live in a primitive fashion."[33] "We climbed to the higher parts of the island and saw a number of cattle which are said to be in direct descent from the cattle which Diego Columbus brought from Spain," Roosevelt wrote. He noted that men are sent to this area with rifles whenever fresh meat is required for a presidential banquet in Port au Prince.

Later, Roosevelt would lead his party and a large contingent of marines and gendarmes on a four-day horseback ride through the steep mountains and the densely overgrown jungles, including a stop at King Henri Christophe's famous Citadelle, a fortress built in the nineteenth century to protect the country from invaders. On 30 January—his thirty-fifth birthday—Roosevelt and his group decided to swim *au naturel* in a cool mountain stream. "We were having a wonderful swim in a state of nature when, on looking up, we found that the entire female population was lining the banks," Roosevelt later recalled. "They had never seen a white man in this condition before and seemed to take it quite calmly. We came out, dried off, and dressed—all except Davis, who insisted on sending for his bathing suit before coming out."[34]

After the horseback ride concluded, Roosevelt and his fellow travelers boarded USS *Hancock,* which was waiting in the harbor. Word was then received that Germany had proclaimed a war zone. "We worked it out on the chart and came to the conclusion that Germany was attempting to exclude every American ship from all of Europe and the eastern waters of the Atlantic Ocean," Roosevelt stated.

Returning to Cuba and going ashore for one last inspection, Roosevelt traveled aboard a little train pulled by an ancient locomotive up a long, steep hill to Santiago. To avoid the train sliding backwards into the Atlantic Ocean, a number of natives ran ahead and alongside, sprinkling sand on the tracks and pushing ties under the wheel. Once atop the mountain, as a safety precaution, they walked down the steep other side.

During dinner in Santiago that night, Roosevelt received an encrypted message from his boss, Secretary Daniels: "Because of political situation please return to Washington at once. Am sending ship to meet you and party at Puerto Planta tomorrow morning." On Sunday, 2 February, USS *Neptune* was steaming toward the mainland with Roosevelt and his party aboard. "[N]o lights were showing, the guns were manned and there was complete air silence," Roosevelt recalled.[35]

Roosevelt loved the seventeen-gun salute he received when boarding a navy vessel as assistant secretary. He even designed an assistant secretary flag to be flown by navy craft when he was aboard. Unfortunately for the youthful and energetic Roosevelt, his new job was more bureaucratic paper shuffling than cruising the oceans. Although he enjoyed the work, finding it both challenging and rewarding, his first love was being afloat. When the United States entered the war in April 1917, Roosevelt—as had Eleanor's Uncle Theodore when war was declared in 1898—asked the administration to assign him to active duty at sea.

Although Daniels declined the request, he did allow his assistant secretary to inspect navy bases and meet with Allied leaders in the summer of 1918. The destroyer USS *Dyer* departed Brooklyn on 9 July, with Assistant Secretary Roosevelt aboard en route to England. During the trip, he was given the privilege of displacing Capt. Edward J. McCauley from his stateroom.

On only his second day at sea, the ship encountered some very rough weather. Roosevelt noted in his diary that "much of the crockery smashed; we cannot eat at the table even with racks, have to sit braced on transom and hold the plate with one hand."[36] During a gun drill at sea, Roosevelt wrote of a "green youngster" who fired a gun near the assistant secretary. After a four-inch shell whizzed a few feet from Roosevelt's head, he wrote, "we thought the end had come."[37]

On one especially rough and squally night near the Bay of Biscay, alarms sounded of a possible enemy convoy in the distance. Although it was a false alarm, Roosevelt sprinted to the bridge in pajamas and bare feet. He apologized to the officers on the bridge for his attire, to which one replied that he felt it made an "excellent and distinctive uniform for a flag officer as long as the Secretary of the Navy does not try to change it to the old fashioned night-gown and carpet slippers." Roosevelt said he wished he could wear a "destroyer costume" of his own invention: khaki riding trousers, golf stockings, flannel shirt, and leather coat. "It does not soil or catch in things!"[38]

On 21 July, the south coast of England came into sight. After landing, Roosevelt began inspecting bases in England, France, Scotland, Belgium, and Italy. He was especially pleased that his assistant navy secretary flag was flown on the British destroyer HMS *Velox,* the first time such an honor had been afforded an American. It also was during this trip, on 29 July, that Roosevelt would have his first contact with another man who loved the sea—Winston Churchill. Years later, they would become the greatest of friends, bound together by their mutual belief in maintaining a strong navy and their battle against the Axis nations.

With his mission accomplished, Roosevelt boarded USS *Leviathan,* which was the former German luxury liner *Vaterland* and reported to be the largest ship in the world, on 8 September, bound for the United States. His arrival in New York, however, was not filled with pomp and circumstance. Bedridden for the entire journey, he arrived on a stretcher, suffering from double pneumonia and influenza. With a high fever and congested lungs and bronchial tubes, Roosevelt nearly died in the mid-Atlantic, according to historian Kenneth S. Davis.[39]

Roosevelt's fell ill when millions around the globe were dying from the influenza pandemic, one of the deadliest in world history. More than five hundred thousand Americans succumbed to the illness, and more than five thousand U.S. Navy personnel died from the flu or its complications.[40]

Roosevelt's sea journey rekindled his deep love of being on the open ocean. So much so that he decided to resign his assistant secretary position when he returned and join the active navy. In a 20 August 1918 letter to Eleanor from Brest, France, Roosevelt wrote: "Somehow I don't believe I shall be long in Washington. The more I think of it the more I feel that being only thirty-six my place is not at a Washington desk, even a Navy desk. I know you will understand."[41] Fortunately for the United States, the war ended before Roosevelt could follow through on his wish to become a full-fledged navy man.

After the war ended in November, Daniels approved another Roosevelt tour to Europe so the assistant secretary could oversee the disposal of surplus property and negotiate the termination of navy contracts. A special dispensation was secured to allow Eleanor to travel with FDR because he had just recovered from double pneumonia. They set sail aboard USS *George Washington,* another former Germany luxury liner, on 2 January 1919, under the command of Captain McCauley, who had commanded *Dyer* on the assignment carrying Assistant Secretary Roosevelt overseas six months earlier.

Although they encountered some rough weather and Eleanor received word of the death of her Uncle Theodore, she fared remarkably well, especially for someone who was not fond of being on the open ocean. In a letter to FDR's mother, Sara, Eleanor described herself as a "marvelously good sailor and attended every meal and all entertainment."[42]

When FDR's duties had been completed, they sailed for home aboard USS *George Washington,* accompanied by President and Mrs. Woodrow Wilson. The president brought back the first draft of the League of Nations charter, which Wilson had managed to have included in the Treaty of Versailles.

As assistant secretary, Roosevelt had two vessels at his disposal for personal as well as business use. *Dolphin* and *Sylph,* both of which had performed presidential yacht duty, were available for him and he made frequent use of them during his seven years in office. The 123-foot *Sylph* served Presidents William McKinley, Theodore Roosevelt, and William Howard Taft. The 240-foot *Dolphin,* a small dispatch boat commissioned in 1885, was one of the first vessels in President Theodore Roosevelt's "new navy," and later carried President McKinley to ceremonies at Grant's Tomb in New York City on 23 April 1897.

On one 1916 inspection trip to Frenchman's Bay in Maine aboard the destroyer USS *Flusser,* a heavy fog was encountered. Roosevelt, knowing those waters extremely well, took control of the vessel. The commander, Lt. William F. "Bull" Halsey Jr., was concerned lest Roosevelt fail to translate his experience sailing schooners and yawls into the much more complicated job of guiding a large destroyer along the fog-shrouded New England coastline, with its dangerous rocks and complex tides. Roosevelt impressed all aboard as he took the destroyer through Lubec Narrows, the strait separating the mainland and Campobello. Years later, Admiral Halsey wrote:

> The fact that a white-flanneled yachtsman can sail a catboat out to a buoy and back is not guarantee that he can handle a high-speed destroyer in narrow waters. A destroyer's bow may point directly down the channel, yet she is not necessarily on a safe course. She pivots around a point near her bridge structure, which means that two-thirds of her length is aft of the pivot, and that her stern will swing in twice the arc of her bow. As Mr. Roosevelt made his first turn, I saw him look aft and check the swing of our stern. My worries were over; he knew his business.[43]

Curtis Roosevelt, FDR's grandson, calls this an extraordinary incident because the captain of a destroyer would not permit an unlicensed pilot to take control of his vessel. "When you're the captain of a ship, you're the captain of a ship, and if you allow someone to be your pilot, you are still responsible." In this instance, however, Curtis says that he has great admiration for Halsey because he allowed his grandfather to "take the helm and literally pilot the destroyer into waters that they were fearful of going into."[44]

During their time together, Secretary Daniels's carefully honed political instincts often helped to temper the sometimes brash and impetuous nature of his young assistant secretary. For example, in 1916, during the worst U.S. polio epidemic, which claimed seven thousand lives, Daniels vetoed Roosevelt's idea to send *Dolphin* to pick up his children at Campobello, where Roosevelt had sent them for the summer to isolate them from the epidemic. He feared that bringing them home by train could expose them to the virus. Daniels, however, said to wait until the Maine primary was over to prevent any public repercussions. *Dolphin* brought the children home in the beginning of October, after the primaries.

Daniels, a landlubber and former North Carolina newspaper editor, was ridiculed for being unprepared for the job because he had little experience in naval affairs. Roosevelt, on the other hand, was an accomplished sailor who worked well with navy officers. Roosevelt was a disciple of Alfred Mahan, who favored a big navy and believed it was important to prepare for war.

One Roosevelt idea, which at first was not well received by Daniels or the British government, involved laying a band of mines in the North Sea, between Norway and Scotland. Roosevelt felt this would help to curtail German submarines from venturing into the North Atlantic, where they were sinking scores of Allied vessels. Later, in February 1918, at the urging of President Wilson, the British agreed to the plan. Unfortunately, it was too late to complete such a monumental project and, although some mines were installed, the war ended before the job was complete. The project was credited by some for demoralizing German U-boat captains, however.[45]

The 1920 Democratic National Convention in San Francisco nominated Roosevelt as its vice presidential candidate on a slate with James M. Cox, Ohio governor, as president. Roosevelt accepted the honor and resigned his Navy Department post. After a grueling race, during which Cox and Roosevelt traveled the country looking for votes, the ticket went down to an overwhelming defeat. The Harding-Coolidge ticket was elected by 61 percent of the popular vote, carrying thirty-seven states.

Demoralized and weary from the campaign, Roosevelt decided it was time to change careers. He accepted a position as vice president in charge of the New York City office of Fidelity and Deposit Company of Maryland, and began work in January 1921. Roosevelt was pleased with his $25,000 annual salary, an amount far greater than what he had received during his decade of public service positions. Even better, the company was headed by Van Lear Black, a millionaire from Baltimore, who shared many of FDR's interests and views. He was a Democrat, a sportsman, and, most important, a fervent yachtsman.[46]

Black's 140 foot power yacht *Sabalo* was a dream come true for Roosevelt and, in the summer of 1921, he agreed to sail with Black to join Eleanor and the children at Campobello. The pair ran into some heavy weather off the coast of Maine. Black was nervous but Roosevelt was at ease, taking the wheel and guiding the mammoth yacht through thick fog and around treacherous shoals. Roosevelt, relishing the chance to show his sailing expertise, arrived unscathed at Welshpool Harbor, Campobello.

The next few days were spent in vigorous and strenuous physical activity with Black and his friends. They fished, sailed, and enjoyed Campobello's glorious August weather. Roosevelt slipped and fell overboard into the icy waters on one fishing trip, and it was reported that the coldness of the water seemed to chill his very soul. After *Sabalo* and its party sailed for home, Roosevelt, although not feeling up to par, took Eleanor and the children out on *Vireo,* his twenty-four foot knockabout purchased the previous year so he could teach his children to sail. They sailed all day, helped put out a forest fire, and then took a dip in Glen Severn, a small freshwater lake where the water is warmer than in the bay. Roosevelt then topped off the swim, as was his custom, with a dip in the cold ocean water. But when he emerged, he did not "feel the usual reaction, the glow I'd expected."[47] The polio virus was about to make itself known.

The next morning, 11 August, he was in great pain, his temperature was 102 degrees, and his legs would no longer support his weight. Within two days, Roosevelt was completely paralyzed from the hips down. He would never again walk without the aid of crutches, or braces and a cane. Doctors were summoned to Campobello and offered a variety of diagnoses, ranging from a heavy cold to a blood clot in the lower spine. Not until a specialist arrived from Boston a full ten days later was Roosevelt diagnosed with polio.

Four weeks later, he was moved to New York City for treatment. Roosevelt's body was stiff, he was still suffering severe pain, and he could not sit up. He was strapped to a makeshift canvas stretcher, was taken down the cottage stairs, out the door, and carried down the steep hill to the wharf. The stretcher was put onto a small motor launch for a two mile trip to the mainland. Roosevelt was placed on the boat's floor, where he could hear the bilge water sloshing a few inches from his head, and gasoline fumes blew in his face. On land again, he was loaded onto a baggage cart and wheeled over cobblestones to a private railroad car. The stretcher was pushed through a window opening, the glass having been removed to accommodate the stretcher. Meanwhile, the press was diverted by Roosevelt aide, Louis Howe, and did not see FDR until he was arranged in his berth, resting on pillows with a cigarette in his mouth.[48]

Eleanor Roosevelt later wrote that the strain of the trip must have been great for her husband. "First of all, a sense of helplessness when you have always been able to look after yourself makes you conscious every minute of the ease with which someone may slip and you may be dropped overboard, in transferring from the dock to the boat. In addition, he had not wanted crowds to witness his departure."[49] This single example shows Roosevelt's extraordinary lifelong ability to carefully orchestrate what the press—and thus the American people—would see and hear. Few Americans in those days ever knew the full extent of his disability and so it would remain for all of FDR's life.

The train pulled out of the station with the Roosevelt family on board. The next morning, FDR entered New York Presbyterian Hospital to begin what would be years of painful and frustrating rehabilitation. Unfortunately, the ravages of polio would never allow him to regain use of his legs, and he would not return to his beloved Campobello for twelve years.

CHAPTER 4

The Water Has to Bring Me Back

Franklin Roosevelt spent the next few years searching for a cure. Although he never found one and his legs remained paralyzed from the hips down for the rest of his life, Roosevelt's search did give him something that may have been even more important than the ability to walk. His polio helped shape the character of the man who would become one of the country's most admired and successful presidents.

"Franklin's illness proved a blessing in disguise," Eleanor Roosevelt later wrote, "for it gave him strength and courage he had not had before. He had to think out the fundamentals of living and learn the greatest of all lessons—infinite patience and never-ending persistence."[1] It also helped Roosevelt, the son of privileged and wealthy New Yorkers, to better understand the plight of those less fortunate than he, whether due to physical infirmity or economic privation.

"He had learned much in the arts of patience and perspective," wrote Arthur M. Schlesinger, a Pulitzer Prize–winning historian, in the first of his three-volume history of Roosevelt. When Roosevelt once was asked whether things worried him, Schlesinger noted, he would reply: "If you had spent two years in bed trying to wiggle your big toe, after that anything else would seem easy!"[2]

Frances Perkins served as New York State industrial commissioner when FDR was governor and, later, was appointed secretary of labor by President Roosevelt, the first woman to hold a cabinet post. She believed that once Roosevelt accepted the humility of his physical disability, he was on his way to greatness. He readily accepted being carried by strong men up back stairs in lecture halls or speaking to constituents while seated in the rear of his automobile.[3]

"Franklin Roosevelt underwent a spiritual transformation during the years of his illness," Perkins noted. "I noticed when he came back that the years of pain and suffering had purged the slightly arrogant attitude he had displayed on occasion before he was stricken." Perkins said Roosevelt emerged from the illness "completely warmhearted with humility of spirit and with a deeper philosophy. Having been to the depths of trouble, he understood the problems of people in trouble."[4]

Slowly, Roosevelt learned to "walk" again, his legs encased in heavy steel and leather braces. The leather brace strap wrapped around his waist and the steel bars traversed the length of his legs, clamping onto the heels of his shoes. The braces were jointed at the knee and had to be clicked in place before Roosevelt could stand. He used crutches or a cane and leaned on someone's arm in order to stand and "walk." Without this assistance, he could not take a single step. Using his powerful arms, chest, and shoulder muscles, however, he continued swimming—a recreational activity that he immensely enjoyed. Franklin Roosevelt took every opportunity to swim and to exercise his legs in warm water, whether it was at Vincent Astor's Rhinebeck, New York, estate called Ferncliff, with its indoor heated pool—the first indoor pool–tennis court complex in the country; or his Warm Springs, Georgia, polio rehabilitation facility; or on a deserted Florida beach; or in the invigorating waters of Cape Cod's Buzzards Bay.[5] Never again would Franklin Roosevelt hike, hunt, or play golf or tennis— activities he greatly enjoyed.

"The water put me where I am," Roosevelt once told a servant, "and the water has to bring me back!"[6] This may have been a reference to the bone-chilling swims he took in the icy Campobello waters just prior to the onset of polio, and which he may have blamed, erroneously, for his illness. He also may have been making reference to the belief that polio virus was transmitted via water. Indeed, some historians have suggested a tired and rundown Roosevelt may have contracted the virus while attending a Boy Scout rally at a Hudson Valley lake several weeks prior to his fever. Nevertheless, Roosevelt traveled the country pursuing every possible "cure" that might allow his legs to return to full use. A great many of these so-called cures involved water.

For two consecutive summers, in 1925 and 1926, Roosevelt spent time in Marion, Massachusetts, and was treated by prominent neurologist Dr. William McDonald, who had devised a treatment plan for polio victims designed to return function to their limbs. Roosevelt swam in Buzzard's Bay and diligently followed Dr. McDonald's treatment regime, which consisted of lengthy, painful, and tedious water exercises, and the use of what was termed a "walking board." Despite Roosevelt's dedication to the regime, he was not successful in regaining use of his legs, although he would later adopt Dr. McDonald's exercise program in his own Warm Springs polio facility, where he believed the Georgian waters possessed special curative properties.

H. Edmund Tripp, a Marion historian, remembers Roosevelt during those days in the 1920s. "He lived in Marion two summers and I remember him well as just an ordinary citizen at the time," Tripp notes. He does recall one instance when Roosevelt revealed his presidential ambitions during a conversation with Dr. McDonald. "While kidding the doctor, he had promised Dr. McDonald that he would be the first visitor at the White House if he ever became president," Tripp recalled. "When that day came, true to his word, Roosevelt invited McDonald to Washington, but the doctor was too ill to accept. So, in June 1933, Roosevelt came to Marion to see the doctor and start his cruise up the Maine coast. He had many friends in Marion, so was able to visit with many of his past neighbors," Tripp said.[7]

Roosevelt, in fact, had dinner with McDonald, his wife, and two other friends aboard *Amberjack II* in June 1933 while the schooner rocked at anchor in Marion Harbor. The next day, only one hundred days after assuming the presidency, he set sail on his famous eleven-day cruise along the New England coast.

Although Roosevelt gained little physically from his hours of grueling exercises in his early days at Marion, he believed differently and followed the doctor's orders to the letter. In one August 1925 letter to his mother, Roosevelt said he swam for one and one-half hours in the morning, followed by several hours of exercises later that afternoon, and then used the doctor's walking board for one-half hour. Designed by Dr. McDonald, the walking board consisted of an oblong piece of wood and two parallel bars. FDR would grip one bar as he used his powerful arms to propel himself along the board. Roosevelt was so pleased with his progress that he extended his Marion stay through December. Then, in a November letter to his mother, Roosevelt wrote: "The walking progresses slowly but definitely and I have walked a block with crutches and only the left leg brace. The Dr. is all right again." In fact, throughout most of his life, Roosevelt never truly gave up believing he would walk again.[8]

Although his days of strenuous sports were over, Roosevelt, his loyal assistant Louis Howe, and his son Elliott built working model sailboats, which they sailed in an annual competition on the Hudson River, during the recuperation period. Roosevelt's devoted mother Sara donated the trophy for the winner.[9] The years 1921 through 1928 were described by his son James as "one of the strangest interludes of father's life."[10] Roosevelt rented a houseboat in Florida in the winter of 1923 and the following season teamed up with a college friend to purchase a seventy-foot houseboat. He and a variety of friends spent their days fishing, sunning themselves, and traveling around looking for secluded beaches where they could swim and where Roosevelt could forget his personal troubles.

Roosevelt kept the ship's log, a record of the daily activities aboard ship, for both *Weona II,* the houseboat he rented for $1,500 for one and one-half months in February 1923, and for *Larooca* (Lawrence, Roosevelt and Company), which he purchased for $4,074 in October 1923 in partnership with John S. Lawrence, a former classmate at Harvard. Although Eleanor was not fond of the water, she did accompany him on some of his houseboat cruises. Despite his infirmity, Roosevelt had a grand time cruising through Florida waters. He and his friends fished and swam, and he even tried his hand writing a little verse. In describing "community life" aboard *Weona II,* Roosevelt wrote:

> You can slack off peak halyards—and eat with your knife—
> You can dine in your shirtsleeves, and so can your wife—
> These are the joys of community life!
> When they first come aboard they think it's so nice,
> With staterooms and bathtubs and comforts sans price,
> Till they suddenly realize that every partition
> Sounds intimate echoes of each guest's condition
> Of mind and of body—for whispers of details
> The wall in its wisdom with great gusto retails
> No secrets or thoughts between husband and wife
> Can safely be had in community life.[11]

Roosevelt clearly enjoyed compiling the logs, ending most of his entries with a line such as "Grog; Grub; good talk and good night."

Roosevelt also took personal charge of provisions for his houseboats. In a 19 February 1925 letter to a Miami grocery store, Roosevelt discusses provisions for *Larooca*. He provides a long list of items that he requests be sent to the houseboat: "twelve grapefruit, four oranges, one cocktail sauce, four dozen eggs, two Fly-Tox [fly killer], two corn flakes, six cans milk, three lbs butter, ten lbs sugar, three anchovie paste, twelve loaves bread, two boxes yellow corn meal, twelve hundred lbs ice, four boxes saltines, three lbs coffee, two guava jellies, two cream cheeses, five lbs sausage (not most expensive ones), eight lbs *very good rump* corned beef, two broilers, twelve pork chops, twelve lamb chops, small ham." Roosevelt continued his letter: "From the last box of fruit which we got we threw away fifteen oranges and six grapefruit, so will you please send us fruit which is not too ripe, and which is good and solid. Also, will you try to get for us a really good piece of corned beef."[12]

Franklin Roosevelt took three cruises on *Larooca*. During the last cruise in February 1926, Eleanor accompanied him part of the way. FDR also made the decision to use his life savings to buy a run-down Georgia resort at Warm Springs; in October 1924 he had first sought treatment in what he believed to be healing waters there. His goal was to develop the resort into a therapeutic center for treatment of polio patients. He believed the warm waters were especially beneficial to polio sufferers, and he wanted to do what he could to help other victims. Eleanor cautioned her husband that if this investment should fail—as had some of his others— his growing family could face financial ruin. He decided to go forward with the purchase, however, but he did put *Larooca* on the market.

Unfortunately, a violent hurricane caused the old houseboat to cut loose from its moorings and be swept inland by the wind, coming to rest in a pine forest far from any navigable water. With salvage impractical, the houseboat was finally sold for junk in 1927.[13]

On 29 April 1926, one month after the last trip on *Larooca* ended, Roosevelt purchased the Warm Springs property and buildings for about $200,000. There he later would become known as "Doctor Roosevelt" to scores of so-called "polios," who came for the same curative waters that first attracted Roosevelt to this remote corner in Georgia's Pine Mountains, about eighty miles southwest of Atlanta. The waters of Warm

Springs are, indeed, warm. For ages, spring water—warmed by the inner earth, has been bubbling up at the base of Pine Mountains. It emerges at temperature of eighty-eight degrees, winter and summer, and never varies by as much as one degree.[14]

Roosevelt, assisted by Eleanor and his ever-faithful aide Louis Howe, started showing renewed interest in politics, and the possibility of returning to public life now seemed an attainable goal. Roosevelt and Basil O'Connor had formed a law firm in New York City and New York Governor Alfred E. Smith had decided to run for president. Smith wanted Franklin Roosevelt to succeed him in Albany's executive mansion.

Roosevelt made the nominating speech for Smith at the 1928 convention, and after resisting strenuous efforts by the governor and others to convince him that he should run for the governorship, he finally gave in. In the end, Smith lost the presidency to Herbert Hoover, but Roosevelt, waging a vigorous campaign, was elected to the first of two consecutive two-year terms as governor. An amendment to the New York State Constitution in 1937 changed the governor's term to four years.

Despite his disability and the demands of his new position, Governor Franklin Roosevelt was not going to be a prisoner in Albany's executive mansion, nor was he going to give up his love of the sea—even though he might have to revise his definition of "sea" to include New York State's numerous rivers and vast navigable canal system. Eleanor Roosevelt explained: "My husband, who loved being on the water, found that the State of New York had a small boat used by State officials for canal travel on inspection trips. He decided to use it himself during the summers for the same purpose."[15] Eleanor sometimes accompanied Roosevelt on inspection trips, often stopping by prisons, mental hospitals, schools, and other state-run facilities.

On 21 March 1929 Roosevelt wrote a letter to Capt. Edward McCauley Jr., who had command of *George Washington* when it returned President Woodrow Wilson and Assistant Navy Secretary Roosevelt from the Versailles Conference in 1919. He had also served as Roosevelt's chief of staff while he was assistant secretary. Governor Roosevelt described one of his upcoming voyages aboard the state boat *Inspector,* a seventy-three-foot wooden hull yacht, which was called a "floating capitol" by some upstate newspapers. The Barge Canal is a 363-mile-long, man-made waterway traversing New York State, connecting the Hudson River with Lake Erie, Lake Ontario, the Finger Lakes, and Lake Champlain.

"This summer I am going on a cruise which makes me laugh whenever I compare it with the Old Navy days. I am taking command of the good ship *Inspector*, which has a glass roof and with the whole family I am navigating the barge canal from Albany to Buffalo, thence to Lake Ontario and the St. Lawrence River and back to the Hudson through the Champlain Canal. It will certainly be a rough and exciting voyage."[16]

Roosevelt took several voyages aboard the two state vessels, *Inspector* I and *Inspector* II, while serving as governor. Tours would routinely last for several weeks at a time and would provide Roosevelt an opportunity to be on the water, which he loved so much. He saw New York's landscape firsthand and met many of the state's citizens and local officials as he traveled over the waterways linking their communities. "I would rather see [the natural beauties of the State] . . . while being seated . . . on the deck of a boat going along at a speed of six or seven miles an hour than I would from the most luxurious automobile ever made traveling along at forty or fifty miles an hour," Roosevelt once remarked during a speech.[17]

Ann Easter of Skaneateles, New York, recalls clearly how much Roosevelt loved being aboard *Inspector*. Easter's father, Guy W. Pinck, was the district engineer and later a commissioner for the New York State Barge Canal, and often took young Ann along with him to see Roosevelt as the governor conducted his summertime tours. She described Roosevelt as a "complete charmer" who loved traveling around the state by boat. She remembers the boat was outfitted with brass rails to help FDR, who had no use of his legs, to move about on deck. Easter recalls swimming with Governor Roosevelt in Seneca Lake near Watkins Glen. A teenager at the time, Easter says "I didn't think too much of it [swimming with the governor]." She continued, "I had a bathing suit on and we were down there in the boat. He [the governor] thought it was a great idea that everybody went swimming—it wasn't anything special." She also recalled Eleanor Roosevelt coming along on several of the trips. Easter said it was clear that New York's First Lady, who had a fear of the water, was not enjoying herself; she did not like being aboard the boat or mingling with all of the local officials and reporters at the various stops.[18]

Roosevelt aide Samuel Rosenman recalls an incident while FDR was taking one of his inspection trips on the Barge Canal. While moored along the canal, Roosevelt noticed a young woman with a small boy at her side standing in the crowd of people gathered around his boat. The boy was crippled in one leg. Governor Roosevelt called them over to the boat and started to question the young boy's mother. The boy had been stricken with polio, leaving one leg crippled. "You are lucky," Roosevelt told the boy, "it has hit you only in one leg. See, both of my legs are gone." Smiling, Roosevelt patted the boy, shook his mother's hand, and then told them not to lose hope because the boy had just as much chance to succeed in life as any other boy. "I have never forgotten," Rosenman said, "the look of courage and faith and self-reliance and affection in the faces of the boy and his mother as they watched this crippled man who had become governor of New York and who already was being mentioned for the presidency of the United States."[19]

Although Roosevelt had a variety of hobbies and interests, he took every opportunity to return to his first love—the water. Whether it was on a gubernatorial boat tour of the state, or—as assistant secretary of the navy—skillfully navigating a destroyer through dense fog along Maine's rocky shoreline, the water is where he most loved to be. He continued his diligent efforts to regain the use of his legs. Over the four years he served as governor, Roosevelt traveled to Warm Springs no fewer than ten times. Years before plane travel would reduce the trip to hours, it normally took Roosevelt more than a full day to reach Warm Springs by train, so he frequently would stay for a few weeks after he arrived.

Years later, Roosevelt founded the National Foundation for Infantile Paralysis with a goal of eradicating polio. Eddie Cantor organized the first fundraiser in 1938, urging people to send dimes to Roosevelt to help fund polio research. The March of Dimes was born, and the United States was well on its way to finding a cure for a disease whose victims totaled almost sixty thousand in 1952.

By 1928, Roosevelt was strong enough to put aside his crutches. He was now able to rely solely on his braces, a cane, and a strong arm on which to lean in order to steady himself. The overwhelming public perception of Roosevelt was that of a young, vigorous governor who, once stricken by polio, had made remarkable progress and soon would have full use of his legs.

James H. Griffith, a Secret Service agent assigned to the White House from 1942 to 1945, was among millions of others in the country who believed the president to be only a bit lame, occasionally using canes or crutches to walk. "I never knew he was totally crippled until I came to the White House," Griffith said. He said Arthur Prettyman, Roosevelt's valet, and Charlie Fredericks, another Secret Service agent, usually had the responsibility of lifting the president into and out of his wheelchair.[20]

Robert Hopkins, son of presidential aide Harry Hopkins, was in the Army Signal Corps serving as a combat cameraman during World War II. He recalls his instructions for photographing the president. "I was told never to take any pictures of him in the wheelchair," Robert remembers. "If his braces showed in the photographs, they were retouched." Hopkins served as Roosevelt's photographer at the Casablanca Conference, the Cairo-Teheran Conferences, and the Yalta Conference. He also accompanied him on cruises, including an afternoon of fishing on the Patuxent River aboard the presidential yacht. Crown Princess Martha of Norway and her daughter, along with Harry Hopkins and his two other children, Diana and Stephen, also were aboard. Although Robert Hopkins said he was determined to catch more fish than the president, only Roosevelt was lucky that day, catching a number of fish while seated on the fantail of the boat. Roberts said that when he complained to his father that only the president was catching fish, Harry Hopkins reassured his young son that the Secret Service, who were circling the yacht in their motorboats, probably were beneath the yacht putting fish on the end of Roosevelt's line.

On a sweltering July 1936 day in New York City, fifteen-year-old Robert Hopkins first learned that Roosevelt could not walk. He first met and photographed the president, and then accompanied him to the dedication of the Triborough Bridge—built under Roosevelt's Public Works Administration (PWA)—and Randall's Island Stadium. Robert remembers: "We stopped at his mother's house, and Sara Delano [Roosevelt] talked to him as though he was a little boy, telling him he should be wearing a sweater. That was the first time I realized he couldn't walk. The Secret Service had to carry him upstairs. I had no idea. It was quite a shock to me that he couldn't walk."[21]

Although most Americans, like Robert Hopkins, were not aware of the extent of Roosevelt's disability, there were some who were quite familiar with it and tried to use it against him during his campaign for governor. A month before the gubernatorial election day in 1928, the *New York Post* ran an editorial addressing Roosevelt's paralysis: "There is something both pathetic and pitiless in the 'drafting' of Franklin D. Roosevelt by Alfred E. Smith."[22] Roosevelt responded immediately, trying feverishly to dispel rumors that he was not physically capable of being governor.

Roosevelt traveled around the state in the backseat of an open car, waving to residents, talking briefly about the issues, and then ending with his invitation to judge for themselves as to whether he is fit to be governor. In one campaign stop, a vigorous Roosevelt sarcastically exclaimed, "Too bad about this unfortunate sick man, isn't it?" The crowd roared with laughter.[23]

Although Roosevelt was elected governor in 1928 and again in 1930 innuendoes and rumors about his health did not end. When he announced in January 1932 that he would seek the Democratic nomination for president, they surfaced yet again. And, this time, they were even more vicious. "This candidate, while mentally qualified for the presidency, is utterly unfit physically," a *Time* magazine story quoted an unidentified observer. This criticism could be considered mild compared with other rumors that Roosevelt was a helpless cripple, whose disease had deranged his mind.[24]

Roosevelt and his advisors forcefully countered all of these rumors and successfully focused his campaign on the economic woes of the country. He spoke with optimism and great strength about his plans to return prosperity and stability to the United States. Yet, words might not be enough. Roosevelt needed to do something spectacular, something that would display him as a vigorous and energetic leader—something, in fact, that would put that vibrant image on the front page of the state's daily newspapers.

So, three days after flying from Albany to Chicago in an unprecedented trip to accept the Democratic presidential nomination, Governor Roosevelt announced to an Albany press conference that he and his four sons—James, John, Franklin Jr., and Elliott—would take a week-long holiday cruise sailing a tiny yawl along the coast of New England. Certainly, this was a needed rest after a grueling struggle to win the nomination but, most important, it was an opportunity for Roosevelt to show the country that he was fit and ready to take the helm in Washington.

CHAPTER 5

Get out of My Wind

"How's everybody this morning," Governor Roosevelt said, greeting the press correspondents gathered in his State Capitol office in Albany on 5 July 1932. Fresh from Chicago where he broke with tradition and personally accepted the presidential nomination of his party, the new Democratic nominee had some more surprises in store.

"Well, here is the news. I'm going on a cruise next week with my four boys and nobody else. We agreed three weeks ago to make this cruise whether I won or lost at Chicago. We are determined that nothing shall interfere this time. My son Jimmy has rented a forty-foot yawl for $150. It was cheap and that's why we could afford it," the governor noted.[1]

In his first press conference since he pledged a "New Deal" for the American people three days earlier in Chicago, Roosevelt made his first order of business the announcement of his plans for a New England cruise. Despite his remark that he would be sailing with his "four boys and nobody else," all of his sons, except Elliott, would go on this trip, along with his old sailing pal, George Briggs, and his cousin Bobby Delano, who signed on as "3rd assistant mess cook." Bobby Delano was a son of FDR's first cousin and Hudson Valley neighbor, Lyman Delano. Bobby's sister Margaret later married A. J. Drexel Paul. Briggs, who in 1937 was appointed by FDR to a high level job in the Bureau of Mine Inspection and Navigation, would keep the ship's log.

"We are going to do our navigation, cooking and washing. I'm going to do the navigating. I want to do a lot of swimming and get some real rest for the campaign that lies ahead," the governor told the newsmen, adding that they would sail from Long Island, but that the exact place of his departure would be kept secret. The cruise, expected to last about a week, would end in New Hampshire, the first state to support Roosevelt's presidential primary bid. Not all would be pleasure, though, as he planned to take along a number of documents pertaining to state and national affairs.[2]

Sarah Powell Huntington of St. James, New York, recalls clearly the piles of documents that Roosevelt ordered put aboard *Myth II,* the thirty-seven foot yawl she and her husband, Prescott Butler Huntington, owned and had chartered to the governor. Mrs. Huntington said there was a great deal of concern on their part because the yawl was not watertight and the documents, stowed in the bilge, might get damaged. "It was an old boat. It leaked, and everybody knew it leaked," Mrs. Huntington said. "When his [Governor Roosevelt's] papers were put in the bilge, we were distressed that they might get wet." However, she said that Roosevelt and his advisors showed no concern.

The first of several boats she and her husband owned, Mrs. Huntington said that *Myth II* was an "ancient" yacht, constantly in need of repairs. She said the yacht was not suitable for FDR and that the head was "impossible for him to manage," but his sons felt it was "dandy" and said "the old man will love it."[3] First Mate Jimmy Roosevelt was concerned, as well, over the condition of the yawl. As he later recalled: "Frankly, I was nervous during the whole trip, because the *Myth II* leaked and I was afraid if heavy weather came out we might be losing ourselves both a father and a presidential candidate."[4]

Mrs. Huntington also remembers hiding the yacht along the Connecticut shore so that snooping reporters could not find it. "We called it the mystery ship," Mrs. Huntington said, because, at first, no one knew its name, its owner, or where it was moored. Mrs. Huntington said it was kept hidden while she and her husband caulked the bottom to stop the leaks. She does recall one reporter snooping around and actually finding *Myth II.* The ship was moored with its stern to the sea, however, so its name was not visible from the water. Mrs. Huntington said the reporter never bothered to go around the rear of the boat, so he never discovered that he actually had found Roosevelt's yawl.[5]

On 11 July 1932—nine days after accepting his party's nomination for president of the United States—Governor Roosevelt set sail from Port Jefferson, New York. Roosevelt said he had sailed those waters for forty years, and had been in almost every harbor from New York to Halifax, Nova Scotia. "I'm going to be navigator this time, but I will wash no dishes." Before departing, photographers asked Roosevelt to pose with his left hand on the yawl's wheel. Expert sailor that he was, Roosevelt balked. "Nothing doing," he laughed, "Don't you fellows know anything about sailing?"[6]

Because *Myth II* had no engine, a launch towed it from the dock and into the harbor. One thousand well-wishers on the shore cheered as the governor took control of his craft and skillfully navigated it into the strong winds whipping across Long Island Sound. "Get out of my wind," Roosevelt cheerfully called to reporters aboard the press boat following behind. His first port of call would be New Haven, Connecticut.

Although Roosevelt hoped to enjoy some private relaxation on the cruise, a public official of his stature could never completely escape press attention, especially after just having been nominated for the highest office in the land. Following in *Myth II*'s wake was *Marcon,* a boat full of reporters and photographers, and *Ambassadress,* a luxurious yacht chartered by political and financial supporters of Roosevelt, including financier and political operative Joseph P. Kennedy.

George Briggs's log of the trip recounted a tale of the press boat approaching *Myth II* a second time that same day, violating Roosevelt's pact with the press that called for only one contact per day. The log states: "Press boat *Marcon* comes up for the second time to take pictures while underway, contrary to agreement, and the Governor riz up and in no uncertain terms, told the swabs where to go. (Note—for the rest of the cruise they kept under heel like good doggies.) No further trouble and apologies and alibis that eve."[7]

Following a choppy sail across the sound, *Myth II* anchored at Morris Cove off the New Haven Yacht Club. After supper, Roosevelt was visited by newsmen, who were forced to row out to meet the governor after their motor boat broke down. Due to the heavy seas, the reporters were dripping wet when they greeted Roosevelt, who laughed and said, "I always wanted a sea-going press."[8] Some of the crew rowed ashore in their dinghy "for supplies, telegrams and various imaginary needs, including Bobby Delano, who joins ship," Briggs noted in the cruise's official log.[9]

The governor and his crew then settled down for an early sleep, to be rested and ready to begin "leg two" of their cruise. The next stop was Stonington, Connecticut, about fifty miles away. Roosevelt would seek the support of New England Democrats who had voted for Alfred E. Smith in the ex-governor's attempt to win the presidential nomination.

The following morning, *Myth II* got off to a later start than Roosevelt liked, and did not arrive at Stonington until near sunset. Roosevelt was greeted by political supporters and those whom he hoped to entice into his camp. Already sporting a deep tan, the governor told those gathered to greet him that he understood their support for Smith, but now that he was their party's standard-bearer, he expected the same kind of loyalty and support.[10] And he would get it.

Roosevelt was a dynamic and strong leader. Whether it was in the world of politics, foreign diplomacy, domestic affairs, or simply in the skippering of a tiny yawl through New England's unpredictable waters, Roosevelt always was in command. Aboard ship, he was a particularly firm taskmaster, as evidenced in Briggs's log entry, made somewhere on the waters between New Haven and Stonington: "By this time, the Skipper and the Mate [James Roosevelt] have struck their true stride, in fact are getting warmed to their work, and the rest of the crew seek relief in sleep, or at least out of earshot."[11]

Followed by a gentle wind, Roosevelt had completed the fifty-mile trip from New Haven to Stonington with ease. Once settled in the quiet harbor, his son John was sent rowing to town to pick up supplies. By the time he returned, steaks were grilling on the two-burner stove and Governor Roosevelt was relaxing on deck.

Ambassadress anchored nearby, with its passenger list sounding like a Who's Who of politics, including Joseph Kennedy; Robert Jackson, secretary of the Democratic National Committee; Frank Walker, assistant treasurer of the committee; and several other political leaders. During the cruise, Kennedy would come aboard the luxury yacht only for strategy sessions in the evenings; he would be ferried away in a seaplane so he could attend to other business, usually in New York City, or spend time with his family at their Hyannisport home.[12]

Despite Roosevelt's sudden emergence on the national political scene, he did not neglect the primary responsibilities of his current office. During the trip, he kept close tabs on his proposal for hydro-power development on the St. Lawrence River. Upon completion electricity would be distributed to New Yorkers via the new New York Power Authority, created when Roosevelt signed the measure into law a year earlier.

Development of the St. Lawrence project, which would not only generate electricity but also provide a navigable link between the Great Lakes and Atlantic Ocean, would require cooperation of the country's northern neighbor. Treaty negotiations between Canada and Herbert Hoover's administration ensued but Hoover, keenly aware of Roosevelt's desire to evict him from the White House, refused to allow Roosevelt's New York Power Authority to play a role in the talks.

In allocating costs for the St. Lawrence project, the Hoover administration set a figure for New York State that far exceeded what the state could pay. It was now clear to Roosevelt that Hoover was delaying completion of the U.S.–Canadian treaty while, at the same time, representing that negotiations between Washington and New York were proceeding smoothly. Hoover probably was hoping this would remove the issue from the upcoming presidential campaign.

But Roosevelt had other ideas. Two days before Roosevelt set sail from Port Jefferson, he sent President Hoover a telegram urging him to move forward expeditiously with the project. He offered to travel to Washington on forty-eight-hours notice to meet with the president. Hoover replied that talks between the United States and Canada were progressing well and it would not be necessary "to interrupt your cruise."[13] The treaty was signed later that year.

After a restful night's sleep in Stonington, Roosevelt weighed anchor the next morning for what would be an exciting sail to Cuttyhunk Island, some fifty miles due east. Roosevelt demonstrated his great skill as a navigator as he guided the tiny yawl through choppy white-capped water around Martha's Vineyard. Dropping anchor at Cuttyhunk, the governor and his crew settled back for a dinner of pork and beans, canned peaches, and—courtesy of *Ambassadress*—roast duckling.

Roosevelt's keen sailing ability did not go unnoticed, according to Briggs's log of the cruise. Briggs praises Roosevelt's "skillful handling" of the yawl. "From remarks gathered from the dock later in the evening, the natives were impressed."[14]

The following day's sail was brief—about twenty miles—and required a tow by a U.S. Coast Guard cutter from Cuttyhunk through a windless Buzzards Bay to Marion, Massachusetts, a Cape Cod seaside community where Roosevelt spent two summers years earlier as he battled to regain use of his legs. "This harbor is no new place to us," Roosevelt said. "We spent a summer here in 1927, and Franklin and John did their first sailing in a twelve foot catboat."

"We had some good sailing today even if we didn't get far. That's the fun of sailing. If you're headed for somewhere and the wind changes, why you just change your mind and go somewhere else," Roosevelt observed. Roosevelt certainly would deftly practice this same philosophy in his new responsibilities as commander in chief. As circumstances changed in domestic and world affairs, Roosevelt simply revised his plans and charted new courses. Rather than be "locked in" to an original and, perhaps, out-dated or politically unworkable plan, Roosevelt would make mid-course adjustments based on current situations and information.[15]

FDR's grandson, Curtis Roosevelt, agreed, adding: "FDR loved the game of life generally, of which sailing and politics are two very good examples. Both are subject to the vagaries of a lot of factors you can't con-trol. Yet both require an enormous amount of skill, particularly in the face of the unexpected."[16]

"The shrewd politician and the sailor, being one and the same, knew that the only certainty in the world is that the unexpected will occur," notes Gaddis Smith, professor of history at Yale University. "As a sailor, he [FDR] was comfortable with uncertainty and knew the necessity of com-promise. You have to tack—sometimes to the right, sometimes to the left. A storm can force you to heave to, remaining in one place or drifting back-ward. Fog can keep you at anchor. The sailor knows the impossibility of predicting the course to be followed on a voyage or the time of arrival."[17]

As the sun rose the next morning over Marion, *Myth II* was hooked up to *Ambassadress* so the yacht could tow the yawl through Cape Cod Canal. After cutting two canal entrance buoys, *Ambassadress* finally found the channel. With a flood tide against them, the vessels slowly made their way through the canal, whose banks and bridges were lined with well-wishers.

Unfortunately, because of the strain of the tow, Roosevelt's yawl started to leak, and the cabin floor began filling with water. After Roosevelt's crew pumped out the water, they were on their way to their next port of call—Marblehead, Massachusetts.

After a full day of sailing—with some very strong head winds—Roo-sevelt planned to anchor near the Eastern Yacht Club at Marblehead for the final night of his trip. With Marblehead in sight, Roosevelt and his crew suddenly were greeted by an unexpected—but welcome—visitor. Briggs's log describes the event:

> Lights of powerboat bear down on us. Proves to be "Seawolf" owned by Mate's father-in-law. Betsey Cushing Roosevelt, Jimmy's wife, and two of her friends had been following the course of *Myth II* all day, and wanted to surprise the governor and the boys with a visit. We are boarded by Mate's Mate and the Bosn of the "Lizzie M" and proceed under tow of the "Seawolf." Just outside Marblehead Light, we get lift off shore, drop tow and sail calmly into Marblehead, just as tho we done it all ourselves. Dropped anchor at 10:48 mid generous welcome considering the hour. Corinthian Y.C. offers to prolong their dance for us and Eastern Y.C. extends courtesies.

That night, Roosevelt and his crew dined on a lobster dinner while the governor conducted a rather unique "press conference" aboard *Myth II,* anchored about fifty feet away from the press boat. Reporters shouted their questions to Roosevelt who, in turn, shouted his answers across the calm waters.

Roosevelt got a late start the next morning on the final leg of his cruise. *Myth II* glided out of Marblehead around noon en route to Portsmouth, New Hampshire, some forty miles away. He visited with friends and well-wishers at Marblehead before taking *Myth II* into Massachusetts Bay. This final forty miles of the three-hundred-mile journey saw perfect sailing weather, with a brisk southeast wind propelling the governor and his crew to their final destination—Little Harbor near Portsmouth, New Hampshire.

The official log notes that the "sea continues to get worse as we get down into the ebb set for Portsmouth Harbor entrance. Just off Little Harbor entrance it was very steep and short. During this run the Skipper and Mate dug deep for the best and last yarns, which results in the Mate going down with colors flying. He could not equal the 'houseboat-hunting lodge-in-the-Pine' and honors go to the Governor," an obvious reference to FDR's houseboat which, in 1926, was destroyed by a hurricane that swept the boat miles from the water, coming to rest in a Florida pine forest. Briggs's final entry in the ship's log reads: "Anchored in Little Harbor and regret the cruise is over. No more cinnamon eggs. No more fires in the galley. Bobby had learned to spell Kutty Sunk. Frank did not get to

Newport but he tried hard. We have one whole batten left in the mainsail, so the cruise is a grand success."[18]

Just how successful the trip was, from a campaign viewpoint, would be left to the judgment of historians. One such Roosevelt scholar, biographer Kenneth S. Davis, believes the cruise achieved two very important goals. It helped to nullify Republican efforts to depict Roosevelt as a helpless cripple, hardly able to care for himself let alone lead a troubled nation. Instead, Davis notes, daily press and newsreel accounts showed a robust, highly skilled blue-water sailor, muscular and self confident, with a sun-tanned vigor and a laughing zest for life. This picture was in sharp contrast to Hoover's formal, buttoned-up demeanor and tense, remote images seen by most Americans.

Second, Davis believes the cruise helped to unify the factionalized Democrats. Roosevelt was now firmly in command. In addition, this unity —along with the urging of his friends—helped convince Smith to accept his loss of the nomination and rally behind the new Democratic nominee.[19]

Curtis Roosevelt, FDR's grandson, took a slightly different view of the cruise and its purpose: "I don't think it was a particular demonstration of his being able to cope with being crippled. I think it was a demonstration of his confidence—somebody that could do something well that required dexterity. It's not something the average person does." Curtis noted that his grandfather "always did things for several reasons," and acknowledged that FDR was not unmindful about answering his critics. "I think he instinctively knew there would be a general sense of admiration for somebody who could sail a boat with his sons that distance," Curtis Roosevelt observed.[20]

Although the cruise was over when he reached Little Harbor, Roosevelt stayed on board the last night and through heavy thunderstorms that drenched the area the following morning. Around noon, he left *Myth II* and motored to Hampton Beach, New Hampshire, where fifty thousand people hailed him as the next president of the United States.

Fittingly, Roosevelt would deliver his first speech of the presidential campaign in New Hampshire, the state that delivered his first primary victory. Hoover, however, would go on to win New Hampshire in the general election. Because it was Sunday, FDR vowed to stay clear of politics; instead he spoke of his recent cruise and memories of the area. "My friends of Maine, New Hampshire, Massachusetts and all points West," began Roosevelt, "this is a delightful welcome home for an ancient mariner. We are just through with a cruise from Long Island and we have had a very wonderful week with no casualties except losing some skin off the ends of our noses and some long hair that almost fouled the main sheet."[21]

After overnighting at Jimmy's Little Boar's Head, New Hampshire, home and visiting with Roosevelt's young granddaughter, Sara Delano Roosevelt, the governor boarded an automobile the next morning, bound for Albany. The vacation cruise was over. The campaign to oust Hoover from the White House, begun a week earlier with the launching of a tiny, leaking yawl from Long Island, would now get under way in earnest.

CHAPTER 6

Ready to Be
Shanghaied

The campaign to unseat Herbert Hoover was vigorous and demanding, leaving little time for Roosevelt to enjoy sailing. Indeed, he was far from the salt air as he crisscrossed the country aboard trains and automobiles in search of votes. When Election Day finally came, almost twenty-three million Americans chose him to lead their nation. Roosevelt won all but six of the nation's forty-eight states; Hoover took Maine, New Hampshire, Vermont, Connecticut, Pennsylvania, and Delaware.

With almost thirteen million Americans out of work, and wages—for those lucky enough to have jobs—falling approximately 43 percent, Americans were putting all their faith into a wheelchair-bound president to lift the nation from economic disaster. Roosevelt had his work cut out for him.

During his campaign Roosevelt did not stop thinking and writing about seagoing adventures. Upon his return to Albany in 1932 after the *Myth II* cruise, Roosevelt wrote to Mrs. Walter Amory, a distant relative, who summered on Naushon Island in Cape Cod's Buzzards Bay. He expressed his regret for not stopping at Naushon Island for the "wonderful feast" she had prepared. Lack of wind prevented them from getting to the island, but he promised that "a similar trip is definitely on the books for next year."[1] True to his word, President Roosevelt made a Naushon Island visit during his New England vacation cruise in June 1933.

Although embroiled in the spirited 1932 presidential campaign, the sea was still on Roosevelt's mind when he wrote his mother, expressing his concern over the deteriorating condition of the boathouse at their Campobello summer home. "This is sad news about my boathouse. It seems to me that if it is about to fall down and not worth repairing, it would be a good idea to have it taken down and chopped into firewood. I take it that *Vireo* is in your boathouse," Roosevelt wrote. *Vireo* was the small sailboat he used to teach his sons to sail.[2]

Ten days after Roosevelt arrived at the White House, plans were under way to build a White House pool so the president could continue swimming and exercising his legs as he had been doing at Warm Springs and Hyde Park. The *New York Daily News* announced a campaign to raise money for the new pool. Other newspapers joined, and by 26 March, almost twenty-three thousand dollars had been raised. Donations of services and equipment amounted to another ten thousand dollars. Congress passed a resolution authorizing construction of the pool on 27 March. During excavation at the year-round pool site in the old west wing of the White House, the floor of an old stable from the days of President James Monroe was discovered. The brick pavers and gutters of the stable were still intact.

At an April press conference, while the pool construction was under way, a correspondent asked whether reporters would be allowed to use the pool as well. The president said they would. He said they also could use the White House tennis courts. The president added: "And the children have a sandpile, too. You boys can play in it, if you like."[3]

The pool was dedicated on 2 June 1933. Speaking from his wheelchair at poolside, Roosevelt told the assembled workers that he once built a pool and "when I had completed it the pool fell in." He said he was confident that this pool will "stand up." The president continued, "I want you men to know that this pool will be a big help to me, and it will be about the only air I can get. It will be one of the greatest pleasures for me during my stay in the White House."[4]

No matter where he traveled, Roosevelt surrounded himself with items that reminded him of the sea. He collected, and sometimes re-rigged, ship models. He purchased nautical prints and paintings. His library of naval books totaled twenty-five hundred volumes; his full library totaled fifteen thousand volumes at his death. He collected ship logs, pamphlets, broadsides, letters, sheet music, relics, and other naval documents.

Roosevelt's collection of naval prints, paintings, and watercolors totaled five thousand. He personally hung them in the White House, Campobello, Warm Springs, and Springwood. Dozens of his prints at Springwood remain today exactly as he placed them. An oil painting commemorating FDR's famous 1933 cruise aboard *Amberjack II* was presented to the president by artist Jonas Lie in 1933; FDR hung it in his study in the White House. Prior to beginning the oil, Lie had visited the White House to study the prevailing light effects on the location where the painting would likely hang. Later, it was transferred to Roosevelt's personal Hyde Park retreat, Top Cottage, and hung over the fieldstone fireplace in the living room. It was still hanging there at Roosevelt's death in 1945. In 2001, the painting, inscribed to Roosevelt by the artist, sold for $149,000 at auction.[5]

Roosevelt collected so many mementos from his sailing and fishing trips that the reception and conference room near the Oval Office became known as the "Fish Room" due to the volume of memorabilia housed there. Every room in the White House had ship model displays and the second floor residence was decorated in a ship model motif. Naval prints hung on the walls of the president's private second floor study, where a two-foot model of the destroyer USS *Bainbridge* was displayed on the mantel along with a model of *Amberjack II*.[6]

Roosevelt had begun collecting as a child, and continued while attending Groton and Harvard. He was most active collecting naval items, however, during his years as assistant secretary of the navy in the Wilson administration and while recuperating from polio. He once said that during his recuperation he owed his life to his hobbies, which also included stamp collecting that he had begun at age nine. At his death, he had assembled more than 150 albums, containing about 20,000 stamps. When his total stamp collection was cataloged, it was found to number more than 1.2 million stamps, with about 80 percent having little value, or what the president called "scrap." Sketches of proposed stamps and final proofs all were personally reviewed and approved by Roosevelt prior to issue during his years in the White House. He often made revisions and corrections to the proofs. After inspecting the proof of the Byrd Antarctic commemorative stamp, he ordered a revision on the location of Byrd's landing in France. "He landed farther north than that," the president observed. Review of the twenty cent transpacific airmail proof was corrected when Roosevelt pointed out that the clipper ship should have three masts, not two. During his administration, 134 new commemoratives and 49 regular stamps were issued.[7]

Although better remembered as a stamp collector, Roosevelt spent as much time and a great deal more money on his naval collection. FDR's purchase of naval prints and paintings declined after 1939 because, as he advised his secretary, "I have practically all of them but I am not buying any more prints. I have no more wall space." One White House visitor in 1938 noted that "there is indeed little wall space in the White House where pictures of the Navy or of the sea do not hang."[8]

While actively collecting, FDR did so omnivorously. Newman McGirr, owner of an antiquarian bookstore in Philadelphia since 1912, said Franklin Roosevelt was one of his best customers. In addition to books, McGirr sold paintings, prints, and manuscripts. He remembers when Roosevelt first came through his door, around 1920. McGirr, who already had sold FDR items through the mail, said Roosevelt bought six original oil paintings by Xanthus Smith, a sailor in a squadron commanded by Adm. Samuel DuPont during the blockade of the Confederate seaports in the Civil War.

McGirr said Roosevelt continued to purchase paintings, books, and other items from him throughout his presidency until his attention was diverted by the war. "He did not confine himself to rarities," McGirr recalled. "He was sort of omnivorous in his collecting." Roosevelt collected things that caught his eye, regardless of whether a painting was by a well-known artist, or a book by a famous author. For example, McGirr recalls, he had an oil painting of the ship *John Adams* sailing into Valparaiso Harbor; it was painted on a piece of sail cloth and crudely framed by the ship carpenter, a McGirr ancestor. "I wrote all the information about it on the back of it and wrote to Mr. Roosevelt about it and he purchased it."[9]

Although known to be a frugal individual with money throughout his life, Roosevelt never questioned the prices of the items, McGirr said. "I don't know whether he ever declined to buy any items because he thought the price was too high, but he never haggled over prices. He always paid the list price without question," McGirr said. "I think he was aiming toward a collection that would give the spirit and the history and the atmosphere of the sea and ships and the Navy," McGirr said. McGirr also noted that Roosevelt purchased books, prints, and paintings from a variety of dealers throughout the country.[10] In addition to ordering through the mail, Roosevelt attended hundreds of auctions prior to being stricken with polio in 1921 or sent Louis Howe, his trusted assistant, in his stead.

From 1921 until his election as New York's governor in 1928, Roosevelt started to catalog his books. He wrote out in longhand some nine hundred cards. He also started to write a biography of John Paul Jones, whose career he admired. Jones, like both Franklin and Theodore Roosevelt, was a firm believer in a strong navy for defense.

In 1962 President John F. Kennedy, a great admirer of Roosevelt and a collector of nautical items himself, stated that he believed Roosevelt's naval collection was intended as a reminder of the "strength and style of our naval tradition—the tradition of daring and devotion which has sustained our Navy in war and which makes it today a mainstay of peace in a troubled world."[11] Kennedy said Roosevelt built his collection by "wary and intelligent choice rather than by laying out great sums of money." In fact, Roosevelt seldom spent more than ten dollars for an individual book, manuscript, or stamp. Kennedy tells of an incident, in the summer of 1933 when a Virginian wrote to Roosevelt offering to sell him two prints of the naval war with Tripoli. Roosevelt returned the letter with "How much?" scrawled at the top. The owner asked $100 each. Roosevelt finally got both for $150. Today the prints are worth several thousand dollars each.[12]

Bookseller McGirr's business began to falter during the Depression and, at the urging of the president, he moved to Washington in 1935. He was appointed to the newly created National Archives, where he helped to set up the Archives' reference library. Although coming from a family of "rank Republicans," McGirr voted for FDR and had a great admiration for him: "[H]e had the welfare of the general public and the small man at heart more than any President that has ever occupied that position." McGirr composed a brief poem, "To Meet His Pilot," to honor his famous customer and, later, his boss:

> Sailing his craft with joy, the happy boy;
> Sailing the Ship of State, the Man grown great.
> Firm hand upon the wheel—an even keel.
> Until the call, and he put out to sea.[13]

After Election Day 1932, Roosevelt could do more than just read and think about being on the water. Now he could make real plans for his return to the sea. He would travel in style aboard Vincent Astor's luxurious yacht *Nourmahal,* a far cry from the tiny, leaking *Myth II,* the yawl he had sailed along the New England coast the previous July. President-elect

FDR chose to rest and prepare for his new job in Washington by taking an eleven-day fishing trip with some of the most powerful and richest men in the country.

After a swing through the south to tout his plans to bring public power to the Tennessee Valley, FDR stopped at Warm Springs and celebrated his fifty-first birthday. Then, it was on to Florida for his fishing trip to the Bahamas. On the evening of 3 February 1933, he boarded a special train for the overnight trip to Florida. The following day he embarked on *Nourmahal,* a 263-foot, diesel-powered, German-built yacht. Joining FDR aboard *Nourmahal* were Kermit Roosevelt, son of former president Theodore Roosevelt; George Baker St. George, a wealthy Republican from Tuxedo Park, New York, whose wife, Katharine, was FDR's first cousin; Frederic Kernochan, a Democratic New York City judge; and Leslie W. Heiter, Astor's physician friend who functioned as the ship's doctor. Vincent Astor, a Dutchess County neighbor of Roosevelt, was related to him by marriage; FDR's half brother James Roosevelt, known as "Rosy," was married to Astor's aunt. Astor was "absolutely devoted to President Roosevelt and looked to him as a father," Astor's wife, Brooke, recalled.[14] Astor was founder and owner of *Newsweek* magazine, which became a great supporter of New Deal programs.

As the luxury yacht was pulling away from the dock, Roosevelt, Astor, Kermit Roosevelt, and the others—Harvard men all—stood at the rail, dressed in blazers and flannels, smoking pipes and cigarettes. Edward Flynn, the Bronx Democratic boss, watched from the pier, and scornfully remarked: "The Hasty Pudding Club puts out to sea."[15] After two days at sea, Roosevelt wrote to his mother, saying that he was "getting a marvelous rest—lots of air and sun." He continued: "Vincent is a dear and perfect host. George and Kermit and Freddie and the young Doctor are excellent companions. When we land on the 15th I shall be full of health and vigor—the last holiday for many months."[16]

Unfortunately, Roosevelt's choice of traveling companions, as well as the luxurious yacht, described as "an ocean liner in miniature," sparked criticism in some quarters, particularly in one Republican newspaper, the *New York Sun*. A portion of the composition, titled "At Sea with Franklin D.," read:

> They were just good friends with no selfish ends
> To serve as they paced the decks;

there were George and Fred and the son of Ted
And Vincent (he signed the checks);
On the splendid yacht in a climate hot
To Tropical seas they ran
Among those behind they dismissed from mind
Was the well-known Forgotten Man![17]

James Roosevelt later would ponder why his father chose such traveling companions, particularly at a time when he was doing so much to
change the sort of world for which *Nourmahal* was a symbol. He noted
that there was not a man in the crowd for whom the president-elect had
any "deep intellectual or political affinity." James concluded, stating that
his father "did not choose the list—he, too, was a guest aboard the
Nourmahal—but he joined in the company voluntarily and accepted its
society. . . . It was as if the company were an escape for him—an escape
back to the world of Groton, Harvard, Fly Club, Hyde Park and other
things far removed from the pragmatic, vital arena in which Father now
was operating."[18]

The post-election *Nourmahal* cruise brought FDR peace and relaxation. Eleven days later, on 15 February, he and his party returned to mainland Florida. Roosevelt's serenity was suddenly shattered by gunfire from
a would-be assassin. The bullets barely missed striking him as he ended a
speech in an open touring car at Miami's Bay Front Park.

The tanned and rejuvenated president-elect had been met at the pier
by a large welcoming committee of dignitaries, honoring the man who
would be president in less than three weeks. An estimated ten to twenty
thousand people gathered at the park to hear Roosevelt. He spoke of
spending winters in Florida in the 1920s aboard his houseboats—*Weona II*
and *Larooco*—where he and his friends enjoyed fishing and swimming in
the warm waters, and sunning themselves. He told the crowd that he
would refrain from telling them any "fish stories" today, but did say they
caught a great number of fish on this cruise. "The only fly in the ointment
on my trip has been that I have put on about ten pounds," Roosevelt told
the admiring crowd. After these brief remarks, he posed for photographers and then settled back into the car's rear seat. The first of five gun-
shots rang out.

The *New York Times* reported that a fearless Roosevelt "except for an
involuntary start backward at the sound of the first shot, showed remark-

able composure. . . . The President-elect, feeling the bullets were intended for him, straightened up, set his jaw and sat unflinching with the calm courage in the face of danger which would be expected of one of his family."[19] Demonstrating his courage and composure, Roosevelt instructed the Secret Service and police to protect the assassin, later identified as Giuseppe Zangara, from the angry crowd. Anton J. Cermak, Chicago's mayor, was fatally wounded in the attack; four others were hurt. President-elect Roosevelt was unscathed. A Miami woman, Lillian Cross, was credited with possibly saving Roosevelt's life when, standing near Zangara, she hit the gunman's arm with her handbag, thereby diverting his aim.

As Secret Service agents quickly started the car to remove the president-elect from further danger, Roosevelt ordered the car be stopped and that Mayor Cermak be placed in the car with him. Roosevelt kept his hand on the mayor's pulse on the way to the hospital, where he valiantly clung to life for almost a month.

Zangara, a thirty-three-year-old naturalized citizen and unemployed bricklayer, said he despised all presidents. He was tried and convicted of Cermak's murder. He was executed in Florida's electric chair thirty-five days after firing at Roosevelt.

Although scheduled to leave Miami by train for Washington that night, Roosevelt decided to spend another night aboard *Nourmahal* so he could check on the condition of Mayor Cermak and the others the next morning. Raymond Moley, a Roosevelt advisor who was with iron-nerved Roosevelt that last night aboard the yacht, later recalled how calm the president-elect appeared after his brush with death. "There was nothing—not so much as the twitching of a muscle, the mopping of a brow, or even the hint of false gaiety—to indicate that it wasn't any other evening in any other place," Moley wrote. "I have never in my life seen anything more magnificent."[20]

This incident provides a clue to how Roosevelt would view the need for protection throughout his presidency. A year later, with the assassination attempt still fresh in the minds of the Secret Service, agents advised Roosevelt to cancel an appearance in Portland, Oregon, because a plot against his life had been discovered. The president vetoed this advice, saying "Every public appearance of a chief executive entails an element of risk; but do you want me to become a prisoner in the White House, more and more apprehensive until I'm afraid to go near a window? If anyone wants to kill me, there is no possible way to prevent him. About all that can be done is to guard against a second shot."[21]

The 1933 pre-inaugural cruise was the first of three lengthy fishing cruises that Roosevelt took aboard the palatial yacht. He also took one brief weekend cruise aboard *Nourmahal* in 1933. In describing *Nourmahal* to a friend, Roosevelt wrote that it was "the only place I can get away from people, telephones and uniforms."[22]

The Roosevelt-Astor relationship would soon take on a new twist, a very strange turn, indeed, as Astor assumed the special clandestine duties of an American spy. Beginning in 1933 and stretching into the early war years, Astor funneled information directly to President Roosevelt. Aside from these secret matters, dubbed "The Roosevelt-Astor Espionage Ring,"[23] the pair also continued their correspondence on a less serious level as well—at least less serious to the nation, although not, perhaps, to them. In a 4 August 1933 letter to Astor, President Roosevelt wrote: "Your deck-hand and his duffel bag stand ready to be shanghaied at the Dutton Lumber Company on Thursday, anytime after twelve noon."[24]

Although this was a brief trip aboard the yacht, it nonetheless took Roosevelt away from the steamy Washington weather. The president was "shanghaied" by Astor at the lumber company dock in Poughkeepsie, New York, for a brief Labor Day cruise aboard *Nourmahal*. With the presidential flag flying from the masthead, the yacht set sail down the Hudson River, around Manhattan, and up the East River to Long Island Sound. Two navy destroyers, USS *Twiggs* and USS *Manley*, trailed the president. USS *Twiggs* later was turned over to the Royal Navy as part of the Roosevelt-Churchill "destroyer for bases" pact; it was one of fifty World War I destroyers transferred to England in return for ninety-nine year leases on several strategic bases in the Western Hemisphere.

The president's mother, his daughter Anna, and his two grandchildren Sistie and Buzzie were among a crowd of well-wishers assembled at the wharf to bid farewell. From Poughkeepsie to the Battery, people lined the shores of the Hudson River, waving and cheering the president as he sailed by.[25] *Nourmahal* anchored in Fort Pond Bay, off Montauk, Long Island, and Roosevelt left the yacht in the small sloop *Orca* to do some fishing. His luck was pretty good; he hauled in sea bass, porgies, and tuna despite heavy swells and stormy conditions. Capt. Herman Gray, who piloted the sloop for Roosevelt, observed, "President Roosevelt has what it takes to be a good fisherman—plenty of patience. They don't bite any faster for a president than for a plumber, you know." Clad only in shoes and white duck trousers, Roosevelt took a sunbath while waiting for fish to bite. "No shirt?" Captain Gray was asked. "No, he's a regular guy, he doesn't need a shirt."[26]

Astor then took his yacht south to Ocean City, Maryland, where he and the president boarded *Orca* for a few more hours of fishing. The next day, outside of Virginia Capes, Roosevelt hooked a one-hundred-pound turtle, which was sent over to the destroyer for inclusion on that night's mess menu. On 6 September, with the brief summer cruise over, Roosevelt returned to Washington and went back to work. That night, he entertained his shipmates at a White House reception.[27]

Meanwhile, storm clouds were gathering around the increasingly unstable world, requiring the sharp attention of the president. Long intrigued by espionage and intelligence work, Roosevelt employed his old friend and neighbor, Astor, to keep him apprised of activities in various parts of the world. According to historian Jeffrey M. Dorwart, Astor served as an intermediary. Most of the information first came from the Caribbean and Panama Canal Zone; later, Astor monitored Latin America, the Galapagos Islands, the Marshall Islands, and other areas that the commander in chief felt were critical. For example, in 1936 Roosevelt was interested in what the Japanese might be doing on the Marshall Islands in the South Pacific. Conveniently, Astor and his sailing pal Kermit Roosevelt planned a "scientific expedition" there as a cover for their espionage work.[28]

On another 1936 trip Astor, a former submariner in World War I, traveled to the Galapagos Islands to investigate rumors that the Japanese might be planning to locate a base there. Upon returning, Astor sent the president a letter, saying that it was a "swell" trip, and thanking Roosevelt for getting the necessary fishing permits for him. He attached a long list of their catch, but didn't mention anything about catching any intelligence. That was better left to a personal meeting, which Astor said he would like to arrange with the president.[29]

In March 1941 Roosevelt formalized Astor's role in providing intelligence to Washington by appointing him as area controller, with responsibility for coordinating intelligence work in the New York area. Accordingly,

Capt. A. G. Kirk, director of naval intelligence, issued a secret directive assigning Astor, a commander in the U.S. Naval Reserve, the job of resolving conflicts or potential conflicts in the intelligence or investigational fields among the Departments of State, War, Navy, and Justice. According to Kirk's order, only he, the commandant of the Third Naval District (and, of course, the president), would know the exact status, duties, and office location of Astor.[30]

However, the issuance of Kirk's directive came in the waning days of Astor's espionage activities. Within a few months, Astor would become ill from stomach problems and then, on 7 December, the United States was thrust into the war as a result of Japan's attack on Pearl Harbor. The picture had changed dramatically and the stakes, suddenly, were much higher. The Roosevelt-Astor connection was much more enjoyable to FDR when they were sailing together aboard *Nourmahal* rather than exchanging espionage secrets.

Washington was damp and dreary in March 1934. Capitol Hill was in turmoil. Roosevelt decided it was time to once again head to the open ocean, in what would be one of the longest absences of a president from Washington while Congress was in session. Nevertheless, promptly at 5 P.M. on 27 March, he boarded his special train en route to Florida, the first time he returned to that state since he narrowly escaped an assassin's bullets the previous year.

Roosevelt embarked from Jacksonville, Florida, once again with his friends—the "*Nourmahal* gang"—aboard *Nourmahal* for a ten-day Easter cruise in southern waters. No White House aides accompanied FDR, although his yacht was trailed by USS *Ellis* with his contingent of Secret Service agents. Marvin H. McIntyre, a presidential aide, set up a temporary White House office in the Miami Biltmore Hotel. Mail pouches with work for the president were flown by seaplane daily from Washington to Miami. McIntyre and a handful of secretaries would sort it before sending it to Roosevelt.

Jimmy Roosevelt later recalled the cruise because it was the first time he was invited to sail aboard Astor's yacht. "It was a rollicking fishing cruise into Southern waters. . . . The trip was memorable because it was one of the few times I recall that Pa lost his temper completely with one of his children—in this case, Elliott—and the only time I ever knew him to display anger over a family matter in front of an outsider." While anchored off Gun Cay Island in the Bahamas, Roosevelt received word that a navy seaplane was on its way to deliver not only the White House mail, but also FDR's son Elliott. Roosevelt apparently became annoyed. Elliott had not been invited and FDR was already upset with him for, as Jimmy put it, "some . . . exploits which had not been in the newspaper." The president ordered Astor not to allow him to board *Nourmahal;* he then went off in a small boat to do some deep-sea fishing. Elliott arrived, according to Jimmy, with a "monumental hangover" from celebrating the night before. Astor quickly took him aboard and hustled him into the shower. When Roosevelt returned, he gave Elliott a stern lecture and sent him back to the seaplane, which was bouncing in the waters off the yacht—not exactly the perfect setting for one suffering the effects of a hangover.

Elliott had his revenge when he returned to land, however. He rounded up some reporters and told them a "fantastic yarn," according to FDR, about the outcome of a fishing contest the president lost. The reporters demanded to come aboard *Nourmahal,* which the president later allowed. Roosevelt then staged a mock trial, in which Elliott was the "absent defendant" and accused him of "gross libel." The president "testified" that he took a sperm whale on a three-ounce hook. The trial was "inconclusive," according to Jimmy, "but everyone went back to Miami in good humor."[31]

Prior to Elliot's arrival, the president had celebrated Easter Sunday services aboard the yacht. A cloudless blue sky greeted Roosevelt on Easter morning while *Nourmahal* was anchored in the warm waters of the Bahamas. Reading from the Book of Common Prayer of the Episcopal Church, the president conducted Easter services on the quarterdeck of the ship. FDR followed the tradition that dictated, in the absence of a chaplain, the senior officer aboard a ship at sea conducts religious services.[32] A longtime senior warden of St. James Episcopal Church in Hyde Park and the product of an Episcopal boarding school, FDR probably relished this role.

Tanned and relaxed, the president was having a grand time sailing and fishing. He decided to extend his vacation cruise another week. Marlin and barracuda started biting for the president when the yacht was anchored in an area of the southern Bahamas known as Elbow Key. The president also enjoyed several pleasant and therapeutic swims in the warm Carribban waters. But, this vacation could not last indefinitely. After seventeen days at sea, a rejuvenated president docked in Miami, and boarded his train bound for Washington.

Later that summer, while Roosevelt was traveling aboard a train in East St. Louis on his way to the funeral of former House of Representatives Speaker Henry Rainey, he wrote Astor a short letter. "The only decent thing for public officials to do is to die at sea and get put overboard without fuss or feathers!" He told Astor that he hoped he could join him in a couple of days in the fall at Newport. FDR was able to visit Astor in September and attended the America's Cup Race.[33]

Roosevelt's final cruise aboard *Nourmahal* took place in 1935 when he embarked from Jacksonville, Florida, on 27 March for a twelve-day cruise in the waters of the Bahamas. Congress, still in session, was in turmoil, and deadlocked on several important matters. Nevertheless, FDR had decided it was time for a little deep-sea fishing. It would be the last time the president would sail with the old *Nourmahal* gang. The original group —Astor, Kermit Roosevelt, Judge Kernochan, George St. George, and Dr. Heiter—was aboard, ready to receive the president upon his arrival. Prior to departure, Roosevelt received word that Louis Howe, who was gravely ill, would likely only live another two weeks. If Howe's condition worsened, Roosevelt was prepared to return to Washington. Howe, however, lingered for another full year before succumbing in April 1936 to a combination of respiratory and cardiac ailments.

Following a ceremonial greeting by Florida's governor, Jacksonville's mayor, and other dignitaries, Roosevelt took a drive through town. Arriving at Commodore's Point, he embarked on the destroyer USS *Farragut III*—the first new American destroyer commissioned in fourteen years. Escorted by USS *Claxton,* the ship set a course for Cat Cay and its rendezvous with *Nourmahal.* According to the official log of this trip, maintained by Roosevelt's naval aide, Capt. Wilson Brown, it was too windy for movies on board that night. "President indicated keen interest in all details of construction and design of *Farragut,*" Brown wrote.

The next morning, *Farragut* arrived alongside Astor's yacht, and the president and two Secret Service agents transferred aboard. Astor had prepared a luncheon for the president, the Duke and Duchess of Kent, and the governor general of the Bahamas and his wife, all of whom had been invited to dine with the party before departure. After lunch, *Nourmahal* set sail for Lobos Cay, where arrangements had been made with Pan American Airways to stop on its regular trip to Miami, to transfer Jimmy Roosevelt to *Nourmahal.*

Roosevelt and the others spent their first full day of deep-sea fishing with moderate success, according to the log. The gang continued to fish and, later that afternoon, *Nourmahal* and its U.S. Navy contingent headed for Great Inagua Island, near the eastern tip of Cuba, about 240 miles away.

Communications to the president were voluminous. Dozens of dispatches were sent daily via the ship's radio; mail was ferried to and from Washington via seaplane and the temporary White House once again set up in the Miami Biltmore, staffed by Marvin McIntyre. After several days of good to excellent fishing, lots of relaxing, and plenty of sun, the president and a small party left *Nourmahal,* at anchor off Crooked Island, to explore a narrow tidal pool that led inland about five miles. When Roosevelt and his party failed to return by early afternoon, a rescue expedition was formed with men from *Nourmahal* and *Farragut.* But the worry was needless; "the rescuers had scarcely cleared the ships when the explorers hove in sight," Brown recorded in the ship's log.

After several more days of fishing, ranging from disappointing to excellent, *Nourmahal* returned to Jacksonville. On 8 April FDR's final cruise aboard this marvelous luxury yacht was over. The deepening international crisis would force the yacht's recreational sailing days to an end in March 1942, when it was transferred to the U.S. Navy. The following year, ownership was transferred to the U.S. Coast Guard for use in ocean station weather patrol in Boston. After the war, the yacht served the James River Maritime Reserve Fleet until it was scrapped in 1964.[34]

Despite nursing a painful sunburn, Roosevelt was content at the conclusion of his twelve hundred mile cruise. He was ready to return to Washington and oversee the next stage of his New Deal, outlined in his State of the Union Message three months earlier. While he was away, Congress adopted a key component of his plan, the Emergency Relief Appropriation Act. It authorized five billion dollars for immediate relief and allowed the creation of the Works Progress Administration, which would eventually put more than eight million Americans to work.

Roosevelt's naval aide summed up the trip: "The cruise was a complete success in that the President had two weeks of rest, recreation and outdoor exercise. The mild climate of the Bahamas was a pleasant break from the raw weather in Washington. The President, while still directing the affairs of state, and being kept constantly informed by radio and mail of the affairs of government and international situation, had a complete break from the normal office procedure. He spent many hours each day in an open boat under the most restful conditions." President Roosevelt issued a final press dispatch: "We hugged azure skies, golden sands, turquoise depths, lush pampas, intriguing inlets, basking lizards, swooping seagulls, winking stars, snapping turtles, lovely doves, verdant seaweeds, and perfect serenity."[35] Franklin Roosevelt's "perfect serenity" soon would be drawing to a close.

CHAPTER 7

Floating
White House

In the summer of 1934, pressures on the White House began mounting. Some twelve thousand longshoremen were striking in San Francisco. Organized labor was calling for a "general strike," the first of its kind in American history. There was a feud brewing among Roosevelt's Cabinet officers over whether there was enough money to continue Roosevelt's relief efforts already under way throughout the country and his commitment to large public works projects.

What's more, Roosevelt also was receiving criticism, some from within his own Cabinet, for proposing that Joseph P. Kennedy head the new Securities and Exchange Commission, authorized by law in June. Secretary of the Interior Harold L. Ickes, a close FDR advisor, called Kennedy a "stock market plunger," but Roosevelt felt the new agency could best accomplish its mission if an insider, someone who knew the ropes in the financial world, guided it.[1] Kennedy had been an early and strong financial backer of FDR in 1932, so some perceived this as Kennedy's reward.

Roosevelt also was starting to sense—and resent—a building public hostility for him and his programs, according to Roosevelt biographer Kenneth S. Davis. The president could not understand why wealthy U.S. capitalists did not realize that he was "the best friend the profit system ever had."[2]

In what would become a routine when things got "hot" in Washington, Roosevelt took off for the open ocean to think, relax, and refresh his spirit. In his fifth Fireside Chat, in which he defended his administration's accomplishments, he asked his listeners: "Are you better off than you were last year?" Three days later, on 1 July 1934, the besieged president boarded the heavy cruiser USS *Houston* and set sail for warm southern waters. The month-long holiday trip took him more than fourteen thousand miles: to Haiti, Puerto Rico, the Virgin Islands, Columbia, Canal Zone, and then through the Panama Canal to Hawaii.

Steaming the first leg of 1,254 miles, Roosevelt arrived at Haiti on 5 July and met on board with Stenio Vincent, Haiti's first freely elected president. Around lunchtime the next day, *Houston* steamed east to Puerto Rico, where FDR disembarked for a motor trip through San Juan with Governor Blanton Winship. The first American president to visit Haiti, he stayed overnight in the governor's mansion.

Continuing his island-hopping tour, Roosevelt next visited St. Thomas, where he toured the island and dined aboard *Houston* with Paul Pearson, the Virgin Islands governor since his appointment in 1933. As the sun rose on Sunday, 8 July, the cruiser steamed thirty-eight miles to its next port of call—St. Croix, where Roosevelt again would leave the ship for a motor tour. He did not stay overnight, but departed around dinner time for the eight-hundred-mile trip to Columbia. After he visited dignitaries there, the cruiser steamed to Cristobal, Canal Zone, where it picked up the president of the Canal Zone for the eight-mile transit through the Panama Canal. After passing through the canal, Roosevelt boarded a small motor launch for some fishing off Cocos Island.

Roosevelt returned to the ship, ate dinner, and went to bed. The next day, *Houston* began the longest leg of its journey—the four-thousand-mile trek to Hawaii. The president again boarded his small motor launch for some fishing before stepping ashore in Hawaii, the first American president ever to visit the Hawaiian islands. Roosevelt toured the islands on 26 July. The president was treated to a luau the following day and then boarded *Houston* for the return trip to the U.S. mainland.[3]

Although Roosevelt did not want to show favoritism for any single naval vessel, *Houston* became FDR's flagship, his "floating White House." Previously, the ten thousand ton cruiser was the flagship of the Asiatic fleet. The president occupied the admiral's commodious quarters whenever he was aboard. During his White House years, Roosevelt took four lengthy cruises aboard the heavy cruiser.

In preparation for his 1934 cruise, a thirty-foot former navy tender was refurbished for use as a fishing boat. It was placed aboard the six-hundred-foot cruiser for use when the president was in good fishing waters. Two wood swivel chairs, each with a swivel socket for the butt of a fishing rod, were built for the fishing boat. Between the chairs, a small water cooler, with receptacles for cups, was installed.[4]

The White House sent along forty Hollywood films, some not yet released to the public, and about three hundred books for the president's onboard library. About fifty books were detective stories, which FDR frequently would read to put himself to sleep. Also included were periodicals from the U.S. Naval Institute.[5]

Four Filipino mess boys, whose cooking FDR enjoyed while he was cruising aboard the presidential yacht *Sequoia*, were assigned to prepare and serve the president's meals while he was on *Houston*. Nothing was spared in transforming the quarters of an admiral into the quarters befitting the president of the United States. While was showing reporters around the ship, one officer stated: "He [President Roosevelt] has done a lot for the Navy, and we wanted to do all we could for him."[6]

President Roosevelt believed in vacations, and preferably vacations involving the sea. Two days before he set sail aboard *Houston*, Roosevelt chatted with Secretary Ickes, urging him to take a vacation. Ickes, who recorded the conversation in his diary: "He was most friendly and touching about it. Here is a man who is probably carrying greater burdens than any other man in the world, and yet he charges himself with the responsibility for seeing to it that a recalcitrant Cabinet member takes a vacation. I told him that I would go away and he remarked that I had made such a promise to him before. He said: 'Go away and take your stamps with you. I am going to take mine with me.'"

This time, Ickes followed the president's orders. On 26 July, he took the 4:10 P.M. train from Washington's Union Station to points west. After traveling by automobile around California and Wyoming, and visiting Yosemite National Park, Yellowstone, Glacier Point, and a variety of other scenic points, Ickes recorded his revised view of vacations in his diary: "I have already begun to feel the benefit of my trip. There isn't any doubt that one should get away once in a while as far as possible from human contacts. To contemplate nature, magnificently garbed as it is in this country, is to restore peace to the mind, even if it does make one realize how small and petty and futile the human individual really is."[7]

Ickes was waiting at the dock in Portland, Oregon, along with Eleanor Roosevelt, James Roosevelt, and a host of dignitaries, for the arrival of FDR from his Hawaiian cruise. A tanned, rested, and relaxed president arrived and, a few days later, boarded the special train heading to the east—and back to work.

Although Roosevelt frequently took both long and short cruises while in office, he never was out of touch with what was happening both in Washington and abroad. Radio channels and seaplanes were kept busy delivering messages and mail both to and from the president. He did take time to fish and enjoy his surroundings, but always allocated sufficient time to keep up with the large volume of paperwork brought to him each day.

Jimmy Roosevelt said that his father was sensitive to the potential public relations problems associated with long cruises.

> Indeed, back in 1934, when Vincent Astor proposed a particularly attractive trip to the Galapagos, Father replied regretfully: ". . . Several jealous females, who would like to go to the Galapagos too . . . suggested that the presidency calls for the presence of the president in the National Capitol for at least a couple of weeks during the year! However, there are two contingencies: either the country may be so prosperous by November first that they will be thinking about profits and not presidents; or that the country will be so busted that they will beg me to go away for a month!"[8]

Roosevelt also kept up with his correspondence, both personal and official, while he floated around the globe. In a 5 July 1934 letter to Eleanor Roosevelt, the president, while aboard *Houston,* wrote: "The Lord only knows when this will catch up with my Will o'Wisp wife, but at least I am proceeding according to schedule, and it is a grand trip thus far. Yesterday we had a good day's fishing, stopping for nine hours in the S.E. Bahamas and F[ranklin Jr.] and J[ohn] and I all got fish—also the people in the other boat—Rudolph and Dick Jervis and Gus. The '3 Musketeers' watched the fishing for awhile." Jervis was a Secret Service agent. Gus Gennerich—a former New York City policeman—was Roosevelt's personal bodyguard. Rudolph Forster was a clerk in the White House. The "3 Musketeers" were reporters traveling in another ship.[9]

If Roosevelt wasn't sailing in style aboard one of the navy's cruisers or destroyers (occupying admiral's quarters), he was cruising aboard one of the presidential yachts—*Sequoia* or *Potomac*. He would regularly take leisurely cruises down the Potomac, usually on Sundays, aboard one of the yachts. He often invited representatives or senators for lunch and a little friendly arm-twisting, sailor-style.

There was nothing like traveling aboard one of the navy cruisers or destroyers, however. When aboard one of these ships, Roosevelt was the commander in chief, with a crew and captain ready and willing to cater to his every whim. His quarters were luxurious—usually two large rooms, one with a bed and private bath and the other with chairs, a dining table, desk, and bookcases. Truly, these quarters befitted an admiral—or a president.

Following his fall 1935 train trip out west to dedicate the Boulder Dam and give an important speech at the San Diego Exposition extolling the virtues of the United States remaining "at peace with all the world," Roosevelt boarded his flagship, USS *Houston,* and departed San Diego for home on 2 October. He was, once again, at sea and content. Most of the cruise would be devoted to fishing and a bit of sightseeing. Roosevelt inspected troops at Fort Clayton, a U.S. Army installation on the west bank of the Panama Canal, and also took an automobile tour of the Madden Dam, which was under construction on the Chagres River. It was completed the next year.

Frank Freidel, a Roosevelt biographer, reported an interesting incident that occurred during a fleet review when Roosevelt was aboard *Houston* while it was still in dock off San Diego. FDR observed the largest naval exercise ever conducted, thus becoming the first American president to actually witness naval maneuvers. *Houston* and accompanying ships represented an enemy sortie from San Diego, according to the official trip log, which states that the exercises included a demonstration of attacks by submarines and the combined fleet. At the conclusion of the exercise, Roosevelt wired his congratulations, applauding the "timing and precision of attacks." He signed the message "Roosevelt, Commander-in-Chief."[10]

The president invited some of his staff and cabinet officials on the 1935 cruise, hoping to improve interpersonal relationships. According to

Elliott Roosevelt, things had not been going well among some of the president's cabinet officers, particularly between Ickes and Harry Hopkins. Hopkins was handling relief efforts for Roosevelt, thus he was competing with Ickes for scarce dollars. Robert Hopkins said his father and Ickes got along reasonably well privately, but he said Ickes was a "rather thorny fellow" who was "very jealous that most of the relief money went to my father's WPA," the Works Progress Administration, instead of to Ickes's projects.[11]

Hopkins and Ickes had plenty of complaints during the cruise, ranging from bad coffee and stale water to lack of fishing success. However, Roosevelt judged the cruise a success, and contributed a few paragraphs to the ship's newspaper, *The Blue Bonnet*:

> The feud between Hopkins and Ickes was given a decent burial today . . . the president officiated at the solemn ceremony which we trust will take these two babies off the front page all the time. . . . Hopkins expressed regret at the unkind things Ickes had said about him and Ickes on his part promised to make it stronger— only more so—as soon as he could get a stenographer who would take it all down hot. The president gave them a hearty slap on the back—pushing them into the sea. "Full steam ahead" the president ordered.[12]

A good deal of preparation was required when Roosevelt traveled aboard a navy ship. In addition to stocking his favorite food and beverages, and a variety of movies and books, the navy also constructed special ramps, elevators, and other aids to assist the president as he moved about ship in his wheelchair. Usually, two strong Secret Service agents lifted FDR from his wheelchair to a specially equipped launch when the president wanted to go fishing. William M. Rigdon, assistant naval aide to the president, described the special "cruise gear" preparations that the navy always installed on ships on which the president was to be a guest. "An elevator had to be put in to facilitate his moving from one deck level to another," Rigdon wrote. "In the president's country—as the area assigned to him was called—ramps had to be built over the coamings and deck obstructions so he could travel about in his wheelchair."[13]

In the president's quarters, additional modifications were required. According to Rigdon, "A bed twelve inches longer than standard was put in his sleeping room, and a bathroom had been especially fitted for him, with a tub that had metal railings around it for FDR to grasp with his strong hands. The toilet bowl had been raised to the level of his wheelchair so that he could move himself from one to the other, and the mirror lowered to enable him to sit in his chair and shave." The president's quarters were freshly painted and a decorative shower curtain was placed around his tub, replacing the stiff canvas curtain usually found on naval vessels. FDR's favorite old leather upholstered recliner also was brought aboard.[14]

The naval aide also had a checklist of items he had to make sure were stowed on board, including a supply of money for the president, corned beef hash for FDR's breakfast, and plenty of coffee, which was served in his four and a half inch diameter cup. The president liked Saratoga Springs bottled water; twenty cases were brought aboard. A supply of long wooden matches, which the president would use to light his cigarettes, also came aboard.[15]

Roosevelt biographer Kenneth S. Davis observed that the moment of transfer from his ship to the fishing boat was a moment of great risk for the president, especially if the seas were choppy. A sudden lurch might send the president flying, exposing him to the potential of great injury. Davis notes, however, that this never concerned FDR, who chatted and joked with the Secret Service agents, never once showing any sign of fear or self-consciousness. His powerful arm and shoulder muscles served him well as he fished, particularly when he had a big one on the line.[16]

Secrecy, particularly during the war years, was strictly observed when equipping a navy ship for presidential travel. The chief of naval operations noted in a 26 December 1943 confidential memorandum to the chief of the Bureau of Ships:

> The Secret Service have pointed out that when a naval vessel goes to a navy yard to receive the elevator and special ramps, a considerable number of people at the yard become aware the president is planning a trip by naval vessel because the boxes are all plainly marked as presidential equipment. The Chief requests that some other marking be placed on the boxes so that the fewest possible number of people will know what is impending.[17]

Unfortunately, information about Roosevelt's travels still found their way out of classified and confidential government circles as evidenced by a 11 November 1944 letter to the president from a loyal ex–army officer in East Hampton, Connecticut. In part, the letter said:

> While lunching in a Middletown, Connecticut, restaurant today, I overheard two men in an adjoining booth engaged in conversation. They mentioned the cruiser, USS *Quincy*. An unusual statement attracted my attention. A toilet bowl on board the *Quincy* had been raised nine inches and the conclusion was that this was done for a certain person who is evidently planning a trip on the cruiser. As I thought it over later, it occurred to me that a loose bit of conversation such as this might be extremely dangerous, if correct, for if a Nazi sympathizer were within earshot he would surmise that the *Quincy* is to be your means of travel to the next big three conference.[18]

Indeed, the cruiser *Quincy* was used by the president for the last of his big three conferences about three months later. Although there were occasional information leaks about the president's travels, apparently none ever resulted in any incidents threatening his safety.

Roosevelt was a first-class fisherman, who usually was successful at netting a good catch even when his fishing colleagues did not. He knew how to handle a rod and reel, and seemed to have a sixth sense as to where the fish would be biting. He also had patience, and would sit for hours in a small launch, trolling and simply waiting to hook a big one. While many deep-sea fishermen used a leather harness to provide additional leverage for them and their rods, Roosevelt did not need one because of his powerful shoulder and arm muscles.

In an October 1935 letter to his mother, while aboard *Houston* in the Cocos Islands, Roosevelt couldn't resist telling her of his fishing luck. "We are having a most delightful cruise, and at this charming spot the fishing is excellent. I have caught two very large sailfish—one on Wed.— 110 lbs. And one today—134 lbs. The result is that my muscles are rather sore, but it is good for my figure and I get lots of sleep and sun and fresh air." The sailfish "put up a magnificent fight" according to the cruise log, which stated that Roosevelt struggled with a light rod before finally landing the nine foot, two inch fish.

During evenings at sea, the president and his guests usually enjoyed watching Hollywood films shown on the deck of the cruiser. One night, while *Houston* was steaming toward the Cocos Islands, the weather turned decidedly squally, with high winds blowing away the screen that protected the president from wind while watching a film. Heavy swells whipped over the rails, flooding the deck with eight to ten inches of water. Roosevelt, however, thoroughly enjoying the film, decided to sit out the storm and watch the movie until the end. By midnight, the winds had picked up, with forty-six miles per hour gusts.[19] The return trip from the west coast took the president through the Panama Canal, with stops at Cocos Island, Panama, and the San Blas Islands, before he disembarked at Charleston, South Carolina on 22 October.

Ickes, who accompanied Roosevelt on the return trip, watched in awe as the president, who had absolutely no use of his legs, moved about the ship, sometimes with the help of others but, often, on his own.

> It was a marvel to me to see the way the president was gotten into and out of his fishing boat. He had a special launch with two chairs in the stern. He always asked one of the party to go with him, but Captain Brown also went with him constantly. Captain Brown, presidential naval aide, and a sailor who had been especially detailed to the *Houston* because he had a lot of experience in deep-sea fishing, stood on the top of the roof that sheltered the stern of the launch. . . . When the *Houston* anchored, a companionway was lowered from the lee side of the ship and the president's fishing launch was brought alongside the little platform at the foot of the companionway. Then two men would carry him sideways down the companionway. They would hand him over to Captain Brown and the other man I have referred to, who would swing him around into his armchair. There he would sit and fish.[20]

A. J. Drexel Paul, who traveled with Roosevelt on his famous June 1933 cruise in the small schooner *Amberjack II*, recalls how well the six foot, two inch Roosevelt, who had the chest and shoulders of a weight lifter, got around on deck. "He had a huge chest, but he was very light," Paul remembered. "Two of us would get on either side of him" when they had to move FDR from topside to below deck. "He got around very well."[21]

Roosevelt was totally at ease on the sea—whether he was traveling in grand style aboard a navy flagship cruiser such as *Houston,* or skimming the waves aboard a small twin-masted schooner, or even skimming the ocean in a tiny, leaking yawl, such as the one he rented in 1932 for a New England cruise. As Harold Ickes recalled, and confirmed by many who sailed with him, Roosevelt's high cheer and buoyant disposition never failed. "Never once," Ickes wrote,

> did he act self-conscious; on no occasion did he seem to be nervous or irritated. Cheerfully he submitted to being wheeled up and down the special ramps that had been installed on the *Houston* for his use, or to being carried up and down like a helpless child when he went fishing. He was an avid fisherman and, with his strong arms and shoulders, he was able to give a good account of himself if he once got a fish on his hook. Fortunately, he was a lucky fisherman also.[22]

Ross McIntire, the president's physician, said the "sun and sea were tonics" for Roosevelt, adding that "good fellowship had the kick of wine, bringing out an almost boyish exuberance in the president that was hard on guests who could not take a ribbing."[23]

Within a month of Roosevelt's 1935 cruise aboard *Houston,* he was on his way to Warm Springs, Georgia. As had been his custom, the president would spend Thanksgiving with the polio patients at his rehabilitation center in Pine Mountain Valley, before returning to Washington in early December.

Meanwhile, the navy was busy readying a new ship for the president. The new presidential yacht—soon to be christened *Potomac*—would replace *Sequoia* and serve Roosevelt for the next five years, transporting him on short, leisurely cruises down the Potomac as well as on longer jaunts to Florida, the Bahamas, and New England.

The wooden-hulled USS *Sequoia* was a former inspection vessel that had been transferred from the Commerce Department to the U.S. Navy. The ninety-nine-foot vessel, built by the Mathis Yacht Co. in Camden, New Jersey, had served as Roosevelt's presidential yacht from 1933 to 1936.

In 1936, President Roosevelt took command of USS *Potomac,* a 165-foot former U.S. Coast Guard patrol boat used to track down rum runners. Built by the Manitowoc Ship Building Company in Wisconsin, it was christened in 1934 as *Electra.* During its 1936 refurbishing for presidential duty, including the installation of an elevator for FDR's wheelchair, some thirty-nine tons was added to the aft deck, raising its center of gravity. As a result, *Potomac* rolled badly when fully loaded.[24]

Whether aboard *Sequoia* or the new presidential yacht *Potomac,* the president relished being on the water; he entertained family and friends in high style. On one bright and breezy Sunday afternoon in April 1935 aboard *Sequoia,* the president invited Margaret "Daisy" Suckley, a sixth cousin, with whom he had an close friendship, and Virginia Livingston Hunt, a distant cousin of Eleanor, to join him, Joseph Kennedy, and some advisors aboard *Sequoia* on a Potomac River cruise. Lunch aboard the yacht consisted of fruit cup, bouillon, shad, new potatoes, chops, peas, mixed green salad with crackers and cheese. Dessert was chocolate pudding with whipped cream and coffee. The meal was served on fine china and glassware, all marked with the presidential naval insignia. Although Hunt was a Republican, she complimented the president and his naval aide, Capt. Wilson Brown, whom she described as a "thorough gentleman." That evening, Suckley and Hunt were invited to return to the White House to hear the president deliver his Fireside Chat. Hunt concluded: "Thus ended another memorable day in the lives of both of us. No matter what one thinks of Mr. Roosevelt, and my thoughts are indeed very conflicting, one must admit he was most kind and thoughtful of us and gave us untold pleasure."[25]

Potomac was available for Roosevelt's use beginning 2 March 1936. Roosevelt used *Potomac* until the war, when it was relieved from presidential duties and assigned to the navy's underwater sound testing station.[26]

For Roosevelt, the new yacht was a dream come true. A far cry from the small yawls and schooners he sailed so well, *Potomac* was much larger. Although a mere midget compared to the giant destroyers and cruisers of the U.S. Navy, the yacht was a bit different from a typical pleasure yacht. It carried two 0.50-caliber antiaircraft machine guns on the forecastle and antimagnetic mine equipment. Propelled by twin diesel engines, top speed was 16 knots. Fifty navy sailors stood at attention as the president was piped over the side by a boatswain.[27]

A collection of Hollywood films and shorts were kept aboard for the president's enjoyment, including *Double Indemnity* with Fred MacMurray and Barbara Stanwyck, *Return of the Vampire* with Bela Lugosi, *Spider Woman* with Basil Rathborn and Nigel Bruce, and *Bathing Beauty* with Red Skelton and Esther Williams.[28]

Potomac also offered the advantage of being the perfect vehicle for a quick weekend getaway down the Potomac River and into the Chesapeake Bay. "Skipper" Roosevelt enjoyed these jaunts immensely during his presidency. He could be aboard less than thirty minutes after leaving the White House. He entertained a number of dignitaries on board including the king and queen of England in 1939, Winston Churchill, Crown Princess Martha of Norway, and Prince Karl and Crown Prince Gustav of Sweden. He even recorded some of his Fireside Chats while on board.[29]

By 1937 it became clear that President Roosevelt considered *Potomac* his personal vessel, when Roosevelt got upset after Secretary of the Treasury Henry Morganthau used the vessel without his specific approval. Morganthau had cruised down the Potomac River with England's treasury secretary. On 24 September 1937 he penned a note to Roosevelt, thanking him for "putting the *Potomac* at my disposal." Three days later, Roosevelt dictated a note to James Roosevelt: "When we get back to Washington, will you check with Captain Woodson and find out why the *Potomac* was used, as permission was given to use *Sequoia* and that under no circumstances is the *Potomac* to be used without direct authority of the President." Woodson replied that there was a mix up; *Sequoia* had been transferred to the secretary of the navy, who had plans to use the vessel that same day, so *Potomac* was used instead. "The present Naval Aide understands thoroughly that the POTOMAC is not to be used except in accordance with specific orders from the President," Woodson stated.[30]

Potomac, more than any presidential yacht before or since, served as a true "floating White House." The yacht provided the country's greatest seagoing president with an instant means of extricating himself from the confines of Washington. Roosevelt could escape to the open water, where he could do some politicking and thinking, or relax and entertain on deck with friends and advisers, or simply throw a fishing line overboard and patiently wait for a bite.

CHAPTER 8
Praying for Fog

Washington was cold and bleak in January 1936, and the outlook for Roosevelt winning a second term appeared bleak as well. He was facing criticism from various factions around the country. He also was reeling from U.S. Supreme Court decisions striking down parts of his New Deal programs. As the campaign season got under way, Republicans were becoming hopeful that Kansas governor Alf Landon, a strong opponent of New Deal programs, could take the White House away from the Democrats.

Despite what many viewed as an uphill battle to retain control of the White House, Roosevelt's desire to be on the open ocean took precedence. In March, a confident FDR announced his intention to take the first long trip aboard his new presidential yacht *Potomac,* for points south. As in previous trips, a temporary White House would be set up in Miami, while the president cruised and fished along the Florida coast and in the warm blue waters of the Caribbean in search of barracuda. USS *Monaghan* and USS *Dale,* with a contingent of Secret Service agents, would accompany the presidential yacht.

Col. Edward "Pa" Watson, a military aide who accompanied FDR on his two-week holiday, caught a thirty pound barracuda near Great Inagua Island. Roosevelt described the fishing as marvelous, the best he had ever experienced in the West Indies. The president attributed his good luck to the fact that "no white men have ever trolled here before & the natives

only catch small fish on hand lines."[1] Roosevelt caught what he called a
"mystery fish" weighing twenty-seven pounds. He could not identify it
and put it on ice for transport to the Smithsonian, where it was identified
as an amberjack. Ironically, this was the name of the schooner he chartered for his 1933 New England cruise. He also said that he "horrified all
hands" by taking Potomac into a shallow bay, with "two feet of water under
the keel & the Navy had a collective fit."[2]

In a letter to Daisy Suckley, his cousin, he included a sketch of a lighthouse near Cat Island in the Bahamas. He wrote: "We anchored off Cat
Island & got out the fishing boats and gear but had very little luck though
we tried two different anchorages—It is too rough to stop at Long Island
this p.m., as the wind is wrong—but I saw our pink lighthouse through the
glasses—I do wish I could draw—perhaps someone will give me lessons."[3]

After his return to land, Roosevelt stopped at Warm Springs, Georgia,
before returning to the White House. A tornado had devastated parts of
Georgia and Mississippi, and the president wanted to see the damage
firsthand. On 7 April, he authorized two and a half million dollars for
relief efforts.[4]

Back in the White House, the shrewd political campaigner, who won a
landslide victory in November 1932, went to work in earnest to make sure
that, come 20 January 1937, his White House lease would be renewed.
He made a few campaign swings to Baltimore, Maryland, Monticello, Virginia, and New York City. In addition, in April he traveled to Fall River,
Massachusetts, to attend the funeral of his good friend and adviser Louis
Howe. This would be the first election for FDR since 1910 without Howe
by his side.

Two months later, Roosevelt traveled to Philadelphia where Democrats once again nominated him, by acclamation, as their candidate for
president. Addressing the delegates on 27 June, the president observed:
"[H]ere in America, we are waging a great and successful war. It is not
alone a war against want and destitution and economic demoralization. It
is more than that; it is a war for the survival of democracy. We are fighting
to save a great and precious form of government for ourselves and for the
world. I accept the commission you have tendered me. I join with you. I
am enlisted for the duration of the war."[5]

Two weeks later, following a pattern he established in 1932 after
accepting the Democratic nomination for president, Roosevelt began
another New England cruise aboard a small, chartered schooner. In re-

marks at Hyde Park before departing by train for Rockland, Maine, Roosevelt commented: "I can look forward now to two or three weeks of freedom from official cares except, possibly, for the reading and acting on
some forty or fifty dispatches a day, the signing of a bag full of mail once
every four or five days unless, of course, I get caught in a fog down the
coast of Maine, and I am rather praying for fog."[6]

Joseph M. Price, chairman of the City Club of New York, was an old
friend of Roosevelt's. Like FDR, he had fought against Tammany Hall.
Price, an avid sailor, summered on Nantucket Island and was a member
of the venerable Wharf Rat Club, which had inducted Roosevelt as an
honorary member when the president visited Nantucket Harbor three
years earlier.

Hearing that Roosevelt would be taking another sailing vacation, Price
wrote the president asking him to make a Nantucket stop, promising he
would have the special "presidential chowder" and another Wharf Rat flag
waiting. The president replied that he would not have an opportunity to
stop on this cruise, but he added, "I shall miss you and the Wharf Rats
and the chowder."[7]

As the president departed Hyde Park by train on the evening of 13
July, he briefly addressed the one hundred residents, including Eleanor,
who assembled to see him off: "I'll be in old clothes and cool by morning—the oldest clothes I've got."[8] FDR slept aboard the train as it made
its way to the Maine Central Railroad Station in Rockland. After arriving
the next day, the president boarded *Potomac,* which carried him twelve
miles to Pulpit Harbor and the waiting fifty-six-foot schooner *Sewanna.*

"I haven't the faintest idea where I'm going except to work to the
east'ard," President Roosevelt told reporters as he set sail from the Maine
coast aboard the chartered schooner, with the presidential flag flapping in
the breeze. "I'm just going to loaf," he said.[9] Franklin Roosevelt loved being
vague, especially when speaking to reporters.

His three sons—James, John, and Franklin Jr.—again would make up
his crew, just as they did during his 1932 and 1933 New England cruises
when FDR and his amateur crew were on their own. This time, however,
two professional sailors would travel with the presidential party. Owned
by Harrison Tweed, an avid yachtsman and New York lawyer who battled
for the rights of the poor and underprivileged,[10] *Sewanna* was more spa-
cious than *Amberjack II,* the vessel FDR chartered for his 1933 cruise. It
had a larger cockpit, with a companionway leading to a private stateroom

that would be used by the president. It included a galley where meals would be prepared and a large main cabin that could sleep four.

There were several other notable differences between the 1936 cruise and the 1932 and 1933 cruises. First, Roosevelt was New York's governor in 1932 and, although trailed by a yacht full of political supporters, and dogged by reporters and photographers, he was not shadowed by the U.S. Navy and a detail of Secret Service agents as he was in 1933 and again on this cruise. In addition, on the 1932 trip, Roosevelt left from Port Jefferson, New York, and sailed to New Hampshire; in 1933, he sailed from Marion, Massachusetts, to his summer home at Campobello.

The 1936 cruise, the last FDR would take as skipper of a small sailing ship, began in Pulpit Harbor, Maine, about twelve miles from Rockland, which is only a short distance southwest of Campobello, his final destination. Three years earlier in Pulpit Harbor, the quick action of his crew saved President Roosevelt from injury when a fire broke out aboard his schooner *Amberjack II*.

Roosevelt would not be sailing directly to Campobello in 1936. Instead, he would be sailing east to Cape Sable, on the southern part of Nova Scotia, and then sail erratically along the Nova Scotia coastline for several days. The president's flotilla would include the presidential yacht *Potomac*, on which Marvin McIntyre, Roosevelt's secretary, and Capt. Ross McIntire, the White House physician, along with a host of other aides traveled; the destroyer USS *Hopkins*, which carried a detail of Secret Service agents; the USS *Owl*, which served as air patrol and air mail tender; and the 114-foot schooner *Liberty*, with the White House press corps on board.[11]

A few days before the president boarded, *Sewanna* was rammed by a fishing schooner that was caught in an eddy. It was pushed against *Sewanna*, denting the bow four feet above the waterline and ripping some rigging. The president's sons, who were sailing *Sewanna* at the time from Portsmouth to Pulpit Harbor, took the schooner into Rockland, for repairs. Fortunately, the damage was relatively minor and *Sewanna* was able to keep its appointment with the president.[12]

On 14 July, with President Roosevelt at the helm, the sleek yacht skimmed what was described as glassy waters for five hours between Pulpit Harbor and his first port of call, Buck's Harbor, where they would spend the night. The next day, the president received a radio message from his son Elliott, who lived in Texas, and who was unable to accompany his father on this cruise: "Elliott Junior born at eleven forty p.m. 14 July. Weight seven pounds, Ruth doing very well, Love to all, Elliott, Fort Worth." By wigwag and radio, the president sent the following reply: "We are all thrilled ever so much. Love to Elliott Junior, Ruth and yourself from—Grandpa and three Uncles Roosevelt."[13]

Later that day, *Sewanna* anchored in Latty Cove. Rear Adm. and Mrs. Richard E. Byrd, their son Dick, and their fox terrier Iceberg came aboard for lunch and an afternoon of sailing. Late that afternoon, the president and his crew departed Latty Cove and sailed aimlessly over the next few hours—fishing, sightseeing, stopping at several additional ports, and even racing an unidentified schooner that challenged *Sewanna,* all in what was described as glorious sailing weather. Roosevelt led the flotilla on an exciting hide-and-seek sail around the isles of the Maine coast. He sailed his schooner into shallow areas where his escorts could not follow. He disappeared for a half hour and then returned, laughing, to take his position as the head of the flotilla.[14] Roosevelt brought his schooner to rest for the night at Seal Harbor, Mount Desert Island.

A little after ten in the morning, in what the *New York Times* reported as FDR's "longest day's sail under canvas since his boyhood," the president made the 108 mile trip from Seal Harbor, Maine, to Stoddard Cove, Nova Scotia, in a continuous thirty-hour sail across the Gulf of Maine and the mouth of the Bay of Fundy.[15] Because the weather turned a bit heavy with rolling seas, Roosevelt ordered two-hour watches during the Bay of Fundy crossing. With the temperature dropping into the fifties and the rocking swells, the crew huddled under blankets provided by *Potomac. Sewanna* made its crossing, at times reaching a speed of 9 knots. Characteristically, Roosevelt included himself on the watch schedule, taking both the 9 P.M. and 3 A.M. watches. Roosevelt did not expect any special privileges even though he was the president of the United States.[16]

Anchored at Stoddard Cove, a deeply tanned FDR—unshaven from his days at sea—donned a black oilskin slicker and his traditional white floppy "Campobello" sailing hat. He boarded a small motorboat with his son Franklin Jr. and went fishing, leaving his schooner for the first time since the trip began. With FDR at the motorboat's wheel, he visited the escort vessels, which had been joined by the coast guard cutter *Ponchartrain,* and then fished for about an hour. A motorboat of sailors kept a discreet distance.[17]

The following day, the president navigated his schooner, in brisk wind, through a light fog bank that at times hid him from his escort. The fog, however, offered no obstacle to Roosevelt, who could sail with great skill through Maine's legendary pea-soup fogs. After a forty-five-mile sail around the southern tip of Nova Scotia, Roosevelt brought *Sewanna* to rest at Shelburne. While anchored, he left his schooner and embarked on the presidential yacht *Potomac*. There, he pressed a button that sent a radio signal, officially opening the frontier celebration in Fort Worth as part of Texas' centennial festivities, marking one hundred years of Texas independence.

> Congratulations on opening of Fort Worth Frontier Centennial Stop I am sending this opening message by wig wag visual signal from the schooner yacht Sewanna to the USS Potomac comma Both in the Atlantic Ocean off the Southern end of Nova Scotia comma and thence by landwire and radio to you stop Best of luck to you all. Franklin D. Roosevelt.[18]

Roosevelt's luck with the weather ended the following day. He spent the sixth day of his cruise under a cold rain while anchored at Shelburne, a community founded by loyalists who fled the United States after it gained independence from Britain. The president again left the schooner, along with his three sons, to board *Potomac*. He caught up on some official paperwork, met with aides, and relaxed in the more luxurious surroundings.

At dinner aboard the presidential yacht, Lt. Comdr. H. Y. McCown Jr., commanding officer of USS *Hopkins,* joined the president and his three sons. According to *Sewanna*'s official log of the trip, "some excellent anecdotes" about the navy and World War I were relayed, as well as a particular one about the return from Europe of President Woodrow Wilson aboard USS *George Washington,* on which then–Assistant Navy Secretary Franklin Roosevelt and his wife Eleanor also were on board. No details on the anecdote were included in the log. "After dinner the President and Secretary McIntyre took Franklin, Jr. and John into camp at bridge. After the game was finished the President inquired, 'By the way, what was the name of that game we were playing?'"[19]

Weather had not improved much the following morning. An impenetrable fog hung over the area, completely blocking Shelburne Harbor. But the president didn't let that interfere with his cod-fishing plans. Roosevelt and Dr. McIntire took off alone in a small fishing boat, traveling down the rocky coast along the fog bank. A guard boat, together with the rest of the escort, followed.

Shortly after reaching the open sea, however, the fog became so heavy that all vessels lost touch with the president's small boat. The president and the White House doctor were alone at sea, out of touch and sight of everyone. The president's guardians scurried feverishly to locate FDR, which they did quickly. He returned to the shoreline and reboarded *Sewanna*. When the fog lifted around dinnertime that night, Roosevelt led the flotilla on the short three-hour cruise to Cape Negro Island, where the flotilla would anchor for the night.

The next day marked the beginning of the second week of Roosevelt's vacation. He awoke to a windless day with heavy fog that blanketed the area. Defying the weather, Roosevelt piloted his schooner, with its sails furled and auxiliary motor running, to Stoddard Cove, where he had anchored four days earlier. Charles J. McDermott, a former Kings County, New York, judge, had a summer home nearby. He came aboard and visited with Roosevelt, who had been a classmate at Columbia Law School. The pair agreed to do some tuna fishing the following day.

McDermott's fishing boat, named *Judge the II*, arrived alongside *Sewanna* the following morning. The president, Franklin Jr., John, and Hall Roosevelt, who was Eleanor's brother and a sailing pal of FDR, went aboard. Roosevelt's bodyguard, Gus Gennerich, went along this time. The president spent the next seven hours trolling for tuna, without success. That night, politics intruded into the president's vacation. Roosevelt boarded *Potomac* to listen to a radio broadcast of Governor Landon accepting the Republican nomination in his effort to unseat Roosevelt during the election four months away.

Now that Campobello had electricity (and telephone service to Roosevelt's cottage would be installed this month, as well), Eleanor Roosevelt was listening to the radio while she awaited the president's arrival. In a letter to her daughter Anna, the First Lady wrote: "We listened to Landon's speech over her (Sara Roosevelt's) radio last night, not well delivered & in spots it faded out but it was effective if you didn't say 'how.' I'm sorry for them if they get in & after all the promises have to do just about what has been done."[20]

Roosevelt's sailing skills were put to a test the next day when he encountered the heaviest seas of the cruise while sailing his small schooner through the treacherous Bay of Fundy, with tides having an average range of forty feet. When the moon and sun are aligned just right, the tides can rise to more than fifty feet, the world's highest tides. Headlines in the *New York Times* conveyed the president's feat: "Roosevelt Sails Dangerous Seas. Scorns Storm Warning." The newspaper described the president's skill: "His seamanship was tested by the sail in rough, white-capped seas. The decks were awash in a run before a stiff southeast wind. The president, at the wheel, clad in oilskin, brought the *Sewanna* through the treacherous Grand passage between Digby Neck and Brier Island, where high seas and cross-currents make navigation hazardous."[21] Crossing a stretch described in the log as "an evil looking piece of water" between Brier Island and Grand Manan Island, which was thirty miles from Campobello, Roosevelt demonstrated to the navy and reporters trailing along in *Liberty* that he was an extremely skillful sailor who possessed great daring and courage.

Roosevelt's naval aide, Comdr. Paul Bastedo, accompanied FDR on *Sewanna*. A "worrying type," Jimmy Roosevelt said his father

> did everything he could to give the commander a difficult time. . . . One evening, when we were completely fogbound, Father became impatient and decided he would take *Sewanna* through the narrows, fog or no fog. "But, Mr. President!" Commander Bastedo expostulated. "You can't do that—it's dangerous!" "But nothing!" Father retorted. "I'm going in tomorrow morning, and that's an order from your Commander-in-Chief."[22]

Jimmy said they took off the next morning in the fog. "One of the escorting destroyers attempted to trail us, hoping to pick up survivors if we hit anything. Thanks to Pa's elegant navigating, we soon lost her, much to his glee."[23]

After arriving in L'Etang Island, Roosevelt—tanned and refreshed from his days at sea—had a beachside picnic, arranged by Eleanor. During the picnic, two navy seaplanes arrived with mail and official documents for the president. He handled the mail while sitting on the island beach, which was just a short sail from Campobello. The next morning, *Sewanna* made its way to the president's summer home.

Roosevelt's arrival at Campobello was in marked contrast to his 1933 arrival aboard *Amberjack II* when he was greeted by a flotilla of ships, thousands of residents lining the shores, and a twenty-one-gun salute from a navy warship. This time, only a Canadian patrol boat met the president, along with Eleanor, Sara Roosevelt, Harry Hopkins, and several friends. The president also surprised his wife as he sported bushy white sideburns similar to those worn by his father James, a mustache, and a heavy beard growth from almost two weeks at sea. When photographers came along *Sewanna* to capture the presidential whiskers on film, Roosevelt chased them away. Charles Hurd, a reporter for the *New York Times*, who accompanied Roosevelt on both this cruise and his 1933 trip, commented on the benefits of two weeks at sea: "Ten days on board the *Sewanna* have not only given the president a heavy coat of tan but a renewed vigor that has put him thoroughly in shape for the rigors of his campaign for re-election."[24]

Jimmy Roosevelt felt the *Sewanna* cruise was his father's "prize cruise" when it came to family participation. In a letter he wrote while aboard *Sewanna,* FDR said he was "re-living some of my boyhood days on a small schooner."[25]

Roosevelt usually enjoyed having reporters along on his trips, provided they kept their distance and only approached him when he wanted to say something. This cruise was no different. Roosevelt regarded the reporters with "tempered affection," while they genuinely admired and supported him. Roosevelt was considered a "reporter's president" and the "best newspaperman who has ever been President of the United States."[26]

Generally, reporters—especially in his first year in office—found Roosevelt to be candid, friendly with answers that were, at the same time, both illuminating and, sometimes, spectacular. He also took care to provide for their comforts, earning him much good will. For example, in preparation for the *Sewanna* cruise, White House Press Secretary Stephen Early wrote to Col. Edmund Starling, head of the White House Secret Service detail, about arrangements for reporters. "As far as I can tell at the present time there will be eight newspapermen who will accompany the President on the cruise up the New England coast," Early wrote. "They will charter their own ship. The charter will be by the day, about $250. The President suggested this morning that you arrange among the cottages there for accommodations for these newspapermen. This will enable them to let their ship go, upon arrival at Campobello."[27]

At one of the stops during the cruise, the wind was so strong that the correspondents in the press boat, anchored less than one hundred yards from *Sewanna,* could not hear the president as he answered reporters' questions. Roosevelt, knowing that reporters had a variety of queries for him, used a megaphone to shout his answers.

After an overnight rest at Campobello, Roosevelt began his automobile/train return to Washington, via a circuitous route through Quebec, New Hampshire, Connecticut, Vermont, and New York, with official stops in each location. With FDR at the wheel, accompanied by his mother, and a Secret Service car following behind, the vehicles were loaded onto an old small ferry boat—which could hold only two cars—for the journey across the bay from Campobello Island to Lubec, Maine.

And so ended the last cruise Franklin Roosevelt would take as the skipper of a small sailing vessel. Now, it was on to his reelection campaign. In November the American people would decide whom they trusted most to steer a troubled nation through the very stormy waters that lay ahead.

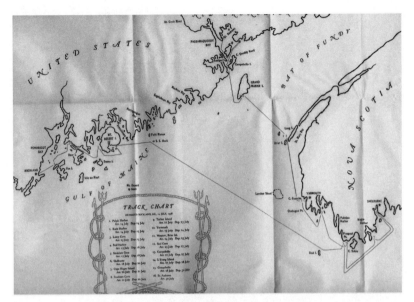

Track chart included in the official log of President Roosevelt's 1936 cruise aboard the schooner yacht *Sewanna*. Accompanied by three of his sons, the president spent two weeks sailing along the New England coastline on the last such trip Roosevelt would take on a smaller sailing vessel.
FRANKLIN D. ROOSEVELT LIBRARY

President Roosevelt used the letters "FDR" to form the upper part of a sailboat on the logo he personally designed for use on his matchbook covers. The Roosevelt Campobello International Park Commission adopted this design for its logo, adding a star and maple leaf to indicate the international nature of the park.
SUPERINTENDENT PAUL B. COLE III AND THE ROOSEVELT CAMPOBELLO INTERNATIONAL PARK COMMISSION

With President Roosevelt at the helm, *Amberjack II* arrives at Campobello, New Brunswick, on 29 June 1933 at the conclusion of a four-hundred-mile cruise. This was FDR's first return to his summer home since 1921, when he was carried out on a stretcher after contracting polio.

FRANKLIN D. ROOSEVELT LIBRARY

Capt. John M. Smealtie, commander of USS *Indianapolis,* welcomes President Roosevelt aboard ship at Campobello on 2 July 1933. The U.S. Navy's new heavy cruiser, on one of its first voyages, returned Roosevelt to Washington following the vacation that included his ten-day New England cruise aboard *Amberjack II.*

FRANKLIN D. ROOSEVELT LIBRARY

Seven-year-old Franklin Roosevelt (left), with a playmate, at the helm of his father's yacht, *Half Moon*, in a stiff wind near the Roosevelt summer home on Campobello Island, New Brunswick. The unpredictable Bay of Fundy, where FDR learned to sail, boasts some of the highest tides in the world. FRANKLIN D. ROOSEVELT LIBRARY

As his mother, Sara, knits, young Franklin navigates the tricky Bay of Fundy waters at Campobello in 1904. Young Franklin Roosevelt spent a good portion of his early years on the sea, both at the helm of small sailboats and as a passenger aboard luxury cruise liners. By age fourteen he had made nine transatlantic crossings with his parents. FRANKLIN D. ROOSEVELT LIBRARY

Franklin Roosevelt paddles his birchbark canoe through the waters off Campobello in 1907. Over the course of his lifetime, Roosevelt was aboard at least 110 named vessels, including luxury ocean liners, canoes, yawls, schooners, sloops, ice yachts, paddle wheel steamers, houseboats, motorboats, destroyers, cruisers, battleships, and even a submarine. FRANKLIN D. ROOSEVELT LIBRARY

Twenty-three-year-old Franklin Roosevelt at the helm of his ice yacht *Hawk,* off Roosevelt Point in the Hudson River in 1905. The twenty-eight-foot ice yacht was a gift from his mother while Roosevelt was a student at Harvard University.
FRANKLIN D. ROOSEVELT LIBRARY

Franklin Roosevelt takes Eleanor, holding baby Anna, and friends on a cruise aboard *Half Moon II* off Campobello Island, ca. 1907.

Franklin Roosevelt at the tiller of *Half Moon II* while sailing through the Bay of Fundy off Campobello Island. This previously unpublished 1909 photograph was taken by Mary Newbold Morgan, a childhood playmate of Franklin and next-door neighbor of the Roosevelt family in Hyde Park.

Assistant Secretary of the Navy Franklin Roosevelt inspects USS *Texas* in Firth of Forth, Scotland, on 29 August 1918. The destroyer USS *Dyer* carried Roosevelt to Europe for his two-month inspection of naval bases. Roosevelt spent most of his return voyage in bed suffering from pneumonia and a bout of influenza, from which he almost died. FRANKLIN D. ROOSEVELT LIBRARY

In 1920 Franklin Roosevelt purchased *Vireo*, a twenty-four-foot sailboat, for seven hundred dollars so he could teach his children to sail. He ordered the destroyer USS *Hatfield* to transport it to his Campobello summer home. FDR, working on model sailboats, is aboard *Vireo* in August 1920 with his children: James (left), Elliott, and Anna (behind the sail). His last sail before polio rendered him paralyzed in 1921 was aboard this boat.

FRANKLIN D. ROOSEVELT LIBRARY

Franklin Roosevelt, his wasted legs clearly visible, is shown here on a Florida beach with friends Marguerite "Missy" LeHand (on FDR's right), Maunsell S. Crosby, and Frances de Rham, all of whom accompanied FDR while he cruised through southern waters aboard the houseboat *Larooca* in 1924. Roosevelt took three cruises aboard the houseboat during his convalescence.

FRANKLIN D. ROOSEVELT LIBRARY

Franklin Roosevelt, with his "catch of the day"—a giant grouper, is cruising in Florida waters in 1924 aboard *Larooca,* a houseboat he purchased in October 1923 with Harvard classmate John S. Lawrence. FDR's son Elliott is standing beside the fish. Roosevelt and friends spent months traveling around Florida in houseboats—fishing, swimming, and sunning themselves.

FRANKLIN D. ROOSEVELT LIBRARY

Franklin Roosevelt, in the pool at his Warm Springs, Georgia, polio rehabilitation center in 1930. Roosevelt purchased the property in 1926, and became "Doctor Roosevelt" to scores of so-called "polios" who came for the same curative waters that first attracted FDR to this remote area in Georgia's Pine Mountains. The water stayed eighty-eight degrees year round.
FRANKLIN D. ROOSEVELT LIBRARY

On 29 July 1930, Governor Roosevelt disembarks from *Inspector* I, a seventy-three-foot wooden-hulled power yacht that sports a glass roof and was dubbed the "floating capitol" by upstate newspapers. Roosevelt used the yacht extensively during his two terms as governor, traveling New York's various waterways including New York's Barge Canal. The boat tours routinely would last for weeks, giving Roosevelt an opportunity to view the landscape and meet New Yorkers along the way. FRANKLIN D. ROOSEVELT LIBRARY

Governor Roosevelt works on a ship model in 1930 at his desk in Albany. Throughout his life, Roosevelt surrounded himself with nautical items. He collected and sometimes re-rigged ship models, purchased nautical prints and paintings, and amassed a library of naval books that totaled twenty-five hundred volumes. His extensive collection of naval prints, paintings, and watercolors totaled five thousand. FRANKLIN D. ROOSEVELT LIBRARY

President Roosevelt prepares to conduct Easter services, Sunday, 31 March 1934, on the aft deck of *Nourmahal,* Vincent Astor's palatial yacht, during a cruise in Bahamian waters. Roosevelt followed the tradition that, in the absence of a chaplain, the senior officer aboard conducts religious services. Astor is in the dark jacket. PRIVATE COLLECTION

President Roosevelt speaks with reporters on the aft deck of the 263-foot *Nourmahal,* during the 1934 Easter cruise. Those traveling with Roosevelt aboard Vincent Astor's yacht included Kermit Roosevelt, son of Theodore Roosevelt; George St. George, a wealthy Republican; Frederic Kernochan, a New York City judge; and Leslie Heiter, Vincent Astor's physician friend. Roosevelt took three lengthy cruises and one brief weekend trip aboard the luxury liner. PRIVATE COLLECTION

In this never-before published photograph, President Roosevelt, aboard
Nourmahal, watches departing destroyer USS *Farragut*. Roosevelt is beginning
his 1935 twelve-day vacation cruise in the waters of the Bahamas. This photo is
only the third known to exist that shows Roosevelt in his wheelchair. It is
unknown whether the wheelchair was brought aboard or was a part of the well-
appointed yacht's furnishings.
PRIVATE COLLECTION

President Roosevelt fishes the Potomac River while aboard the presidential yacht USS *Sequoia*. Gus Gennerich, a former New York City policeman and trusted FDR bodyguard, is standing behind the president. *Sequoia* was a former inspection vessel transferred from the Commerce Department to the U.S. Navy. It served as Roosevelt's official yacht until it was replaced in 1936 with USS *Potomac*. FRANKLIN D. ROOSEVELT LIBRARY

The presidential yacht USS *Potomac* sails on 9 June 1939 to Mount Vernon with the king and queen of England aboard. *Potomac,* a former U.S. Coast Guard patrol boat used to track down rum runners, was refurbished for presidential duty in 1936. It became Roosevelt's "floating White House" until the United States entered World War II. At that time, the Secret Service decided it was too risky for the president to be traveling on this small vessel.
FRANKLIN D. ROOSEVELT LIBRARY

In July 1936, two weeks after traveling to Philadelphia to accept the Democratic nomination for a second term as president, President Roosevelt boarded the chartered schooner *Sewanna* in Pulpit Harbor, Maine, for a two-week cruise along the New England coast. John, Franklin Jr., and James (left to right), came along, as well as FDR's old sailing pal, George Briggs. This would be the last cruise FDR would take aboard a small sailing vessel.

FRANKLIN D. ROOSEVELT LIBRARY

Standing on the deck of USS *Indianapolis* on 17 November 1936, President Roosevelt reviews the Argentina naval fleet. Reelected to a second term, Roosevelt traveled to South America to deliver his personal "Good Neighbor" message to an Inter-American Conference in Buenos Aires, Argentina.

FRANKLIN D. ROOSEVELT LIBRARY

USS *Houston* prepares to disembark President Roosevelt in Pensacola, Florida, on 9 August 1938 following a two-week cruise to the Galapagos Islands. Fishing from a small whaleboat, Roosevelt caught several record-size fish, as well as a 230-pound shark. In addition, thirty new species, subspecies, and varieties of creatures were collected during the voyage.

Gen. Douglas MacArthur (left) and Adm. Chester Nimitz flank President
Roosevelt aboard USS *Baltimore* in Pearl Harbor on 26 July 1944. Roosevelt
sailed aboard the heavy cruiser from San Diego, California, to Hawaii, where he
inspected facilities and met with military leaders. The cruiser followed a zigzag
pattern across the Pacific Ocean and was darkened from dusk until dawn to
avoid being a target for enemy aircraft and submarines.

FRANKLIN D. ROOSEVELT LIBRARY

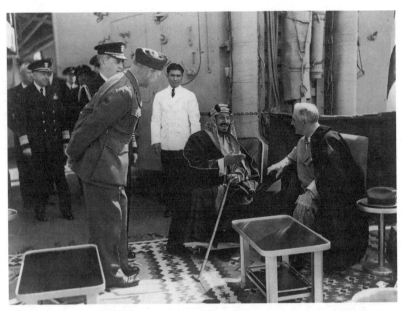

Aboard USS *Quincy* on Valentine's Day 1945, President Roosevelt confers with King Ibn Saud of Saudi Arabia at Great Bitter Lake, Egypt. Ibn Saud slept in a tent set up aboard USS *Murphy,* the destroyer FDR had dispatched to pick up the king. The king also brought live sheep aboard so he could dine on fresh meat daily. The president would soon be departing for home now that he had concluded Yalta Conference discussions with Winston Churchill and Joseph Stalin. This was Roosevelt's last sea voyage; two months later the president died.

FRANKLIN D. ROOSEVELT LIBRARY

CHAPTER 9

Davy Jones, Peg Leg, and Senior Pollywog Roosevelt

"I am beginning to come up for air after the baptism by total submersion on Tuesday night last! The other fellow was the one who nearly drowned," Franklin Roosevelt wrote to Josephus Daniels, his ex-boss and former secretary of navy, after his reelection victory in November 1936.[1]

Roosevelt's "other fellow" was Kansas governor Alf Landon, who was trounced by the president on Election Day. Despite earlier fears that Roosevelt might not be reelected, Americans went to the polls on 3 November and returned the fifty-four-year-old Democrat to the White House in one of the largest landslides in American history. Roosevelt received nearly five million more votes than he had received in 1932. He captured 523 electoral votes, compared to Landon's 8 electoral votes (Vermont and Maine). The Democrats also maintained their majority in the Senate and the House.

The president had actively campaigned throughout the country. Although not endorsed by most major newspapers, public opinion polls showed that he was the favorite among voters all across the United States. After his return from his two week cruise aboard the chartered yacht *Sewanna* in August, the president's official White House schedule called for heavy campaigning; the chief executive crisscrossed the nation by rail aboard the presidential special.

Roosevelt actually had started his campaign as the new year dawned.

In an unprecedented personal appearance before a joint evening session of Congress, he delivered his State of the Union address on 3 January 1936. Previously addresses were delivered in writing. The only president to deliver such a message personally to a joint evening session was President Wilson, when he asked for a declaration of war against Germany. "Why this departure from our former dignified practice?" asked the House Minority Leader.[2] Roosevelt had broken precedent in 1932 as well, when he flew from Albany, New York, to Chicago to personally accept the Democratic nomination for president. The master campaigner and political strategist had, once again, emerged victorious.

With the reelection campaign behind him, Roosevelt turned his attention to South America, where an Inter-American Conference was being held in Buenos Aires, Argentina. Roosevelt decided to go himself and deliver his "Good Neighbor" message personally to the delegates. The president's goal was to promote his "Good Neighbor" policy in Latin America, and to merge all Western Hemisphere nations into a unified group, which would make up an anti-Axis bloc to oppose aggression in Japan, Germany, or Italy.[3]

His mode of travel, once again, would be the sea, where he also could rest after the grueling campaign. The heavy cruiser USS *Indianapolis,* which had returned FDR from Campobello after his 1933 New England cruise, carried him to South America in the company of his son Jimmy; Dr. Ross McIntire, the White House physician; Comdr. Paul Bastedo, naval aide; Col. Edward "Pa" Watson, military aide; and Gus Gennerich, his bodyguard.

Grace Tully, Roosevelt's long-time secretary, observed many years later that the president decided to attend the conference himself because it afforded him an opportunity to combine "his favorite relaxation of a sea trip with the business at hand."[4] And some sea trip it was—a twelve-thousand-mile ocean voyage that lasted a month. There was plenty of time for fishing, sunning, and relaxing; movies were projected on the ship's bulkhead each night.

USS *Indianapolis* departed Charleston, South Carolina, on 18 November 1936. In a letter to his mother while en route, Roosevelt said: "We have had three restful days and sleep and sunlight have done us all good." He noted that the following day he intended to troll to the north of Trinidad "where there are some rocks with some deep water around them."[5] But the fish weren't biting on this trip. In a letter penned to Miss Suckley, FDR's cousin and close friend, he wrote that he

> received the Deputy Governor (of Trinidad), the Am. Consul & wives & the press, & went fishing while the two cruisers took on fuel oil—we traveled about twenty five miles escorted by a British Colonel—he may have been a good colonel, but he didn't even get one bite for any of us! It is always thus—if we take any local guide who-knows-all-about-it with us, the fish disappear—& when we go alone, with no local knowledge, we always do well.[6]

As they were about to cross the Equator, an elaborate "Crossing the Line" costumed ceremony was held aboard, in which two hundred people were issued "subpoenas," including FDR, for trial and initiation into King Neptune's Court. Roosevelt was nominated as "Senior Pollywog" and, along with the other neophytes, was given an "intensive initiation" that included ducking in tanks of water from tilted chairs, running a gauntlet, and being spanked, put in a coffin, "electrocuted," and tickled. The fun lasted from noon until 4 P.M. Roosevelt got off easy; all he had to do was make a speech in his defense.[7] Roosevelt thoroughly enjoyed this frolicking and good-natured horseplay. It helped him relax and clear his mind of the troubles he faced at home and around the world. Roosevelt wrote to Daisy Suckley:

> Monday 23—All is preparation for the Crossing of the Equator—I am Senior Pollywog & this afternoon I set "watches" on top No 2 Turret & on the bow, two officers & two enlisted men changing at one-half hour intervals (all of them also Pollywogs)—dressed up in ridiculous costumes—watching for Davy Jones or Peg Leg to come on board over the bow—Sure enough at 7:30 tonight there was a loud beating of drums and blowing of bugles & they appeared with their retinue in splendid costumes & all of us witnessed the ceremony of announcing that at noon tomorrow Father Neptune & his court will come on board to initiate all Pollywogs into the mysteries of the deep & make them into Shellbacks![8]

Later in the cruise, *Indianapolis* passed by an old German battleship, which fired a twenty-one-gun salute to the presidential flag flying on Roosevelt's vessel. "Tonight," Roosevelt wrote to Suckley, "the *Graf Zeppelin* flew over us & around us on the trip from Rio Pernambucco & thence home. She was most lovely in the moonlight & lights blinked from her cabin 1,000 feet above us—I sent a message of 'gluckliche reise' [happy journey] in answer to her greeting."[9]

Although the fishing was not great, the trip did provide an opportunity for Roosevelt to rest from the exertions of the campaign. He basked in the adoration of thousands who lined the streets of Rio and Buenos Aires and cheered, "Viva la democracia! Viva Roosevelt!" Roosevelt was possibly "more highly esteemed throughout Latin America than any foreigner who had ever lived."[10]

Roosevelt considered the trip a diplomatic success, but others felt that the appearance of the U.S. president was successful merely from a public relations viewpoint because the overall goal of the conference—an anti-Axis bloc—was not achieved.

On a personal note, Roosevelt suffered a great loss on this trip. His bodyguard, Gus Gennerich, suffered a heart attack and died while dining in a Buenos Aires café. Gennerich had served Roosevelt since his first campaign to be New York's governor in 1928. More than a bodyguard, Gennerich had assisted FDR in dressing and undressing, as well as in and out of bathtubs, swimming pools, boats, and automobiles.[11] He was a close friend and Roosevelt felt his loss deeply. "The tragedy of poor Gus hangs over all of us," FDR wrote his wife, describing Gennerich as the "kind of loyal friend who simply cannot be replaced."[12]

Roosevelt returned to Washington, rested and tanned, on 15 December. He started inaugural preparations for his second term as president. This would be the first year that the inauguration would occur on 20 January, rather than 4 March, as had been the previous custom. The change was dictated by the Twentieth Amendment to the Constitution adopted in February 1933.

A torrential rain pounded the Washington area as Roosevelt took the oath of office in an open pavilion in front of the Capitol. As he read his second inaugural address, thousands of rain-drenched admirers listened as the president proclaimed that the nation had come far from the "days of stagnation and despair," but stressed that there still were serious economic problems facing the country. He challenged Americans to fight injustice and to fight for the basic necessities of life for all Americans.

"Many voices are heard as we face a great decision," Roosevelt said. "Comfort says, 'Tarry a while.' Opportunism says, 'This is a good spot.'

Timidity asks, 'How difficult is the road ahead?'" Roosevelt said that despite all the progress made over the past four years, "I see one-third of a nation ill-housed, ill-clad, ill-nourished."[13]

Following the inaugural address, the Secret Service and Dr. Ross McIntire insisted FDR ride back to the White House in a covered car to avoid the driving rain. Roosevelt declined. "The people have been standing in the storm for hours, waiting to see me," the president said. "I can do as much."[14]

Roosevelt strongly believed that government can and should be the agent for social and economic change in the country, and he was seeking the support of the American people to implement his vision. Not everyone in the United States agreed, however. Members of the U.S. Supreme Court already had struck down important parts of Roosevelt's economic recovery program. So, emboldened by his landslide reelection victory, Roosevelt sent a plan to Congress on 5 February that called for the reorganization of the federal judiciary. Roosevelt believed that the Supreme Court was comprised of "nine old men," all of whom were over sixty years old—and some over seventy—and all with a decidedly conservative bent. His new plan, among other changes, would add a new justice to the high court for any justice still serving after reaching seventy years of age. Under the plan, six new justices would be appointed, all by Roosevelt and all, presumably, sharing his political viewpoint.

Roosevelt's plan was seen as an attempt to "pack" the Court with justices who could be counted upon to support the president and his programs. The president failed to garner the support, even from his own longtime backers, and subsequently abandoned the plan. A compromise plan, the Supreme Court Retirement Act, was passed by Congress; it allowed justices to retire at seventy years of age, with full pay.[15] As a result, one conservative justice did retire, and several of Roosevelt's New Deal programs were approved by the Court in the spring of 1937.

Roosevelt also was shifting his attention to the international scene, which was becoming more unstable and dangerous with each passing day. Despite the pressures facing the president, both at home and abroad, he found time to take to the open water, although all future trips would be aboard either his presidential yacht or a navy vessel, accompanied by a full contingent of aides and security personnel. He remained in constant contact with the White House.

USS *Potomac*, Roosevelt's new presidential yacht, received plenty of use after it was delivered to him in January 1936. The former U.S. Coast Guard patrol boat was taken by the U.S. Navy and converted for the president's use. It was not as luxurious as some might have expected, according to the president's son, Elliott. "He [FDR] slept below decks in a stateroom that few admirals would have looked at twice. On the main deck, there was a combination saloon-dining room, with direct access to the galley. The cushioned fantail provided a spot where visiting dignitaries could be entertained," Elliott Roosevelt wrote.[16]

Anthony W. Lobb, a Secret Service agent assigned to the White House during 1941–1942, accompanied President Roosevelt on several of his cruises aboard *Potomac*. Lobb eventually left the White House to join the army because "they weren't going to have a war without me." He served in the army's Counter-Intelligence Corps (CIC), and headed the unit that discovered Adolf Hitler's Last Will and Political Testament. Lobb clearly recalled guarding the president and how much Roosevelt enjoyed his cruises aboard the presidential yacht. "The president would sit back in his deck chair, smoking a Camel." Lobb said the president used to smoke at least two packs of Camel cigarettes each day, and always appeared relaxed when he was aboard a ship. "He was a very cheerful man. I never saw him get angry," Lobb said.

On one weekend cruise to Chesapeake Bay, Lobb was sitting in the bow of the boat fishing off its deck. The agent was having pretty good luck, but the president wasn't catching anything. "What is that young man using for bait?" Roosevelt asked another Secret Service agent as he noticed Lobb reeling them in. Lobb's good luck continued, but they just weren't biting for the president.

Lobb said five Secret Service agents usually accompanied Roosevelt on these weekend cruises. Two would go along with him on *Potomac,* and the others would follow behind in *Calypso,* a navy boat used by the Secret Service and later sold to Jacques Cousteau. The Secret Service also used USS *Cuyahoga,* the same vessel used to trail FDR during his famous 1933 New England cruise.

Lobb said preparations for these weekend cruises were quite extensive. They would depart the White House on Friday evening or by noon on Saturday—the president in his car, with a Secret Service car in front and one behind. The Maryland state troopers were put on alert and would meet the entourage once they crossed the state line. *Potomac* would depart from Annapolis, or sometimes the Washington Naval Yard, with the president on board. It would, travel down river to southern Chesapeake Bay, usually anchoring overnight around Tangier Island, in the vicinity of a sunken battleship. The president liked it there because the fish usually were biting.

Lobb said the presidential yacht had ramps and an elevator so Roosevelt could move about the vessel easily in his wheelchair. The lavatories were on the first level and were handicap accessible, long before such accessibility was standard. Cabinet officers, aides, and political friends would frequently accompany the president on these weekend trips, according to Lobb. A mail pouch with the president's work would be flown in by navy seaplane on Sunday morning. *Potomac* normally would return to the Washington Naval Yard by late Sunday afternoon.[17]

In addition to frequent weekend fishing trips on the Potomac River and in the Chesapeake Bay, Roosevelt took the yacht on cruises to Florida and the Carribbean as well. He even took it on a clandestine—and later famous—trip in August 1941 up the New England coast.

Early in the Roosevelt administration, the navy had prepared a paper outlining the best fishing spots on the Potomac: "The president, secretary of the Navy, and assistant secretary of the Navy are all interested in getting the latest news of good fishing in the Potomac." The memorandum stated that they were interested in learning "exact localities, kind of fish, bait to use, or type of spoons if trolling, depth of water and best fishing at what stage of tide."[18]

Roosevelt always liked to have the very best advice and background information before undertaking an endeavor, whether it was a governmental decision affecting millions of his fellow citizens or finding the exact spot where the fish were biting. In the end, however, this seasoned old sailor relied mostly upon his own judgment and intuition, which seldom failed him throughout his remarkable life.

CHAPTER 10

Clearing Away Personal Cobwebs

Before U.S. entry into the war sharply curtailed President Roosevelt's seagoing travels, he logged thousands of nautical miles cruising up and down the eastern seaboard, to the Florida keys, the Bahamas, the Galapagos Islands, and the west coast—inspecting, fishing, "gaining perspective," and just plain relaxing.

Roosevelt continued to visit Warm Springs, Georgia, as well, where he enjoyed laughing, exercising, and swimming with other "polios." He provided a shining example of the heights to which someone afflicted with such a disease can aspire. From 1924 to 1945 Roosevelt made forty-one trips to his Georgia rehabilitation facility, most of the visits lasting a week or two. Short visits were impractical because it took the better part of a day of train and automobile travel just to get to his Pine Mountain cottage. Sixteen visits were made during his presidency.

Roosevelt provided extraordinary inspiration to hundreds of patients struggling to recover from the debilitating effects of the polio virus. He enjoyed joining them during daily exercises and water games. Roosevelt believed that individuals afflicted with polio had just as much opportunity to excel in life as those who had been spared the ravages of the disease.

The president's own words provide a glimpse into one possible motivation for his personal animus toward Adolf Hitler's quest for the "master race." In a letter to Marjorie Lawrence, a singer with the Metropolitan Opera Company as well as a polio victim who had shown improvement from the disease, Roosevelt wrote: "[T]oday, when all we love and cherish is jeopardized by those who take their rules of life from the brutality of barbarism, and preach and practice that all but the physically perfect should be summarily liquidated, your victory exposes with the light of truth the godlessness of the lie they teach."[1]

During a 1938 visit to Barnesville, Georgia, the president spoke about his favorite mountain retreat:

> Fourteen years ago, a democratic Yankee, a comparatively young man, came to a neighboring county in the State of Georgia, in search of a pool of warm water wherein he might swim his way back to health; and he found it. The place—Warm Springs—was at that time a rather dilapidated small summer resort. His new neighbors there extended to him the hand of genuine hospitality, welcomed him to their firesides and made him feel so much at home that he built himself a house, bought himself a farm, and has been coming back ever since. And he proposes to keep to that good custom. I intend coming back very often.[2]

The president loved to swim and took every opportunity to get into the water. Eleanor Roosevelt Seagraves, his oldest grandchild, remembers swimming with her grandfather in the White House pool and during the warmer months at the Hyde Park pond at Val-Kill, Eleanor Roosevelt's cottage. "It was a lot of fun. We just had the family around." Although FDR's legs were visibly atrophied by polio, Seagraves recalled, "We were so used to the handicap that we didn't even notice it."[3]

Seagraves, known as "Sistie," and her brother Curtis, nicknamed "Buzzie," lived in the White House from 1933 to 1937 and from 1943 to 1945. They were photographed constantly and became the "darlings of the public," Curtis Roosevelt recalls. "We were very much exposed to the press because my grandmother thought the country, in its great depression doldrums, needed any amusement it could get. . . . Whatever we did caused a fuss."[4] FDR thoroughly enjoyed his grandchildren, visiting with them each morning to find out their plans for the day. They provided a source of escape and relaxation, as did sailing, to a president who faced an array of problems far more complex and serious than any American leader had confronted.

Roosevelt sought the sea as the place where he could recharge himself, clear away his "personal cobwebs," and find a new source of creativity and innovation.[5] About two months after the 7 December 1941 Japanese attack on Pearl Harbor, Roosevelt explained: "I try to get away a couple of times a year on these short trips . . . there is a chance . . . for thinking things through, for differentiating between principles and methods, between the really big things of life and those things of the moment which may seem all important today and are forgotten by the world in a month."[6]

Boarding the special presidential train around midnight on a balmy April 1937 Washington evening, the president traveled by rail to Biloxi, Mississippi. He transferred to a car, and motored to New Orleans. His son Elliott and his new presidential yacht *Potomac* were waiting. A two week fishing cruise to the Gulf of Mexico began.

In a letter penned to his mother while on board, the president wrote: "Here we are at Point Isabel, near the mouth of the Rio Grande and the Mexican border, and so far the trip has been a complete success. We have had good fishing and lots of sunlight and sleep . . . we are leading a quiet existence and there is no news outside of an occasional tarpon."[7] The presidential escort consisted of two destroyers: USS *Moffett* and USS *Decatur.*

The White House set up a temporary headquarters, with Marvin McIntyre in charge, at a Galveston hotel. The press corps did the same because, on this trip, the president did not invite reporters to come along, as had been customary on most previous trips. Roosevelt agreed to "cover" himself for the press, and did send wireless messages to the correspondents. In one message, which was not very newsworthy, he wrote: "Spent a quiet Sunday aboard *Potomac*. Comfortable anchorage off Port Aransas. Got grand rest in preparation for tomorrow's fishing. Sea rough this morning but much smoother tonight. Governor [James V.] Allred visited me this afternoon."[8] In 1939, Roosevelt named Allred, a strong supporter of New Deal programs, a federal judge after the completion of his second term in the White House.

The following day at Port Aransas Roosevelt landed his first tarpon, a ninety pound silver king, after playing him for twenty minutes. He sent a press update to reporters back in Galveston: "Returned after dark this evening, Monday. Total catch fourteen tarpon, everyone in party contributing. Splendid day's sport. Plans for tomorrow depend upon conditions at sea. Everyone in fine spirits." Toward the end of the cruise, Roosevelt invited reporters aboard for a press conference. Gathered on *Potomac*'s deck, they witnessed a tanned president, dressed in dark trousers and open-neck blue shirt, land his second tarpon. It was bigger than the first and was brought into the boat after a one-hour-and-twenty-two-minute vigorous fight between fish and president.[9]

The president received and sent important papers via seaplane, as had been the procedure on other voyages. Roosevelt signed thirty-two minor bills into law on the deck of the yacht just as his voyage was ending.[10] He boarded the presidential special in Forth Worth for his return to Washington.

During a 13 May press conference aboard the train, Roosevelt, aware of criticism of his frequent seagoing trips, expanded on their purpose, perhaps a bit disingenuously. "The object of these trips, you know, is not fishing. I don't give a continental damn whether I catch fish or not. The chief objective is to get a perspective on the scene which I cannot get in Washington any more than any of you boys can," the president said. "You have to go a long way off so as to see things in their true perspective," the president continued. "Because if you sit in one place, right in the middle of the woods, the little incidents that don't mean a hill of beans get magnified by a president just as they do by a correspondent."[11]

Four days later, Roosevelt was back in Washington's stifling heat. But criticism of his trips continued. Also, because he would not allow reporters to accompany him on this latest cruise, speculation about the president's health became an issue, especially from some of his harshest critics. During a press conference in his office, the president, in an off-the-record moment, read from a publication of the McClure Newspaper Syndicate to reporters assembled around his desk:

Unchecked. A New York specialist high in the medical field is authority for the following, which is given in the strictest confidence to editors: Towards the end of last month, Mr. Roosevelt was found in a coma at his desk. Medical examination disclosed the neck rash which is typical of certain disturbing symptoms. Immediate treatment of the most skilled kind was indicated, with complete privacy and detachment from official duties. Hence the trip to southern waters, with no newspaper men on board and a naval convoy which cannot be penetrated.[12]

The correspondents asked whether the president intended to sue the newspaper syndicate. Roosevelt replied that he had no such plans. Steve Early, the president's press secretary, told the reporters that the editor of the McClure Syndicate said they would retract the reference to the coma if the White House would issue an official denial. A White House statement would lend credibility to the news syndicate, it was thought, which Roosevelt did not wish to do.

Roosevelt traveled more than any previous president in American history, much of it on the sea. Roosevelt took frequent trips down the Potomac and on Chesapeake Bay aboard his presidential yacht. Over the course of the 1937 summer, Roosevelt took at least seven weekend cruises aboard *Potomac,* escaping both the political as well as the atmospheric Washington heat. Although these trips were brief, they provided the president with needed rest as well as time to think through his ideas in an environment he loved.

The summer saw a number of developments on the legislative front, including extension of the Neutrality Act, which Roosevelt signed while cruising aboard his yacht. Among other provisions, the act prohibited exporting of armaments to so-called "belligerent" nations. Aviation also lost one of its earliest pioneers when Amelia Earhart disappeared during her round-the-world flight. Some speculated that she was on a secret espionage mission for President Roosevelt, spying on Japanese-held islands in the Pacific. Others discounted this theory, indicating that there is no solid evidence for it.[13] Earhart and her navigator, Fred Noonan, were never found; it appears unlikely the spy theory will ever be proved or disproved.

After Congress adjourned in August 1937, Roosevelt finalized plans for yet another cruise, this time a little closer to home. At the end of August, Roosevelt traveled to his Hyde Park home via New York's Hudson River, where he completed work on bills passed during the session. On 2 September, Roosevelt boarded *Potomac,* at anchor in the Hudson, near Poughkeepsie. The ensuing week-long cruise was in Long Island and Block Island Sounds. Accompanying the president were his son Jimmy as well as Harry Hopkins, Dr. Ross McIntire, and Capt. Paul Bastedo. FDR's recently promoted naval aide, Bastedo had traveled with FDR on several earlier cruises.

The yacht traveled down the Hudson, past the Battery, then up the East River into Long Island Sound. The navy destroyer USS *Selfridge* shadowed *Potomac,* as did several U.S. Coast Guard vessels with Secret Service agents on board. The presidential party made fishing stops at Fort Pond Bay on the eastern tip of Long Island, Montauk Point, then Great Salt Pond on Block Island and Fishers Island. FDR and his party landed thirty-six striped bass in choppy waters on the final day of the cruise. Gale force winds delayed the president's Block Island departure, so he summoned reporters to an impromptu press conference aboard *Potomac.*

Back in Washington, the president addressed the deepening international crisis, especially with regard to hostilities that had broken out between Japan and China. On 14 September, he issued an executive order prohibiting U.S. merchant vessels to transport any arms, ammunition, or other implements of war to China or Japan. The president stated that any merchant vessels flying the American flag that attempted to transport such items to the Far East "do so at their own risk."[14]

After discussing additional business, the president announced that he would depart near the end of September for the Pacific coast on a "perspective" trip. He wanted to "take the pulse of the West" with regard to the success of his New Deal programs that aimed at putting people to work. The trip, with stops in Iowa, Wyoming, Idaho, Oregon, Montana, Minnesota, and North Dakota, would be primarily aboard his special presidential train, although he would sail aboard the destroyer USS *Phelps* from Seattle to Victoria, British Columbia.

In Chicago on 5 October, Roosevelt spoke about the dangers of war and the hope that the United States would not have to do battle.

> War is a contagion, whether it be declared or undeclared. It can engulf states and peoples remote from the original scene of hostilities. We are determined to keep out of war, yet we cannot insure ourselves against the disastrous effects of war and the dangers of involvement. We are adopting such measures as will minimize our risk of involvement, but we cannot have complete protection in a world of disorder in which confidence and security have broken down. . . . America hates war. America hopes for peace. Therefore, America actively engages in the search for peace.[15]

On his way back east, Roosevelt spoke to a radio audience from his railroad car in Cleveland. He spoke in great clarity about the need for the president, as well as all Americans, to travel frequently around the country in order to see how the average citizen lives. Roosevelt said, "I knew a man once who, after graduation from college with a Bachelor of Arts Degree, kept right on by taking a degree in Science, a degree in Law, a degree in Medicine and several graduate degrees in other subjects. When I knew him he was forty-five years old and had been in college for more than a quarter of a century. He was a walking encyclopedia but had never been outside of his home town, and he was about the most bigoted, narrow-minded, unsophisticated and generally impossible person I have ever met." Roosevelt offered this man this advice: "Take a second-hand car, put on a flannel shirt, drive out to the Coast by the northern route and come back by the Southern route. Don't stop anywhere where you have to pay more than $2 for your room and bath. Don't talk to your banking friends or your Chamber of Commerce friends, but specialize on the gasoline station man, the small restaurant keeper and the farmers you meet by the wayside and your fellow automobile travelers."[16]

Returning to Washington in early October, Roosevelt took to the air-waves to outline to the American people his plans for a special session of Congress, which he was calling for 15 November. In this Fireside Chat, the president said that, based on his recent trip, he found Americans were pleased with the substantial gains in prosperity, but they still were not fully satisfied. "I have taken trips to all parts of the country. Last spring I visited the Southwest. This summer I made several trips to the East. Now I am just back from a trip all the way across the continent, and later this autumn I hope to pay my annual visit to the Southeast," Roosevelt told his radio audience.[17] Roosevelt was proposing a variety of measures to help make the recovery more permanent and to forestall the spread of the ever-deepening recession. The mood of Congress was not supportive, however, and Roosevelt failed to gain backing for his legislative proposals, including those dealing with wages and hours, regional planning, governmental reorganization, and agriculture.

Stymied by Congress' reticence on these issues, Roosevelt planned a trip to Florida for a little fishing and relaxing. He was forced to postpone his travel when he suffered a seriously abscessed tooth that, despite its extraction, left the president bedridden with pain and a fever. About a week later his doctor pronounced him fit to travel. Before departing Washington for warmer climes, the president was asked during a press conference which tooth had caused him the trouble. He replied, using his best nautical terminology: "Number 3 hold, starboard side aft."[18] Roosevelt boarded the presidential special on 27 November, bound for Florida. Meanwhile, Congress continued to argue over what should be done.

Arriving in Miami two days later, Roosevelt was greeted by thousands of cheering residents lining the street, only a few blocks from the site where a would-be assassin in 1933 fired five bullets at Roosevelt, narrowly missing the then-president-elect. FDR next boarded *Potomac* and headed out through Biscayne Bay to the open Atlantic. The destroyer USS *Selfridge* again provided presidential escort services. A temporary White House was set up in a hotel in Coral Gables, Florida.

The presidential party fished at the Dry Tortugas, about sixty-five miles west of Key West. Roosevelt caught the first fish of the trip, which was described by son Jimmy as a large mackerel. The president spent the next day trolling for sailfish and barracuda. Unfortunately, Roosevelt's tooth problem recurred, forcing him to cut short his cruise by two days. He returned to Washington for treatment of his sore gums.

On 12 December, the U.S. gunboat *Panay*, assigned to remove the remaining Americans from China, was fired upon by Japanese planes. Three men were killed and many others were wounded. *Panay* sunk in China's Yangtze River. The Japanese government apologized, paid a large indemnity, and promised no such further aggressive attacks would occur.

Over the course of the next four months, Roosevelt saw little of the sea. His vacation trips were land based—a week at Hyde Park in February 1938, and ten days in Warm Springs over Easter. Around this time, the president started making arrangements to build a repository for his public and private papers at his boyhood home in Hyde Park, which would become the nation's first presidential library.

Despite the toils in Washington and FDR's preoccupation with how the New Deal would be viewed by future historians, thoughts of the open seas were never far from his mind. In April 1938, he embarked at Charleston, South Carolina, aboard the fifteen million dollar cruiser USS *Philadelphia,* the first light cruiser authorized in the Roosevelt administration. A twenty-one-gun salute to the president pleased him as the ten-thousand-ton vessel left the dock, to head in the general direction of the Caribbean for ten days of sun and fun. Roosevelt brought along Thomas Qualters, a personal aide; Marvin McIntyre; Col. "Pa" Watson; and Ross McIntire, his physician. The destroyer USS *Fanning* provided a presidential escort.

As the cruiser was pulling away, the president spotted the dilapidated USS *Hartford,* the Civil War–era flagship of Adm. David Glasgow Farragut, hero of the 1864 Battle of Mobile Bay, tied up at another pier. Edward Delano, one of Roosevelt's ancestors, had a hand in constructing the old screw sloop, now unpainted and rotting at the pier.

"It looks awful. It's in horrible shape," Roosevelt shouted to Adm. William Henry Allen, commandant of the navy yard. "Why don't you get a WPA project down here and fix it up?" Roosevelt questioned.

"Well, we have not any money for that sort of thing down here," the commandant shouted in reply.

"You just send in a request for the appropriation and I'll see that it goes through," the president responded.[19]

About six months later, *Hartford* was towed to Washington, where it remained until 19 October 1945. It was towed to the Norfolk Navy Yard and classified as a relic. *Hartford* sank at its berth in 1958, and was subsequently dismantled.[20]

Foul weather and choppy seas prevented Roosevelt from fishing early during his spring 1938 trip. As conditions improved he did have some good luck, landing a twenty-pound pompano near Sombrero Island. Later in the cruise, the president took top honors in reeling in a twenty-pound barracuda off Caicos Island.

In one odd twist, this Roosevelt cruise made a bit of navigation history: existing ocean charts to the Eastern Bahamas, depicting the location of the lighthouse on Sombrero Island, were incorrect. The lighthouse, according to data collected on Roosevelt's trip, is actually two miles east of the location shown on the existing charts of the day. Charts were revised to reflect FDR's coordinates.

On the president's last night at sea, USS *Philadelphia* received a wireless SOS from *Marathon,* a Norwegian freighter en route from Montreal to New Orleans. Roosevelt ordered *Philadelphia* to reverse course and find the freighter. Approximately two hours later, *Marathon* was spotted and the ship's surgeon was lowered overboard, using the president's motorized fishing boat. After reaching the freighter the surgeon removed a steel splinter from a seaman's eye. The doctor back on board *Philadelphia* and the mission of mercy over, the cruiser headed north. It returned the president to Charleston docks the next evening, ending the twenty-seven-hundred-mile fishing cruise.[21]

Philadelphia had sprung a leak while transporting the president; it took on more than thirty-five tons of water. In an accident near Samana Bay the ship's anchor damaged a hull plate. Subsequently, the ship's sound room flooded. The vessel returned to the Philadelphia Naval Yard for repairs after disembarking the president.[22]

In July 1938 Roosevelt was aboard the presidential special heading west for a series of campaign speeches in Colorado, Utah, and Nevada— among other states—in support of primary candidates backing his New Deal programs. Roosevelt's efforts were partially successful; some of the candidates he backed achieved victory in the primaries. After the western leg of the train trip was completed, the president boarded the cruiser USS *Houston,* which was waiting for him in San Diego. Roosevelt was looking forward to some peaceful fishing in the Galapagos Islands. With conservatism on the rise in the country, this was one holiday cruise the president really needed for "relaxation, recreation (and) restoration of body and spirit," according to Roosevelt biographer Kenneth S. Davis.[23]

From his White House staff, the president took his congenial and relaxed military aide, Pa Watson, along with Stephen Early, Dr. Ross McIntyre, and Basil O'Connor, a former law partner. Roosevelt also invited Dr. Waldo L. Schmitt of the U.S. National Museum of Natural History at the Smithsonian Institution. He wanted Schmitt along so he could help to identify fish and other marine species encountered. On 16 July, *Houston* left San Diego with the president and his party on board. The destroyer USS *McDougal* accompanied the presidential cruise.

In a letter to Marvin McIntyre from somewhere at sea, Roosevelt wrote, "All goes well on board—except that Pa got a sailfish today—the only one & he is asking to succeed Pershing as General of the Armies. We miss you much. I take it you have a screamingly funny time over primaries. Here we don't care who wins!" Roosevelt, fishing from a small motorized whaleboat at Cedros Islands, 250 miles from San Diego, took a thirty pound yellow tail tuna after a fifteen minute battle. Next, he landed a prize thirty-eight-pound tuna while Pa Watson took a sixty-pound grouper at the entrance of Magpalena Bay, Baja California.[24] Obviously, the much needed R&R was working.

A little past noon on 24 July, President Roosevelt's ship crossed the equator, and briefly anchored at Darwin Bay in the Galapagos Islands. As he had during his Good Neighbor cruise in 1936, Roosevelt engaged in a light-hearted "crossing the line" ceremony in honor of the ship crossing the equator. This time, however, Roosevelt was no longer "Senior Pollywog" (someone who had not crossed the equator), but was now "Senior Shellback," the designation given to someone who had previously crossed the imaginary line dividing the earth. Senior Shellback Roosevelt ordered official watches stood in a military manner in the places he designated: the top of the turret, No. 2, and in the "eyes of the ship." During the ceremony, "presidential party pollywogs on the watch wore flying helmets, goggles, fur-lined flying suits and Sam Browne belts. Officer pollywogs went on duty wearing overcoats with upturned collars (in tropical summer), side arms, binoculars, and enormous diving shoes especially designed for the occasion. . . . Strange and ominous-looking objects began appearing on deck, including scaffolds, an electric chair, coffins, operating tables and stocks such as the Pilgrim fathers never knew," to be used on the pollywogs.[25] Some three hundred pollywogs were turned into shellbacks during the ceremony. Roosevelt had an uncanny ability to dismiss the serious concerns facing his presidency and the country, and thoroughly enjoy this type of frolicking good fun.

About an hour later, the ship began moving sixty miles further southwest; it anchored for the night at Sullivan Bay. Roosevelt found the fishing excellent and left the cruiser in his motorized whaleboat frequently over the next week. After a week in the Galapagos, a rested and satisfied president gave the order to weigh anchor. *Houston* departed the Galapagos en route to the Cocos Islands, nearly four hundred miles to the northeast. Arriving August 1, Roosevelt and his party spent the next week fishing the shark-infested waters of the Cocos Islands. The sharks gave the anglers some real trouble as they took them off their hooks. Roosevelt landed the "grandaddy of them all" when he caught a 235-pound tiger shark that had put up a monumental struggle for more than ninety minutes.

One day Roosevelt took his small whaleboat into the waters on the unprotected windy side of the island. He snagged a twenty-pound rainbow runner. He also reeled in albacore, wahoos, and a thirty-eight-pound blue crevally. Both the rainbow runner and the crevally were the largest of those species on record, according to Dr. Schmitt, the curator for such species in the national museum. Nine species collected were not in the museum's study collection.[26] In addition, nearly thirty new species, subspecies, and rare varieties of creatures were collected during the voyage. Some of the new species, including a new kind of royal palm, a crablike creature, and a species of sponge, were named after Roosevelt because he was the sponsor of the trip.[27]

While *Houston* was at anchor off Panama, Roosevelt decided to invite the queen of the San Blas Indians out to tea, according to Michael F. Reilly, a Secret Service agent traveling with the president. Reilly described the San Blas Indians as a people proud of their longstanding policy not to mingle with white men. Roosevelt sent his motorized launch out to get the queen, and she enjoyed her tea with the president. She then re-boarded the launch to return to shore. Reilly says the tide had fallen, so Secret Service agent Bob Clark "gallantly lifted the Queen from the boat and carried her ashore so that her gaudy ceremonial gown would not get wet." Reilly later wrote, "As he sat her down, the Queen's subjects raised a hue and cry and began stoning the lady and her gallant escort. Her Majesty retreated rapidly down the beach and Bob got back into the whaleboat as quickly as possible." The queen had committed the "unforgivable sin" of touching a white man.[28]

Hearing that a hurricane was heading northward, *Houston* cleared the Panama Canal and headed home at top speed. Suddenly, one night, the ship "seemed to turn upside down," according to Agent Reilly, who was stationed outside Roosevelt's cabin door. "I grabbed a steam pipe and hung on," Reilly recalled. Tables, sofas, and chairs went flying across the room. Reilly quickly opened the president's door and found Roosevelt had been thrown out of bed and was sitting on the deck, struggling to climb back into bed.

"What's the matter?" the president asked. "Did we ram or go aground?" At that moment, a marine appeared with a message from the captain that "we have hit heavy weather." Reilly said, "We pitched and tossed and seemed on the verge of capsizing all night, but old seaman Roosevelt made himself secure in his bed and slept perfectly."[29]

In his final personal letter written while aboard *Houston*, Roosevelt told his wife: "All goes well. I caught a 230 lb. Shark yesterday—1 hr. and 35 minutes—so I win the pool for the Biggest Fish."[30] A rejuvenated and bronzed Franklin Roosevelt, along with his cargo of fish and marine species, would soon be back home.

CHAPTER 11

Storm Signals from across the Seas

"There comes a time in the affairs of men when they must prepare to defend, not their homes alone, but the tenets of faith and humanity on which churches, their governments and their very civilization are founded," President Roosevelt said in his annual message to the Seventy-sixth Congress on 4 January 1939.[1] Roosevelt warned of "storm signals from across the seas," stressed the need for a strong national defense, and urged the United States to put its "own house in order" to prepare to meet what he described as undeclared wars raging around the world.[2]

As Hitler's army prepared to invade Czechoslovakia, the United States took steps to test its own defenses along the Atlantic seaboard, stretching all the way to South America. Roosevelt, long a devotee of the navy, elected to supervise personally the "war game" exercises scheduled to begin in February at an undisclosed location somewhere in the Caribbean. Recovering from the flu, the president would receive some much needed rest.

Before departing Florida for the Caribbean, Roosevelt took to the airwaves to deliver a stern warning to foreign dictator aggressors who might be eyeing the Americas for expansion. Addressing his radio audience from the back seat of his automobile, the president declared: "We say to all the world that in the western hemisphere—in the three Americas—the institution of democracy—government with the consent of the governed—must be maintained."[3]

Embarking USS *Houston* in Key West, Roosevelt traveled in the admiral's quarters to the secret site where the two week winter exercises would be conducted. Almost 150 ships, 600 planes, and about 60,000 officers and enlisted men would participate in what was said to be the largest contingent in each category engaged in U.S. naval games.[4] A temporary White House was set up in Miami to get messages to and from the president.

Although Roosevelt had hoped to get in a bit of fishing during the two weeks at sea, the war games occupied most of his time, leaving little freedom on this cruise to play with his rod and reel. The president had done a little fishing with his physician, Dr. McIntire, and others before boarding *Houston;* he even contributed one dollar to a pool for the person catching the biggest fish.[5]

Roosevelt actively participated in the war games, and surprised both the public and the press when he announced that the goal of the games was not simply to protect the Panama Canal, but rather the entire Western Hemisphere from a transoceanic attack. In what was described as the most elaborate naval maneuvers ever staged in American waters, the games got under way promptly at midnight on 19 February. The fleet had been divided into "white" and "black" teams, with the white forces attempting to seize a U.S. base, probably the Panama Canal. The president was part of the black forces, whose role was to defend the base from attack.[6] All forces had sealed orders, and even the president was not familiar with every detail of the battle plans.

After sailing thirty-nine hundred miles, observing, and actively participating in the successful war maneuvers, Roosevelt returned to the White House on 4 March. Rested and refreshed from two weeks of sun and salt air, he was confident the navy was ready to defend the nation.

Although Roosevelt visited Warm Springs around Easter for ten days and took several trips to Hyde Park, he would not take any lengthy cruises for the next five months. In mid-August he would embark on one of the country's newest cruisers, USS *Tuscaloosa,* which would carry him on a twenty-five-hundred-mile trip in the North Atlantic. Until then, however, he would have to be content with brief weekend getaways aboard his presidential yacht, mostly on the Potomac River.

Two weeks after returning from the war maneuvers in the Caribbean, Roosevelt took the first of many weekend trips aboard *Potomac.* The sleek craft, with the presidential flag snapping smartly in the wind, ferried FDR and some of his friends downriver to Mount Vernon. The president returned to the White House that night. Later in the spring Eleanor Roosevelt joined the president and some of their friends—including new Supreme Court Associate Justice William O. Douglas, the youngest Supreme Court justice since 1810—for an overnight cruise down the Potomac. At least two additional spring trips were taken aboard the presidential yacht. On one Roosevelt brought along some salt water fishing gear, so he could try his luck on the Chesapeake Bay. During the cruise, FDR took time to review the Hatch Act legislation, which had been passed by both houses of the Congress and forwarded to the president for signature. This legislation would restrict federal employees from active political campaigning.

Meanwhile, the president also had been working on detailed plans for the upcoming visit by King George VI and Queen Elizabeth of England, a visit that was designed to strengthen the bonds between the United States and its mother country, especially as storm clouds continued to develop around the globe. The royal couple would arrive in early June 1939, spend time with the president and first lady in Washington and Hyde Park, then return home. Roosevelt personally managed the visit, even small details. In January, the president had sent a lengthy letter to the king; it was packed with detailed schedules, and offered a variety of options for the visit. He even advised that, due to the usual hot and humid summer weather, the royal party should bring thin and lightly colored clothing. The president did a remarkable amount of hands-on planning.[7]

The royal visit proceeded without a hitch, complete with a Sunday afternoon picnic at Roosevelt's new personal retreat, Top Cottage, in Hyde Park. The president drove the king and queen from his Hyde Park home to his new cottage using his hand-controlled Ford convertible. Picnic fare for 150 guests consisted of hot dogs, potato salad, baked beans, beer, and strawberry shortcake. Simple old-fashioned picnics were a favorite of the Roosevelt family.

After the king and queen departed for Canada before heading back to England, Roosevelt returned to Washington. As an especially sweltering July day drew to a close, the president gathered his fishing gear—and some friends and advisors—and boarded *Potomac*. He was headed out to sea for some angling off Ocean City, Maryland. He had heard that the white marlin were running. However, after a weekend of attempts, Presidential Assistant Harry Hopkins took top honors, reeling in a sixty-five-pound fish.

On 5 August, an unusually fractured and hostile Congress began to close up shop. In the final hours of the session, Roosevelt collected the three hundred bills and left town, heading again for his home along New York's Hudson River. He would review the bills in his comfortable boyhood home, and veto or approve as he wished.

When the work was completed, he boarded the cruiser USS *Tuscaloosa,* anchored at pier 32 in New York City, and headed to the North Atlantic for two weeks at sea. The destroyer USS *Lang* would accompany the president on the trip. In a letter to his son Jimmy, Roosevelt said he would "be on the *Tuscaloosa* somewhere near the North Pole for the next ten or twelve days."[8] His plans called for only one scheduled stop on the cruise, at Campobello Island, where he would meet with his son Franklin Jr., who was staying at the Roosevelt family summer home.

Traveling at much greater speeds than Roosevelt was accustomed to in a sloop or tiny yawl, the cruiser reached Portsmouth, New Hampshire, the following day. *Tuscaloosa* anchored off the coast near the Isles of Shoals to observe the navy's efforts to salvage a sunken submarine, USS *Squalus.* Roosevelt, peering through binoculars on the cruiser's bridge, watched the operation and also received a report from the admiral in charge of the project. The new U.S. submarine, which came to rest in 240 feet of water, had plunged to the bottom of the North Atlantic during a test dive, killing twenty-six crew members. Miraculously, thirty-three were rescued using the McCann rescue chamber, a revised version of the diving bell invented by Comdr. Charles B. "Swede" Momsen, who supervised the *Squalus* rescue efforts.

Continuing its northward journey, the cruiser encountered heavy fogs, typical for this stretch of the New England coastline, and was delayed a few hours in reaching Campobello. The president was besieged by reporters when he arrived; he was asked whether he had decided to seek an unprecedented third term in the White House. They told him that Edward J. Kelly, Chicago's mayor, said it was "Roosevelt or ruin" as far as the Democratic Party was concerned. FDR replied, "No comment."[9]

Roosevelt's own Campobello cottage was not open, so he rested at his mother's adjoining house, his boyhood cottage. He visited with Franklin Jr., his wife Ethel, and their year-old son, Franklin D. Roosevelt III. After his brief seven-hour stay FDR embarked again aboard *Tuscaloosa.* The cruiser steamed out of the inlet, bound for Halifax, Nova Scotia, where it briefly would lay at anchor. Roosevelt tried his luck at some trolling, but was unable to land any fish.

As darkness fell, *Tuscaloosa* got under way for an overnight run to Cape Breton Island, where a navy seaplane was waiting with important papers from Washington. But the fog rolled in and the plane was not able to make connection with the president. Despite the continuing fog, the next morning *Tuscaloosa* weighed anchor and sailed 225 miles to Bay of Islands, Newfoundland, which is said to be the farthest north Roosevelt had visited since he took office in March 1933. Roosevelt wanted to try the fishing grounds, known to be teeming with salmon.

After fishing all day, and getting drenched by an evening rainstorm, the only catch was made by the recently promoted Gen. Pa Watson, who reeled in an eighteen-pound salmon. Roosevelt, commenting on his military aide's catch, noted, "His unique specimen, while not the fattest known, excels all I have seen in my long experience. It is, in fact, the Adonis of salmon. Its regular features, its pink complexion and its rippling muscles make it a fit comrade for the general."[10]

Bonne Bay, Newfoundland, the famed tuna fishing grounds, was Roosevelt's next port of call. *Tuscaloosa* steamed through dense fog to reach the small fishing village, where the president hoped to try his luck. He also hoped to receive his Washington mail, which had still not been delivered. Unfortunately, the weather continued to prevent the seaplane from ferrying important papers to the president.

One chilly day in August 1939, while the president was bundled up and sitting on deck, fishing rod over the stern, he received a radio message that broke the contented peace he was feeling as he fished the Grand Banks. Germany and Russia had signed a nonaggression economic assistance pact. Roosevelt's mood turned grim as he acknowledged to Secretary of State Cordell Hull that Hitler obviously had decided on war. "He has secured his eastern flank and now need only worry about the western front—Poland doesn't count," Roosevelt said. "He always said that Germany should never fight a war on two fronts."[11] Roosevelt ordered *Tuscaloosa* to head home.

The White House mail finally reached Halifax while *Tuscaloosa,* en route home, was held captive once again by heavy fog. The president now had his mail and paperwork from Washington, even though he continued to be fogbound. The next morning, the cruiser steamed through the fog and out of the harbor, heading for the Gulf Stream. Roosevelt took some time to troll the warmer waters on his way to Sandy Hook, New Jersey, where he docked at the trip's end.

Within a few days of FDR's return to the White House, the situation in Europe took a decidedly bad turn. Germany invaded Poland a week after Germany and Russia signed their nonaggression pact. Germany justified the invasion by saying that the Poles had attacked first. Within two days, Britain and France declared war on Germany. Shortly thereafter, the British ocean liner *Athenia,* en route home from Europe, was torpedoed by a German U-boat, killing twenty-eight Americans on board en route home from Europe. The United States was slowly, but inexorably, being drawn into the maelstrom.

In his fourteenth Fireside Chat to the nation on 3 September 1939, President Roosevelt again pledged that the United States would remain a neutral nation, although he said he could not ask every American to remain neutral in thought, as well. "Even a neutral has a right to take account of the facts. Even a neutral cannot be asked to close his mind or close his conscience," Roosevelt told a predominantly isolationist nation. "I have said not once, but many times, that I have seen war and that I hate war. I say that again and again. I hope the United States will keep out of this war. I believe that it will. And I give you assurance and reassurance that every effort of your government will be directed toward that end. As long as it remains within my power to prevent, there will be no blackout of peace in the United States," the president concluded.[12]

Six days later, President Roosevelt declared a limited national emergency, thus expanding his powers to act in the event of an emergency. Americans were cautioned to limit travel to Europe. The American Federation of Labor adopted a resolution opposing U.S. involvement in the war, but proposed a boycott of goods from Germany, Russia, and Japan.

Two weeks later, the president announced that submarines of unknown nationality were spotted off the southern boundary of Alaska, off the coast of Boston, about sixty miles off the tip of Nova Scotia, and halfway between that point and the Nantucket Shoals. Surprisingly, when questioned by a reporter, the president said that the waters on the eastern seaboard were patrolled from Maine to the Caribbean, but no patrols were maintained in the Pacific, off the west coast of the nation.[13]

Meanwhile, the army already had ordered work speeded up at its six government-owned arsenals, with double shifts working at some. Eight new battleships were in varying stages of construction and a number of other vessels, including two aircraft carriers, thirty-eight destroyers, twenty submarines, six light cruisers, eight motorized torpedo boats, and four submarine chasers. Since Roosevelt took office in March 1933, 106 new naval vessels had already been commissioned.[14]

Over the next few months, the European situation deteriorated even further, and its repercussions began to be felt across the Atlantic. German U-boats prowled the waters off the North Atlantic, torpedoing British ships and ships belonging to its allies. By February 1940, some estimates place the loss to Allied shipping from the U-boats at more than four hundred thousand tons. The threat to the United States continued to increase. Roosevelt finally issued a proclamation on 18 October 1940 that closed U.S. territorial waters and ports to submarine and armed merchant vessels from belligerent nations, including France, Germany, Poland, the United Kingdom, India, Australia, Canada, New Zealand, and the Union of South Africa.[15]

In February 1940, a weary Roosevelt decided he needed some rejuvenation. He announced that he would embark on a two week vacation cruise in southern waters. This time, however, the trip was shrouded in mystery; the president refused to comment in any detail on his plans. One report in the *New York Times* stated that the president's physician, Ross McIntire, reportedly concerned about his health, advised Roosevelt to get away from his routine duties, and take a southern vacation as soon as possible.[16]

Dr. McIntire urged FDR to take as many vacations as possible, preferably in his favorite environment—the sea. The White House physician credited his sea vacations with keeping the president "trim." However, McIntire noted, "Despite our bargain about regular vacations, I doubt, however, if he would have kept the agreement except for his love of the water and fishing. Not even Izaak Walton was ever more the Compleat Angler. After a day of battle with deep-sea big fellows, he would turn to me with a wheedling grin and say 'We've got another hour, so what about a bit of bottom fishing?'"[17] Walton was the seventeenth-century English angler who wrote the literary classic, *The Compleat Angler*.

Dr. Howard Bruenn, who began assisting McIntire in the care of President Roosevelt in March 1944, agreed that the water brought the president peace and relaxation. "He loved to watch the water," Dr. Bruenn recalled. "He would sit in his chair on deck and just watch the water. He enjoyed it."[18]

On Valentine's Day in 1940, in the middle of a Washington blizzard, Roosevelt left aboard the presidential special. En route to Pensacola, Florida, he once again boarded USS *Tuscaloosa*, putting out to sea, on what the newspapers described as a mystery cruise. Speculation was rampant that Roosevelt was going to meet with officials of the British, French, and Italian governments while he was at sea. Roosevelt cautioned correspondents to not go too far "out on a limb" in their speculation, lest it be sawed off.[19]

In a letter to Eleanor, written while aboard *Tuscaloosa,* the president said he would inspect the Atlantic defenses and cross through the Panama Canal the following day. He hoped to get in some fishing. He said it had been "choppy and windy but warm since yesterday a.m. and I've already had lots of sleep and sunlight."[20]

The U-boat threat mandated absolute secrecy and security greater than on previous trips. Two destroyers, USS *Lang* and USS *Jouett,* escorted the president's ship. When Roosevelt reached the Canal Zone, U.S. navy planes and eighteen U.S. army bombers formed an escort through the canal. Roosevelt inspected the Atlantic defenses at the canal, lunched at the officers club, and boarded the cruiser again. *Tuscaloosa* sailed into the Pacific Ocean by early evening.

Roosevelt fished along the Panama coast. He caught a small blue crevally and an amberjack; his shipmates reeled in two amberjacks, two crevallies, and one "mystery" fish. Roosevelt also held a news conference aboard the cruiser, dispelling speculation that he was meeting Allied officials at sea. He said the defenses at the Panama Canal had been doubled since his first official visit in 1934, and expressed satisfaction with the work under way there.[21]

The next day, Roosevelt did a bit more angling for sailfish off the coast of Costa Rica and, later, fished for red snapper. But the fish were not biting for Roosevelt on this trip, although Dr. McIntire reeled in a forty-pound red snapper. In a letter to his mother from the Canal Zone, Roosevelt wrote of "a good cruise and a fine rest but not many fish."[22]

After two weeks and four thousand miles of sun and salt air, *Tuscaloosa* returned Roosevelt to the Pensacola docks. FDR boarded the presidential special, bound for cold and snowy Washington. He would resume day-to-day control as the United States became more and more involved in the ever deepening crisis abroad.

In addition to the monumental international task, Roosevelt was facing another challenge as well. Should he abandon his personal wish to retire from public life and, instead, seek an unprecedented third term in the White House?

CHAPTER 12

Rattlesnakes of the Atlantic

President Roosevelt stayed close to home after his two week vacation in February 1940, mulling the prospects of seeking a third term while also keeping a close eye on the escalating European crisis. Over the next several months, Italy's Benito Mussolini joined Adolf Hitler in the war against England and France, and Germany invaded Norway, Denmark, Luxembourg, the Netherlands, and Belgium. In England, sixty-six-year-old Winston Churchill replaced the discredited Neville Chamberlain as prime minister.

In response, Roosevelt sought an increase in his defense budget and established the Office of Emergency Management to be prepared if war came to the shores of the United States. By June 1940 France fell to German forces, and Congress authorized $1.5 billion for naval defense and $1.8 billion for other military defense efforts. In July lawmakers approved Roosevelt's four-billion-dollar request to establish a two-ocean navy.

But what about Franklin Roosevelt and his wish to retire? Was he ready to abandon his personal desire to return to Hyde Park? Would he fight to win an unprecedented third term at 1600 Pennsylvania Avenue? As he pondered his choice, the deteriorating world situation helped to subordinate personal wishes to the national interest. As Hitler continued to invade countries and win victories, Roosevelt relented. As the Democratic Convention opened in Chicago on 15 July 1940, FDR allowed his name to be put into nomination.

When Roosevelt's name was mentioned during the convention, a loud voice was heard throughout the hall: "We want Roosevelt! . . . The world wants Roosevelt!" When the speech concluded, the voice boomed again, sparking an hour-long demonstration for the president. Later, it was discovered that the voice was coming from Chicago's superintendent of sewers; he was speaking from a microphone in the hall's basement. "The voice from the sewer" went down in history, according to the *Almanac of Presidential Campaigns*.[1]

Roosevelt, age fifty-eight, was nominated on the first ballot, and Wendell L. Willkie, a Republican businessman and lawyer ten years FDR's junior, would run hard against him into November. Willkie proved to be Roosevelt's strongest challenger yet.

Roosevelt had curtailed any lengthy travel for the last several months. He did take a quick train trip to Charlottesville on 10 June to address the University of Virginia graduation exercises, where Franklin Jr. would later receive his law degree.

Four days before Hitler invaded France, Roosevelt left the White House amid what was referred to by the press as "unusual precautions," en route to the naval yard, where he embarked on the presidential yacht *Potomac*. Motorcycle police rode ahead and on both sides of the president's closed car. FDR customarily rode in an open car, especially when it was warm, such as this June day. Two Secret Service cars followed immediately behind the presidential car.[2]

During the summer, the president embarked on an ambitious schedule to personally inspect military installations, shipyards, and factories involved in the production of guns and other weapons of war. However, because of the rapidly changing world situation, the president limited his travels to locations from which he could return to the White House quickly, usually within twelve hours.

He inspected facilities in Norfolk; Portsmouth, New Hampshire; Boston; Watertown, Massachusetts; Newport, Rhode Island; New London, Connecticut; Norwood, New York; and South Charleston, West Virginia. He also inspected the Philadelphia Navy Yard and Army Depot; Aberdeen Proving Ground, Maryland; Glenn-Martin Aircraft Plant, Baltimore; Fort Meade, Maryland; and the Watervliet Arsenal, near Albany,

New York.[3] He used his presidential yacht *Potomac* for some inspection trips, including trips to New England naval yards, Fort Meade, and the Martin Aircraft plant.

As often was the case with Roosevelt's actions, his trips served several purposes. The president had a chance to personally inspect facilities, as well as demonstrate to the accompanying press contingent that the United States, indeed, was getting ready in case hostilities spread across the ocean. The inspection visits also inspired the swelling workforce with the importance of their work to the nation. And, perhaps, most important, the trips allowed Roosevelt to campaign without really appearing to campaign.

In September, while aboard the presidential special bound for Washington, Roosevelt announced to reporters traveling with him that he had worked out an arrangement with England. Fifty old "four piper" World War I destroyers would be traded to England in exchange for the right to construct American naval and air bases on Crown colonies in the Western Hemisphere, including bases on the islands of Bermuda, the Bahamas, Jamaica, St. Lucia, Trinidad, Antigua, British Guiana, and Newfoundland. Roosevelt characterized this so-called "destroyers for bases" pact as necessary for "preparation for continental defense in the face of grave danger" and essential for U.S. "peace and safety."[4]

Ten days later, the president approved the "Peace Time Universal Selective Service Act," which required young men to register for the draft. Roosevelt set 16 October as the deadline date for every male between the ages of twenty-one and thirty-five to appear at neighborhood draft boards to register.

Despite being challenged by Willkie, the toughest opponent he had yet encountered, Roosevelt decided the unsettled world situation would allow him to forgo active campaigning and not "engage in any purely political debate." Instead, he would deliver only five campaign speeches to correct any "misrepresentations" from the Willkie camp. Willkie, a vigorous campaigner, traveled more than thirty thousand miles, crisscrossing the country; he delivered more than 540 speeches, attacking Roosevelt as an incompetent warmonger.[5]

The president decided he had better respond to these intense attacks. In the last few weeks of the campaign, he came out swinging. Roosevelt traveled to New York City, New Jersey, Connecticut, Massachusetts, Buffalo, and Cleveland. He stressed the same message: Republicans had consistently voted against increasing defense spending to ensure the security of the nation, as well as against helping Great Britain battle the Nazi onslaught. During a campaign appearance at Madison Square Garden in New York City, he accused the Republicans of playing politics with the country's national security. He coined the catchy phrase "Martin, Barton and Fish," ridiculing three Republican congressmen who voted consistently against a variety of measures introduced in support of Roosevelt's foreign and domestic policies.[6]

Roosevelt boasted about the preparedness of the U.S. Navy, which he called "as powerful and as efficient as any single navy that ever sailed the seas in history." However, he warned that as powerful as the U.S. Navy was, it might not be able to win against a combination of powerful naval forces. Roosevelt declared that, as a result, more needed to be done to enhance U.S. fighting forces.[7]

During a campaign stop two days later in Boston, Roosevelt described the U.S. Navy as the country's "outer line of defense," noting that he had worked to build a big navy since taking office in 1933. Roosevelt was one of the best friends the navy has ever had. His cousin, Theodore, years earlier had brought the U.S. Navy of age with his "Great White Fleet," thus making it the second most powerful force in the world.

By 1933, however, the navy was demoralized from years of meager budgets and lack of new ship construction. Navy brass hoped the new president would reverse the record of President Herbert Hoover; he did not authorize construction of a single naval vessel during his entire four years in the White House. The U.S. Navy's wish was about to come true, although not quite as quickly as it had hoped.

In what has been described as creative "backdoor financing," Roosevelt allocated $238 million from the National Industrial Recovery Act, passed by the Congress in June 1933, to build thirty-four new vessels, including cruisers, destroyers, carriers, and submarines. Roosevelt also authorized additional funding for dry docks and other naval facilities. He ably convinced an isolationist Congress that putting people to work building new ships was an important public works program. Two goals were accomplished: Jobs were created for the country's unemployed, and strengthening of the U.S. Navy began to restore badly sagging morale.

The following year, Congress passed—and Roosevelt signed—legislation to bring the navy up to "treaty strength." Navy officials had been pleading for the number of ships allowed the United States under terms of an international arms limitation treaty, but they had been ignored both by President Hoover and a wary Congress. The pace of the build-up to treaty strength would be slower than the navy had hoped, however. It would pale in comparison to the monumental ship construction program that ensued following the attack on Pearl Harbor on 7 December 1941. Naval historian Samuel Eliot Morison lists the following vessels constructed during the period 1934 through 1939:

> 1934: four cruisers, one destroyer
> 1935: one cruiser, six destroyers, one floating dry dock
> 1936: one cruiser, two destroyers, four submarines
> 1937: twenty-four destroyers, one cruiser, two gunboats, six
>   submarines, one cargo ship, three fleet tugs
> 1938: two carriers, five cruisers, twelve destroyers, six submarines
> 1939: four cruisers, eight destroyers, four submarines, two
>   minesweepers, one cargo ship, one fleet tug

Overall, during the period 1933 through 1940, Roosevelt, in a campaign speech in Boston, boasted that the number of commissioned ships increased from 193 ships in 1933 to 337 ships in 1940. In addition, 119 new ships were under construction. The number of navy personnel had almost doubled, from 106,000 sailors in 1933 to 210,000 in 1940. Six times as many men were employed in the country's navy yards in 1940 as compared to 1933.[8] Roosevelt's "new" U.S. Navy was starting to take shape. To calm the ever growing number of isolationists, however, Roosevelt stressed that these actions, along with securing new American naval and air bases in the Atlantic Ocean, were not preludes to war, as the Republicans were arguing, but were measures taken to keep potential attackers away from U.S. shores.

On 5 November, Americans went to the polls and returned Roosevelt to the White House. He became the first—and only—president to serve more than two terms. Although the popular vote for Roosevelt was less than it was in either 1932 or 1936, Roosevelt's Electoral College win was a landslide—449 votes for Roosevelt and 82 votes for Willkie.

Following a brief cruise on the presidential yacht *Potomac,* a victorious but weary president made plans for his first real fishing vacation since early in the year. On 2 December, he departed aboard USS *Tuscaloosa* for a cruise to southern waters, including Florida and the Caribbean. His new Scottish terrier, Fala, a gift from his cousin Daisy Suckley, traveled with Roosevelt. Fala was to become the most celebrated presidential pet in American history and would play a key role in the president's next campaign.

In addition to eight-month-old Fala, FDR was accompanied by Brig. Gen. Pa Watson, Dr. Ross McIntire, Harry Hopkins, and Capt. Daniel J. Callaghan, the president's new naval aide. Although the fish were not biting particularly well on this trip, Roosevelt had time to rest and relax. During this cruise Roosevelt conceived of one of the most important programs to assist England with its fight against the Nazis.

While USS *Tuscaloosa* was at anchor, a navy seaplane landed nearby and delivered a letter from Prime Minister Winston Churchill. The 7 December 1940 letter, later described by the prime minister as one of the most important letters he had ever composed, explained to Roosevelt that England was in dire need of cash. "The moment approaches," Churchill wrote, "when we shall no longer be able to pay cash for shipping and other supplies." England had permitted the United States to inspect its financial records; the British government had only two billion dollars on hand to pay for more than five billion dollars in orders from American factories.[9]

In response, Franklin Roosevelt conceived the beginnings of the Lend-Lease program, a creative and ingenious means to circumvent a 1934 law that forbade the United States from trading with any warring nation, except on a cash basis. The overall goal of Roosevelt's program was to provide material aid to countries whose defenses were vital to the defense of the United States.

Later, during a press conference in his White House office, President Roosevelt explained the program by using the analogy of a garden hose: "Suppose my neighbor's home catches on fire, and I have a length of garden hose four or five hundred feet away," the president said. "If he can take my garden hose and connect it up with his hydrant, I may help him put out the fire. Now what do I do? I don't say to him before that operation, 'Neighbor, my garden hose cost me fifteen dollars; you have to pay me fifteen dollars for it.' What is the transaction that goes on? I don't want fifteen dollars—I want my garden hose back after the fire is over."

The president continued: "All right. If it goes through the fire all right, intact, without any damage to it, he gives it back to me and thanks me very much for the use of it. But suppose it gets smashed up—holes in it— during the fire; we don't have to have too much formality about it, but I say to him, 'I was glad to lend you the hose; I see I can't use it any more, it's all smashed up.' He says 'How many feet of it were there?' 'There were

150 feet of it.' He says, 'All right, I will replace it.' Now, if I get a nice garden hose back, I am in pretty good shape."

Four days after Christmas 1940, Roosevelt took to the airwaves and delivered his sixteenth Fireside Chat. He stressed the need to assist Great Britain in that country's fight against Hitler, as well as to ensure U.S. security. "We must be the great arsenal of democracy," the president declared. "For this is an emergency as serious as war itself."

"If Great Britain goes down," Roosevelt warned, "the Axis powers will control the continents of Europe, Asia, Africa, Australia, and the high seas—and they will be in a position to bring enormous military and naval resources against this hemisphere." Roosevelt also said that some argued that the expansive Atlantic and Pacific Oceans would protect Americans from totalitarian aggression. But the "width of those oceans is not what it was in the days of the clipper ships"; modern bombers can make the trip from England to the United States without refueling. Edward R. Stettinius Jr., selected by Roosevelt to administer the Lend-Lease program, later observed that it was a "vital mechanism" that allowed the Allies to combine all their resources to fight the Axis powers. Stettinius said this sharing, or "pooling," of resources worked both ways. "In Britain, American soldiers were receiving millions of tons of war supplies with no payment by us. . . . American ships were being repaired with no cost to us in British ports all over the world. In Australia and New Zealand, almost all the food our soldiers ate was being given to us by those countries."[10]

Despite grumblings that the Lend-Lease program was giving Roosevelt a "blank check," Congress approved the proposal two months after it was submitted and appropriated the seven billion dollars requested by the president. Roosevelt signed it into law on 11 March 1941. Churchill was relieved.

In conjunction with the new Lend-Lease program, Roosevelt announced a $350 million shipbuilding initiative in early 1941. Merchant ships would be mass produced by using prefabricated materials and all-welded parts instead of riveted ones. These ships would be used to move troops and convey supplies, equipment, trucks, and jeeps purchased from the United States.

The so-called "Liberty" ship was a "dreadful looking object," according to the president. He described them as a type of ship built by the yard or foot. "Nobody that loves ships," Roosevelt said, "can be very proud of them; but it gets them out, and the difference, roughly speaking, in time between building a ship that is built like a square, oblong tank and a ship that is really a ship is six or eight months." Between 1941 and 1945 a total of 2,770 Liberty ships were constructed. Delivered at the rate of one ship per day, they were built by thousands of assemblers, many with absolutely no experience in shipbuilding. They worked double and triple shifts to get the job done. Liberty ships formed FDR's "bridge of ships" across the oceans, and were manned by the U.S. Merchant Marine in wartime status. Later in the war, shipyards began producing a newer ship, the so-called "Victory" ship. It was faster and bigger than the Liberty. Armaments were similar to those installed on Liberty ships. The hulls of the Victory ships were strengthened to prevent the type of fractures experienced on Liberty ships. Victory ships also could easily converted to other uses after the war. There were 534 Victory ships built between mid-1944 and mid-1946.[11]

Roosevelt, suffering from a head cold, was ready to escape a cold and snowy Washington to get some much needed rest. On 19 March 1941, Roosevelt boarded the presidential special en route to Port Everglades and the east coast of Florida. His yacht *Potomac* rocked at anchor awaiting the president. There was a good deal of concern about Roosevelt taking a fishing trip at this time, particularly with reports of German U-boats prowling North American waters. Nevertheless, Roosevelt decided to go.

Destroyers accompanying *Potomac* manned antiaircraft guns twenty-four hours a day. Depth charges and torpedoes were ready in the event of any U-boat sightings. In an 18 March Secret Service memorandum, Col. Edmund Starling, chief of the White House detail, outlined security precautions that would be taken en route to Florida and while the president was at sea. Three reporters were permitted to accompany the president, but had to travel aboard the destroyers.

Three Secret Service agents drove to Jacksonville on St. Patrick's Day to handle advance work there as well as at Port Everglades where the presidential yacht was waiting. Six agents were assigned to travel with Roosevelt aboard the train to Florida, including Michael Reilly, who later would succeed Starling as head of the White House detail. Reilly and Tommy Qualters traveled aboard *Potomac* with Roosevelt, while the other four would trail the presidential yacht aboard USS *Benson,* one of newest U.S. destroyers.[12]

Unfortunately, high winds and heavy seas delayed Roosevelt's departure from Port Everglades. Heavy security surrounded the dock where the presidential yacht was moored. Ironically, about twenty-two yards away, the Nazi freighter *Arauca* lay at anchor after putting into port about fifteen months earlier after a confrontation with a British cruiser. The freighter's flag, bearing the Nazi swastika, snapped in the breeze. The Secret Service ordered a U.S. Coast Guard sentry stationed nearby to watch over the ship and its crew of forty-four men. Roosevelt frequently rested on deck, so such lax security seems unthinkable in retrospect.[13]

While on shore, Roosevelt had an opportunity to inspect the navy's air training base at Jacksonville, and expressed amazement at the progress achieved in little more than a year. Finally, after more than a thirty-six-hour delay, Skipper Roosevelt ordered *Potomac* to weigh anchor and put out to sea on Sunday morning, 22 March. Harry Hopkins, Harold Ickes, and Attorney General Robert Jackson were on board. Unlike Roosevelt's other southern vacation cruises, the world situation dictated that, on this trip, he venture no more than eight hours from port. Three cars of his special train would remain on stand-by in Miami, in case he had to beat a hasty retreat to Washington.

While Roosevelt was fishing one day, *Benson*'s crew honed their skills by firing imaginary torpedoes at the presidential yacht. If real, *Potomac* would have "capsized" and immediately "sank."[14] Neither FDR's luck with the fish, nor his luck with the weather, was very good on this trip. When he reached the Bahamas, the yacht, whose instability eventually would result in it being condemned as unfit for presidential duty in open waters, pitched back and forth on the heavy seas, causing the president to wonder what might happen if a stiff wave should hit the stern.[15]

In his diary, Harold Ickes said he feared for his life and the life of Roosevelt and others on board one night while *Potomac* was anchored off Great Bahama. The small craft listed thirty-two degrees in the rough water, Ickes recalled. Ickes and Jackson, who shared the cabin next to Roosevelt, lay in their beds watching the waves wash up over their portholes. "If the *Potomac* should capsize, there wasn't a chance for a single one of us," Ickes thought.

Ickes, who feared for the president's safety, said he "felt angry" that Roosevelt would take such chances with his own life. Even though the destroyer *Benson* kept an eye on the presidential yacht that night, Ickes said it would have been impossible for the ship to come close enough to shore, where *Potomac* was anchored, to rescue the president and others. He also believed that sailors in smaller boats could not have gotten to the yacht in time to save everyone if the yacht capsized.[16]

After a week at sea, *Potomac* returned to port, once again mooring near the Nazi freighter. By the time Roosevelt left his yacht, the Nazi freighter was flying the Stars and Stripes, a result of an order from the president interning all German and Italian ships.[17]

While in port, a radio hookup was made aboard the yacht, so that Roosevelt could address Democrats attending Jackson Day dinners around the country. The next day, he boarded his presidential special bound for Washington. Inspection stops were made at Camp Jackson, South Carolina, and Fort Bragg, North Carolina.

Over the next few months, Roosevelt's seagoing trips were restricted to weekend getaways down the Potomac River and into Chesapeake Bay. The Secret Service was particularly diligent in preparing for the trips, working closely with the Metropolitan Police, Park Police, and Maryland State Police. The police departments provided guard duty on the bridges under which the presidential yacht would pass. Agents always traveled with Roosevelt aboard *Potomac*. Other agents were aboard *Calypso*, which accompanied the president. The president traveled on dry land, to and from Hyde Park, with one side trip to Staunton, Virginia, to speak at the Woodrow Wilson Memorial.

Then, on the morning of 3 August 1941, Roosevelt began a train trip that, once again, would find him on the sea. The president left Washington's Union Station aboard the Pennsylvania Railroad, bound for New London, Connecticut. *Potomac* was waiting for him at the New London submarine base. The yacht set sail due east and anchored that night at the Harbor of Refuge at Point Judith, Rhode Island. The following morning, the yacht got under way, anchoring briefly in Apponagansett Bay. It next sailed to Buzzards Bay, where it cruised back and forth until 7:30 that night, when it dropped anchor at Negro Ledge. Within half an hour, Roosevelt left the yacht and piloted a Cris Craft speedboat. He cruised to the Yacht Club Landing in South Dartmouth, Massachusetts, and returned to *Potomac* around 8:15. Later that night, *Potomac* stood out to sea, finally dropping anchor for the night in Menemsha Bight, off Martha's Vineyard.

This was the beginning of what would become a monumental charade, designed by Roosevelt himself, to convince everyone that he was on one of his fishing holidays, instead of what was to be the first of the great wartime summit conferences between Franklin Roosevelt and Winston Churchill, Britain's prime minister. The real purpose of the trip was a closely guarded secret; not even the head of the Secret Service's White

House detail or Grace Tully, Roosevelt's devoted personal secretary, knew what was happening. Reporters were not permitted to travel with the president, as had been the custom on previous fishing trips. Instead, they were left at the New London docks and had to rely on routine navy press releases, which noted that the fishing was good and the presidential party was enjoying some fine weather.

The charade even extended to Roosevelt's mother, Sara. In a 2 August letter he wrote while aboard the train to New London, the president spoke of his desire to "sleep under a blanket" for the first time since May, which was when Washington's sweltering heat had set in. He said that he would cruise away from newspapermen and photographers. He would probably be gone for ten days, and that she would read "short daily reports from the *Potomac*."[18]

Before dawn the next morning, *Potomac* moved alongside the cruiser USS *Augusta,* which had overnighted in Menemsha Bight as well. President Roosevelt transferred to the cruiser.

David Robinson was a young naval ensign assigned to *Augusta.* He was present during the historic cruise. "The *Augusta* threw a special gang plank with railings over to the *Potomac*," Robinson recalled, "and the president walked slowly and stiffly, supported by his steel braces, followed by his party and various pieces of luggage. They proceeded directly to the admiral's quarters, using the special elevator from the well deck to the communications deck where flag quarters were located."[19]

Augusta, with the president of the United States now on board, made its way east past the Nantucket Shoals Lightship, plotting a course for Ship Harbor, Newfoundland. Meanwhile, back in Menemsha Bight, a Roosevelt look-alike was stationed on *Potomac's* deck. With a cigarette holder in his mouth, he cheerily waved to onlookers on shore. Roosevelt wanted to make sure everyone believed he was continuing his fishing cruise. The presidential yacht slowly navigated the Cape Cod Canal and onlookers continued waving to "President Roosevelt."

At the same time, the "real" President Roosevelt and his party—including his sons Franklin Jr., a navy ensign, and Elliott, an army captain; Pa Watson; Dr. Ross McIntire; Harry Hopkins; Sumner Welles, assistant secretary of state; Averill Harriman, a presidential assistant; and, of course, FDR's Fala—were steaming toward Argentia Bay, Newfoundland, one of the bases that the United States leased through FDR's "destroyers for bases" swap with Great Britain. Roosevelt was heavily protected; USS

Tuscaloosa, USS *Madison,* USS *Moffett,* USS *Sampson,* USS *Winslow,* and USS *McDougal* provided the armed escort.

While aboard *Augusta,* Roosevelt did share his secret with his cousin, Daisy Suckley, one of his closest and most trusted friends. In fact, Suckley may have been the only individual, outside of his immediate entourage, whom he trusted with the secret; even Secretary of State Cordell Hull was not told beforehand that Roosevelt would meet the British prime minister at sea.

"Strange thing happened this morning," Roosevelt wrote to Suckley, who lived in Rhinebeck, a short distance from Springwood, FDR's boyhood home.

> Suddenly found ourselves transferred with all our baggage & mess crew from the little "Potomac" to the Great Big Cruiser "Augusta"! And then, the Island of Martha's Vineyard disappeared in the distance, and as we head out into the Atlantic all we can see is our protecting escort, a heavy cruiser and four destroyers. Curiously enough the Potomac still flies my flag & tonight will be seen by thousands as she passes quietly through the Cape Cod Canal, guarded on shore by Secret Service and State Troopers while in fact the Pres. will be about 250 miles away.[20]

During one early morning operation, Fala, the president's Scotty, barely escaped serious injury. The crew was preparing paravanes, steel shells with fins that, when suspended from the ship, are designed to cut enemy mines. Suddenly, as they were ready to unravel the steel cable, allowing the devices to go overboard, Fala trotted out right next to the cable. If the cable had unraveled, it could either have cut the dog or entangled him, throwing him overboard. "Commander Bibby ordered a couple of sailors to remove Fala from the area, an act they performed promptly. He was not allowed out on the deck again without a leash and someone to walk him," Robinson said. During the rest of the cruise, Pa Watson usually was assigned "Fala duty."[21]

Roosevelt arrived at Ships Harbor, Newfoundland, two days before Churchill. The president thus had time for a little deep-sea fishing from a small motorized whaleboat, which he piloted. He reeled in an unidentified fish that he had pickled and sent to the Smithsonian Institution.

Ensign Robinson also remembers being shocked at the appearance of Roosevelt when the president was being wheeled out on deck one morning to join a group fishing on the fo'c's'l. Roosevelt, dressed in an old sweatshirt and trousers, was wearing his floppy white fishing hat, and clenching his cigarette holder between his teeth. "However, I was somewhat shocked at his appearance. I had become accustomed through the years of seeing [photographs of] a healthy, husky Roosevelt sitting at a desk or in a car. Now as I looked at him, his face seemed severely drawn, his shoulders looked shrunken, and his whole body seemed to sag toward the middle. His crippled legs seemed to just hang and his upper thighs were seemingly flat," Robinson remembered. "It was a tribute to the man that, despite his crippled lower body, he had accomplished so much."

Robinson said that the assembled fishermen weren't having much luck. But as soon as the president's hook hit the water, Robinson said, he had a bite. His first catch was an "exceedingly ugly dogfish with a tremendous head and mouth and a short fat body." The president remarked, "It looks like Catfish Smith [the senior senator from South Carolina]. In fact, it reminds me of several senators I know—all mouth and no brains."[22]

Churchill arrived aboard *Prince of Wales,* a camouflaged English battleship. It still showed damage from its battle with Germany's warship *Bismarck* on 24 May. Roosevelt liked the prime minister immediately. In another letter to Daisy Suckley, he described him as an English version of Fiorello LaGuardia, New York City's mayor. He cautioned his cousin, "Don't say I said so!"[23] Roosevelt and Churchill met for three days. They hammered out an agreement, which later became known as the Atlantic Charter. It stated the shared goals of England and the United States. More important, perhaps, than the document, was the obvious display of cooperation and alliance between the two nations.

Roosevelt visited the British ship for church services and lunch on 10 August. Capt. T. R. Beardall, Roosevelt's naval aide, outlined procedures to be followed during the president's visit in a memorandum to Churchill's personal assistant:

> The president will embark in USS *McDougal* at 1030. *McDougal* will proceed alongside HMS *Prince of Wales,* bow to stern, *McDougal* starboard side to starboard quarter *Prince of Wales.* Using *Prince of Wales* crane, brow will be swung from *McDougal* to *Prince of Wales,* and the president will proceed on board. At the termination of the anthem, after the guard of honor has sloped arms, the president will walk aft, thus reviewing the guard, and will proceed aft

inboard of the mixed ranks of enlisted personnel to his chair on the fantail, near the after hatch. During divine services moving pictures may be taken. Following divine services, still pictures and movie close-ups of the president, prime minister, and their staffs may be taken. After the pictures have been taken, the president will inspect the top side in his wheelchair, and I understand ramps will be provided to facilitate this.

Following lunch, the brow was rigged from the deck of the British ship to the superstructure deck of *McDougal*. Roosevelt walked across to the superstructure deck of the American ship. Beardall also explained the president's photo policy. "For your information, the president is never photographed when walking, or in his wheelchair. However, it is perfectly all right to take pictures when he is standing still or sitting in a large chair."[24]

Before the historic conference ended, Roosevelt decided to send a special gift to all the sailors aboard the British ship. He ordered two thousand cardboard boxes prepared, each containing a half pound package of cheese, several pieces of fruit, and a carton of cigarettes. Forty sailors were assigned to carry out the assembling process. Ensign Robinson, assigned to organize the work, was allowed to head the detail of men who would deliver the gifts to HMS *Prince of Wales*.

H. V. Morton, a British journalist selected by Churchill to accompany him on the mission, remembered the gift boxes. "The afternoon of Saturday was enlivened by President Roosevelt's generosity to the ship's company," Morton wrote a year after the historic voyage.

We saw approaching in motor boats, a pyramid of something like one thousand five hundred cardboard cartons, which a chain of American sailors had soon stacked on our deck. Each carton contained an orange, two apples, two hundred cigarettes, and a half pound of cheese. There was a box for every sailor in the *Prince of Wales*, and inside each one was a card with the words: "The President of the United States sends his compliments and best wishes." It was a kindly thought which was enormously appreciated by our men.[25]

The historic conference outlined a new world order based upon "certain common principles" shared by both countries. Drawing to an end,

Roosevelt and his party laid a course to rendezvous with *Potomac,* which had anchored at Blue Hill Bay, Maine. *Prince of Wales* weighed anchor and stood out through the U-boat–infested waters of the North Atlantic; sixty-three Allied ships already had been sunk by the Germans since the previous October. Four months after *Prince of Wales* carried Churchill to his meeting with Roosevelt, the battleship was sunk by the Japanese, and nearly one-half of its crew, including the captain, perished.

On August 14, Roosevelt penned another letter to Daisy Suckley:

At 11 A.M. we picked up the high hills of Mt. Desert—our experimental ship the "Long Island" appeared & went through her exercises. At 2 we anchored off Blue Hill Bay, the little Potomac came alongside, we said goodbye to the Augusta, transferred, a run in to the mouth of Eggemoggin Reach, safe from submarines & are anchored in a protected cove trying to catch some flounder & buy some lobsters. The radio talks & talks of the conference & commentators are mostly very silly or very mendacious! Why can't they stick to the facts? It was funny to [see] a paper again—borrowed from a fisherman!

The next day, Roosevelt did a little more fishing at Deer Isle and then anchored overnight in Pulpit Harbor, which he described in another letter to Suckley as "the loveliest tiniest 'hole in the wall' on the whole coast." He continued, "Tomorrow we have only a dozen miles to Rockland where we take the train—I fear that 50 newshawks will meet us. That part will be harder than the conference itself."[26]

Secret Service Agent Anthony Lobb was assigned to stay in the White House during the Atlantic Charter trip; he had no idea that the president was doing anything except taking a brief fishing vacation. "They left me in the White House to guard the silver," Lobb joked. He confirmed that the trip was so secret that his boss, Col. Edmund Starling, head of the White House detail, did not know its true purpose. "We thought it was just another cruise."[27] "I learned about the Atlantic Charter Conference through the newspapers and on my birthday, August 9, while I was still at Westhampton Beach," Grace Tully wrote a few years later. "I almost toppled out of my chair when I read the headlines and it was my first intimation that the Boss was not simply having a nice quiet cruise on the yacht *Potomac* while catching 'the first fish,' 'the biggest fish' and 'the most fish,' which was the way the betting ran about the presidential yacht."[28]

Shortly after this historic meeting, there occurred an event that was profoundly disrupting and emotionally distressing to the president. His beloved mother, Sara, died on 7 September. Franklin Roosevelt wore a black armband in mourning for his mother for the next twelve months.

The first shots were fired in the country's battle in the Atlantic on the morning of 4 September 1941, when a German U-boat fired upon USS *Greer,* a destroyer making a routine mail run from Newfoundland to Iceland. The destroyer had tracked and possibly provoked the submarine with its sonar for three hours before the U-boat commander decided to fire a torpedo. Both the first, and then a second, missile missed the destroyer.[29]

The incident prompted Roosevelt to order escorts for all future shipments, as well as to issue a directive to shoot all German submarines on sight. Escort ships played a dangerous cat-and-mouse game with the U-boats lurking below. In a Fireside Chat to the nation on 11 September, the president called the *Greer* incident "piracy legally and morally" and warned the German government that the United States would not be intimidated; the country stood ready to defend freedom of the seas. Roosevelt said, "[W]hen you see a rattlesnake poised to strike, you do not wait until he has struck before your crush him. These Nazi submarines and raiders are the rattlesnakes of the Atlantic. They are a menace to the free pathways of the high seas. They are a challenge to our own sovereignty. They hammer at our most precious rights when they attack ships of the American flag— symbols of our independence, our freedom, our very life."

When Roosevelt, wearing his black armband, finished his radio address in the Diplomatic Room of the White House, the national anthem was played, bringing to their feet all those assembled in the room to hear the president. Roosevelt succeeded in stirring the emotions of patriotic Americans everywhere that night, and proceeded to go forward with his plan to defend aggressively the country's right to sail the high seas. The president, however, never mentioned in his speech that *Greer* had locked its sonar on the German submarine and tracked it for three hours.[30]

Two more incidents occurred within the next month, with more disastrous results for the United States. On 16 October, German U-boats fired upon USS *Kearny* while it was escorting a convoy of Canadian merchant ships. Many casualties occurred, along with the death of eleven crew members. *Kearny* was the first U.S. destroyer damaged in World War II. Despite a hole ripped in its starboard side, the ship was able to steam to Iceland under its own power. In a Navy Day address to the Navy League on 27 October, Roosevelt declared that the *Kearny* "is not just a Navy ship. She belongs to every man, woman and child in this nation." As the audience cheered, Roosevelt continued: "We Americans have cleared our decks and taken our battle stations."[31]

Two weeks later, a U-boat fired upon the U.S. destroyer USS *Reuben James*. The torpedo tore the vessel in two, sinking the first American vessel and killing 115 crew members. Only forty-five crew members survived.[32]

A little after lunchtime on a quiet Sunday, 7 December 1941, Secret Service Agent Anthony Lobb was chatting with Howell Crim and Wilson Searles in the White House Usher's Office. The telephone rang. "Wilson Searles answered it," Lobb recalled. "He handed it to a naval attache who was on duty in the Usher's Office." Suddenly, a look of shock came across the naval officer's face. "Oh my God," he exclaimed, "They did it, they bombed Pearl Harbor." Quickly turning to the others in the room, the naval aide cautioned "Don't say anything about it." Chief Usher Crim laughed, adding, "Everybody knows about it now."

Lobb said Roosevelt was upstairs in the White House working on his stamp collection when the call was received. He was advised immediately. "It was utter confusion," Lobb remembered. The White House was sealed off and agents were stationed on the roof with machine guns. The normal presidential detail of sixteen agents was instantly increased to forty; the White House became an armed camp.[33]

The United States was at war.

CHAPTER 13

New Secret Base at Shangri-La

During a White House dinner party in the spring of 1942, President Roosevelt was asked by a guest about the recent air strikes over Tokyo that were led by Lt. Col. James H. Doolittle. It was the first time American bombers had penetrated deep into Japan since the attack on Pearl Harbor four months earlier. "Mr. President, couldn't you tell us about that bombing? Where did those planes start from and go to?" the guest inquired. The next day, at a White House press conference, the president relayed his answer to the correspondents assembled in his office. "Yes," he said in reply to the guest's questions, "I think the time has come to tell you. They came from our new secret base at Shangri-La."[1]

As FDR adviser Sam Rosenman later observed, Roosevelt's response was a polite way of saying that he was not going to reveal that the bombers, each armed with four 500-pound bombs, took off from the aircraft carrier USS *Hornet* in stormy seas less than seven hundred miles off the Japanese coast. Rosenman, who was with Roosevelt when the president received word of the successful Tokyo air strike, described FDR as being "overjoyed" at the news. He believed it would demonstrate to U.S. citizens as well as the country's allies that the war could be won despite a series of recent spectacular Japanese victories—and demoralizing Allied losses—in the Pacific.

The direct attack on Japan, long desired by President Roosevelt, was a tremendous boost to sagging morale. It provided some satisfaction that the United States was striking back in retaliation for Pearl Harbor. In fact, as naval historian Nathan Miller points out, the daring Tokyo air raid plan was accompanied by a verse among sailors aboard *Hornet:*

> An eye for an eye
> A tooth for a tooth,
> This Sunday, it's our turn to shoot.
> —Remember Pearl Harbor.[2]

Doolittle's raid was regarded as a great success, especially because neither Doolittle nor the pilots of the other fifteen B-25s were able to practice takeoffs from the deck of a carrier. Instead, they had a month of training at Eglin Air Base in Florida; the carrier's deck dimensions were marked off on the airstrip.[3] Air support for the top-secret operation was provided by USS *Enterprise,* commanded by Franklin Roosevelt's old friend, Adm. William F. "Bull" Halsey. Halsey, showing uncommon confidence in Roosevelt when he was assistant navy secretary, had allowed him to pilot a destroyer through treacherous New England waters off the coast of Maine.

Shangri-La, Roosevelt's name for the "secret base," also became the name of the president's new retreat. Built at an 1,800-foot elevation in the Catoctin Mountains, it was near Thurmont, Maryland, sixty miles north of the White House. Roosevelt took the name, Shangri-La, from the mythical place in James Hilton's 1933 novel, *Lost Horizon.* Shangri-La would later be named Camp David by President Dwight D. Eisenhower.

After Pearl Harbor, the protection of the president took on the greatest importance. The Secret Service restricted Roosevelt's travels on the sea, and even on inland water, because of the danger posed by German U-boats traveling the North Atlantic within sight of New York City. FDR, however, believed this threat to be "more fancied than real."[4]

Roosevelt still needed somewhere to relax and recharge. If he could not take to the water, he preferred a cool mountain location where he could escape the steamy summers of Washington. On the advice of his physician, Ross McIntire—now commissioned as a rear admiral in the navy—Roosevelt ordered that a site be found within a one-hundred-mile radius of Washington.

Shangri-La, a two hour drive from the White House, was the ideal getaway for Roosevelt. The remote facility had been used as a recreational camp. It would be refurbished, rebuilt, and then furnished with a collection of furniture. Some of the furnishings were from the White House attic, and several colonial-style pieces were from *Potomac*. After being relieved of presidential yacht duty, *Potomac* was refitted with special equipment and reassigned to the navy's underwater sound testing station. The only military that could be spared during the war, the yacht staff was assigned to service the new retreat.[5]

President Roosevelt made frequent use of Shangri-La to relax in a secure and secluded setting. Although he preferred being on the water, sailing aboard his yacht—even on the Potomac River or Chesapeake Bay —was thought too risky. Roosevelt refused to remove a navy ship from the fleet to help protect him. Roosevelt, however, was going to make sure his new retreat took on a nautical flair. The president kept a logbook for visitors to sign just as they would when boarding one of his sailing vessels. On his first official visit in 1942, the president wrote in the book: "U.S.S. Shangri La. Launched at Catoctin. July 5, 1942."[6] Each succeeding visit to Shangri-La was recorded as a "cruise" in the logbook. An examination of the logs shows various entries in the president's own handwriting, including "Commissioned," "Full Steam," "First Trial Run," "Another Cruise," and "Re-commissioned."[7]

Protected by Secret Service agents and a contingent of U.S. Marines, Shangri-La offered the type of secure setting that satisfied Roosevelt's protectors. Only one incident threatened the president's personal safety. William M. Rigdon, assistant naval aide to the president, described an early Sunday morning car ride around the secluded red clay back roads. Roosevelt was at the wheel of his hand-controlled Ford, with a single Secret Service agent accompanying him. They drove onto a private road through a large estate. Approaching the caretaker's cabin, a small woman emerged with a shotgun slung over her arm. "What are you doing up here?" she asked. "Don't you know this place is posted?"

Roosevelt identified himself as the president of the United States. The Secret Service agent also identified himself, placing himself between the woman and the president. "I don't care who you are!" she said. "If you don't have something in writing from Mr. Payne you'd better get out of here." She lifted her shotgun menacingly. The president backed up his

Ford, turned around, and drove off. The next morning Mr. Charles Payne, owner of the estate, was summoned to the White House. After the incident was relayed to him, he expressed his regret and provided the president with a written permit to use the private road on his property.[8]

While at Shangri-La, FDR regularly met with staff to review wartime activities. Beginning a practice that would be carried on by future presidents, he invited foreign heads of state to visit the retreat. British Prime Minister Winston Churchill made two visits to Shangri-La during the war. Each sitting on a canvas chair next to the pond, Churchill spent time fishing with the president. Other times, the president would board a rowboat with a military aide and spend the afternoon trout fishing in Hunting Creek. The National Park Service had stocked the creek's pond with plenty of brook trout prior to the president's arrival.

Roosevelt, who fancied himself to be somewhat of an architect, made rough drawings in April 1942 showing how the new retreat should be laid out—including enlarging and screening the porch of the main cabin. He suggested other improvements to the former Catoctin Recreational Demonstration Area, which was a camp established in the early years of the New Deal to demonstrate the feasibility of developing parks from worn-out agricultural land. It also had been used as a family camp by federal employees.[9]

The president ordered certain diseased and misshapen trees removed, but the dogwood and other shrubs were to remain near his cabin to provide shade and privacy. President Truman later ordered all the shrubs removed to provide him with a better view from the window. Roosevelt said the former craft shop should be converted into sleeping quarters for the Filipino mess boys, who were being re-assigned from *Potomac* to Shangri-La.

Secret Service agents would sleep in nearby tents, according to the president's sketch. They actually stayed both at a local hotel and, later, at a cabin near the president's "Bear's Den" cabin. Mike Reilly, head of the Secret Service unit protecting Roosevelt, slept in a nearby abandoned Civilian Conservation Corps barracks, dubbed by Roosevelt as "221B Baker Street" after Sherlock Holmes' address. There even was a rustic doghouse constructed for Fala, although there is no evidence that the presidential pup ever slept anywhere except in the president's bedroom.[10]

There were twenty separate duplex cabins, once construction had been completed, and each carried a descriptive name. In addition to

"Bear's Den" and "221B Baker Street," other names included "Baker Street Urchins," where additional Secret Service agents were assigned to sleep; "One Moment Please," the communications cabin; "The Pill Box," where Lt. Comdr. George Fox, the president's physical therapist was housed; and "Breadbasket," the appropriate name for the mess hall.[11]

A special inclined bridge from the floor of the president's bedroom to the ground outside was cut into the wall to allay Roosevelt's fear of fire. With pressure from inside, the emergency exit could be activated, allowing Roosevelt to escape if fire ever engulfed his cabin.[12]

Security at the facility was paramount. A ten-foot barbed wire fence surrounded the perimeter; flood lights and sentry booths were scattered throughout the 143-acre grounds. A contingent of one hundred marines, housed at nearby Camp Misty Mount, provided perimeter security. They supplemented the Secret Service protection inside the compound.

On 8 August 1942, following Roosevelt's "1st trial run," he pronounced Shangri-La "accepted" by the navy. He commended the navy stewards who had hung the naval prints he sent, while—in an aside to the guests accompanying him on this visit—he confided: "I may make a few changes tomorrow." That weekend, his guests re-hung the prints, under the personal direction of the president.[13]

As Roosevelt and his guests were getting ready to enjoy the quiet of the Catoctin Mountain retreat, the bodies of six executed Nazi saboteurs were being loaded into army ambulances in Washington. They had secretly entered the United States to blow up defense plants. In June 1942, Hitler invaded America's shores via the North Atlantic; saboteurs entered the United States along the east coast.

U-boats discharged eight Nazis off the coasts of Long Island and Florida. Discarding Nazi uniforms, they changed into civilian clothing. Their goal was to blend into American cities and work on plans to blow up defense factories and transportation facilities in the United States. They brought along enough explosives to last two years, one hundred thousand dollars in American cash, and forged identification cards.[14]

Thanks to alert coast guardsmen and an investigation by the Federal Bureau of Investigation, the plot was thwarted. All the Nazis were apprehended. President Roosevelt directed that the saboteurs be tried by a military tribunal, rather than through the regular American court system. The defendants appealed to the U.S. Supreme Court. They argued that the president lacked the authority to require trial by tribunal, rather than through the regular court system. The high court denied the appeal, ruling in President Roosevelt's favor.

The military commission met in July. After completing its hearing, it rendered a judgment that all eight Nazis should be sentenced to death. The tribunal's report and record of testimony were submitted to Roosevelt for review. The president upheld the findings. Six of the prisoners were electrocuted in August, less than two months after they secretly came onto American shores. The president commuted the sentence of two prisoners because they assisted the government in apprehending the other six. One was sentenced to hard labor for life, while the other received a thirty-year sentence.[15]

During dinner at Shangri-La the next evening, talk turned to the fate of the Nazi saboteurs when Dorothy Rosenman asked where they would be buried. Although Roosevelt indicated that plans were incomplete, the bodies of the executed saboteurs had been driven to Blue Plains in the District of Columbia the previous afternoon. They were each buried in a pauper's grave.[16]

In addition to the rest and relaxation Roosevelt enjoyed at Shangri-La, the retreat also afforded him an opportunity to enjoy some of the old-fashioned rich cooking, similar to what was prepared in his mother's household, rather than the fare produced by Henrietta Nesbitt, housekeeper at 1600 Pennsylvania Avenue. Nesbitt's rule was "plain foods, plainly prepared," which Roosevelt said "would do justice to the Automat." Secret Service Agent Anthony Lobb said Roosevelt "hated" Mrs. Nesbitt's cooking because the meals she prepared were "poor" and "she did a poor job of nutrition." "The most powerful man in the country, he could not command a good dinner," noted historian Arthur M. Schlesinger Jr., who said Roosevelt "spent his years in the White House in a state of ill-suppressed dissatisfaction."

But it was different at Shangri-La. The Filipino mess boys reassigned from *Potomac* always wanted to please their boss. They served him delicious dishes, such as oyster crabs with whitebait and peach cobbler with thick cream. This was hardly the type of food of which Nesbitt would approve.[17]

While at Shangri-La, the president enjoyed sitting on the screened porch, pasting stamps in his albums, playing solitaire, or working on paperwork. In the evenings, after the customary dry martinis during cocktail hour, followed by dinner prepared by the mess boys, he often would play poker or gin rummy with his guests. Grace Tully, his longtime private secretary, remembered the president's chagrin one evening after she continued winning at gin. Roosevelt composed and hand printed a sign, which he ordered hung on the door of the sitting room:

VISITORS WILL BEWARE OF GAMBLERS
(ESPECIALLY FEMALE) ON THIS SHIP[18]

Shangri-La would be the only "ship" FDR would be on for some time to come. In fact, after his clandestine meeting with Winston Churchill in Newfoundland in August 1941, Roosevelt would not take to the sea again until 1943. Security concerns by the Secret Service as well as the need for Roosevelt to stay close to the White House to monitor the war would dictate that his travels be kept to a minimum, and all would be on dry land. Roosevelt, however, still kept his mind on the water and, specifically, on the U.S. Navy.

In May 1942, in a statement commemorating "Maritime Day," the president said that the United States, at no time in its history, had been more dependent upon the productivity of the nation's shipyards and efficient operation of cargo vessels. "We are engaged in what is largely a war of ocean transportation," Roosevelt said, "We must carry to the corners of the earth the men and materials for war; for our armed forces and for those of our allies."

"A little more than a year ago," Roosevelt continued, "we embarked upon the greatest shipbuilding program in history. No other nation ever had attempted so vast a maritime enterprise." He described ship production as a "near-miracle" adding that the nation's shipbuilding capacity had increased 500 percent.[19]

Roosevelt once had hoped to attend the U.S. Naval Academy at Annapolis. His father vetoed the move, but FDR had enjoyed and learned much during his term as assistant secretary of the navy in the Wilson administration. Most important, he believed in a big navy, as had his cousin Theodore. Building a big navy took time, however. Roosevelt gradually moved ahead with his plans after he took office as the president in 1933.

The unsettled world situation and then U.S. entry into the conflict resulted in a dramatic increase in shipbuilding, at speeds never before accomplished here or abroad. Besides the 2,770 Liberty ships used to transport supplies, vehicles, weapons, and troops, that were constructed in four years, Roosevelt succeeded in convincing Congress to approve construction of dozens of new battleships, cruisers, destroyers, submarines, aircraft carriers, and naval airplanes.

Roosevelt also liked to tinker with designing ships himself. Naval historian Thomas C. Hone pointed out that sometimes FDR's designs were "remarkably perceptive." FDR encouraged the development of destroyer escort vessels and escort aircraft carriers; both were tremendously helpful during the war.[20] An early advocate of such antisubmarine vessels, Roosevelt had recommended their construction to the Wilson administration during World War I. But his suggestions were discounted at the time. Even though Roosevelt now was commander in chief, his ideas for antisubmarine ships still met with opposition from navy officials; they preferred to invest in new destroyers.

"President Roosevelt initiated the destroyer escort (DE) program as early as June 1940," notes naval historian Samuel Eliot Morison. Although the Bureau of Ships produced designs for the first two experimental ships, the general board of the navy rejected them because they deemed them too costly. Instead, the board authorized construction of new destroyers and "the DE program was shelved for many more months," Morison points out.[21]

Following the attack on Pearl Harbor, the DE program got off the ground. Ironically, the navy board authorized their construction for England, not the United States, under terms of Roosevelt's Lend-Lease program. Many of these vessels, however, did end up flying the stars and stripes. Although approximately one thousand DEs were authorized, many were never built because of the delay in moving forward with construction and then the decline in U-boat activity later in the war.

The destroyer escorts, described by Roosevelt as "speedy and dangerous," were tough little warships, built specifically for fighting the German U-boat menace in the North Atlantic.[22] By late 1940, twenty-six Allied ships were being sunk for every U-boat destroyed. Maneuverability was a key feature of the DEs. Their narrow turning radius of four hundred yards, compared to the eight hundred yards required by a destroyer, was critical for tracking U-boats. Armed with depth charges every bit as powerful as those found on destroyers, they also had short-range antiaircraft guns and torpedoes, along with sonar and radar for detecting the enemy below. They cost one-third less to construct than destroyers, and could be produced in considerably less time.

In June 1944, destroyer escorts were involved in the capture of German submarine U-505, the first enemy warship captured since the War of 1812. Altogether, destroyer escorts destroyed twenty-eight German U-boats during the course of the war. They quickly became a weapon greatly feared by the Nazis.

Between 1942 and 1945, 563 destroyer escorts were constructed; 78 were transferred to England under the Lend-Lease program.[23] Today, USS *Slater* is the only DE to remain afloat in the United States. Commissioned in 1944, it has been faithfully restored, is listed on the National Register of Historic Places, and is operated as a museum ship by the Destroyer Escort Historical Museum, a not-for-profit educational organization. *Slater* is moored on the Hudson River in Albany, New York, a short automobile ride from FDR's Hyde Park home.

In August 1942, President Roosevelt turned over an American "submarine chaser" to the Netherlands' Queen Wilhelmina and her government—in exile in England—"as a symbol of friendship and admiration" to assist that country's war effort. In accepting the vessel, the queen remarked that it was "fresh evidence of the excellent spirit of friendship which ever since the days of John Paul Jones has existed between our two navies." In referring to Roosevelt, the queen continued: "May your love of the sea and of seamanship pervade this vessel and inspire those on board."[24]

The next month, Roosevelt turned over a similar vessel to Norway. In accepting the vessel, Norway's Crown Princess Martha thanked the American people, and especially her friend, President Roosevelt, whom she described as "one whose clear vision and unfailing courage have contributed immeasurably to rally the forces of freedom."[25]

Ten months after the attack at Pearl Harbor, Roosevelt was still confined to dry land. He embarked on a two-week inspection tour of the United States war plants and training camps. The twelve-state tour, from Washington to California and back, would be aboard his special train. He departed Washington on 17 September. To ensure his safety, three reporters were allowed to travel with the president but were not permitted to file any reports until the trip was concluded.

Roosevelt spent every one of the fourteen nights on his special train—with "not one night ashore." During the days, he toured training camps, navy yards, and manufacturing plants around the country. He was impressed by the number of women working in the plants, especially on machines requiring great skill and accuracy. After returning to Washington, Roosevelt stated that he was pleased with what he saw, and pronounced that wartime production was nearly up to his goal.

Roosevelt was especially happy with the "spirit" of the people. "That is the main thing that I saw on my trip around the country—unbeatable spirit," the president told the nation during a Fireside Chat in October. "If the leaders of Germany and Japan could have come along with me, and had seen what I saw, they would agree with my conclusions. Unfortunately, they were unable to make the trip with me. And that is one reason why we are carrying our war effort overseas—to them."[26]

Soon Roosevelt again would make history. When he takes his war effort overseas, he becomes the first American president since Abraham Lincoln to travel to the frontlines where war is raging.

CHAPTER 14

Greatest Man
I Have Ever Known

Fala, President Roosevelt's three-year-old Scottish terrier, had become quite a national celebrity since he moved into the White House in 1940. He was a constant companion to the president, traveling on most presidential trips whether on land or sea. He even earned the Secret Service code name "Informer" because Americans knew that when they saw the little terrier the president wouldn't be far behind.

One Saturday morning in early January 1943, Fala must have been a bit confused. Preparations were under way at the White House for his master to take another trip, but suddenly he was handed over to Daisy Suckley, the president's cousin—leash, harness, and muzzle. Obviously, this was one trip that the presidential pup would not be taking.

Suckley, who lived near the Roosevelts in Hyde Park, was working as an archivist at the new Franklin D. Roosevelt Library. As she prepared to take Fala, Suckley told the president that she would leave him in an outside dog pen when she went to work each day. "Oh don't," the president declared. "He hates to be left behind—take him to the library with you every day, and walk him during lunch."[1]

Roosevelt seldom left Fala behind, but this trip was top secret and would involve a different mode of transportation from any he had taken since he first took up residence at 1600 Pennsylvania Avenue in March 1933. FDR was about to become the first sitting U.S. president to leave the country during wartime. He would also be the first U.S. president to fly to a foreign land, although he personally disliked traveling by air.

The next morning, under extremely tight security, the president left Washington aboard the "Ferdinand Magellan," a specially built armored Pullman railroad car that was designed to provide maximum protection for the president while traveling. Purchased in 1942 at the behest of the Secret Service, the 142-ton car, with three-inch-thick green tinted glass capable of stopping a machine gun bullet fired at point blank range, and two escape hatches in case of emergency, was the heaviest passenger car in the United States. The first railroad car built exclusively for a U.S. president, the Magellan consisted of the president's master bedroom, three other bedrooms, a dining room, kitchen, lounge, and shower. Sixteen Secret Service agents usually accompanied FDR on board.[2]

After the United States entered the war, Roosevelt's travels were strictly controlled. Even routine train trips to Hyde Park entailed extensive security precautions, including the checking of every mile of track over which the president's train would travel. Army guards or state policemen were posted at all overpasses, culverts, and switching yards. The president's train had right of way over all other trains, which had to either stay clear of it by at least twenty minutes or move off to a siding while the presidential train passed.[3]

The train departed from the hidden railroad spur within the Bureau of Engraving and Printing, heading north as though bound for Hyde Park. At Fort Meade, Maryland, however, the train stopped, waited an hour, and then turned around, heading south. No longer "the presidential special," the train was simply tagged "special" even though the country's thirty-second president was still on board. The regular Pullman staff of porters and cooks was replaced on this trip by the Filipino mess staff, previously from the presidential yacht *Potomac* but now on duty at Shangri-La.

Two days later, the train arrived at an isolated railroad siding in Miami. President Roosevelt was whisked in the dark by automobile to a waiting Pan American Boeing "clipper" flying boat that was under lease to the U.S. Navy. Within a short time, Franklin Roosevelt was airborne, en route to Casablanca and the first major wartime conference outside the western hemisphere. Winston Churchill would be attending but, despite FDR's pleadings, Joseph Stalin would pass on the opportunity to meet with the two Allied leaders.

Secret Service Agent Michael Reilly was deeply concerned about the president's safety, especially because German submarines had been actively shooting down bombers and other planes crossing the Atlantic. In addition, Roosevelt was going to an active war zone full of Nazi spies, all of whom would be hailed as heroes if they assassinated the commander in chief of U.S. fighting forces.[4]

Roosevelt was adamant about going; he told Reilly that he would comply with whatever security precautions the agent felt were necessary. "I do not care where we stay," Roosevelt told Reilly, "out in the desert in tents if you think that is necessary."[5] Reilly made the arrangements necessary to take the president to Africa, and to ensure his safe return to the United States when his business was concluded.

Roosevelt's plane first made a stop at Trinidad, one of the American bases secured from the British in the destroyers-for-bases agreement. The aircraft then stopped at Belem and Natal, two Brazilian seaports, before beginning the crossatlantic journey. Following a long and tiring plane ride, Roosevelt's aircraft—met at sea by an escort of American fighters—landed in Gambia. He boarded a small boat for a brief cruise in the Gambia River Harbor. Upon returning, USS *Memphis* was waiting in port, and the president was hoisted to the deck of the cruiser. Unfortunately, one of the men carrying FDR slipped on the deck and fell; the president landed hard "on his rear," according to Harry Hopkins' recollection of the incident.[6] Roosevelt had dinner and rested overnight aboard the cruiser. The next day, he was flown aboard a C-54 army transport plane over the snow-capped Atlas Mountains to his Casablanca destination.

Robert Hopkins, Harry's son, whom FDR had met previously and liked, was summoned by Gen. Dwight Eisenhower and told to leave the fighting in Tunisia and travel to Casablanca to photograph the historic event for the president. Actually, Casablanca proved to be somewhat of a family reunion for both Roosevelt and Hopkins because not only Robert Hopkins but FDR's sons Elliott and Franklin Jr. also arrived.

Elliott had met his father at the plane, which landed about fifteen miles from Casablanca. They were hurried into an armored automobile, whose windows had been blackened with mud to provide security for Roosevelt during his visit to an active theater of war.

Secret Service Agent Reilly, who arrived at Casablanca in advance of the president, left nothing to chance in protecting Roosevelt. All the food and liquor that would be consumed by the president was tested and placed under tight security. Reilly even constructed a bomb shelter near the president's villa. Armored plates, sandbags, and cement were used to convert the swimming pool into an air raid shelter. When Reilly proudly showed Roosevelt the makeshift bomb shelter, the president replied: "If you expect to get me into that thing, Mike, you had better come in swinging."[7]

The conference proceeded without a single security hitch. Before returning to the United States, Roosevelt insisted on inspecting and taking a brief cruise aboard HMS *Aimwell,* an American tugboat built for England under the Lend-Lease program. Next, he traveled to inspect troops at the front line at Rabat, about eighty-five miles to the northeast. Traveling by armored car and jeep, Roosevelt met with twenty thousand soldiers. He dined with them in the field on boiled ham, sweet potatoes, string beans, fruit salad, bread, jam, and coffee, as the Third Division Artillery Band serenaded the diners with "Chattanooga Choo-Choo," "Deep in the Heart of Texas," and "Alexander's Rag Time Band."[8]

Two days later, Roosevelt and Churchill visited Marrakech, about 120 miles south of Casablanca. Roosevelt was very satisfied with the results of the wartime meeting when the conference ended. Churchill was satisfied as well. They had agreed on the timing of the cross-channel invasion of France, as well as the timing for the invasion of Sicily. FDR had announced that the Allies would accept only an unconditional surrender from Germany, Italy, and Japan.

Now, it was time to go home. Franklin Roosevelt had a cough and a fever. He was extremely tired from the exhausting traveling, endless meetings, and, especially, the late-night sessions with the prime minister. Early in the morning, before Winston Churchill was even out of bed, Roosevelt's plane was readying for takeoff. Churchill hurried out to the runway in his bed clothes to say goodbye to his friend, the president. As the plane lifted off through the fog-covered ground, Churchill looked away, saying that he was too nervous to watch the Roosevelt's aircraft take off. "If anything happened to that man, I couldn't stand it. He is the truest friend; he has the farthest vision; he is the greatest man I have ever known."[9]

Before heading for the United States, however, Roosevelt had his plane divert to Liberia for lunch with the African country's president. He next flew to Brazil for a conference aboard the American destroyer USS *Blackhawk* with President Getulio Vargas. They pledged cooperation against the rising U-boat attacks on Allied ships. The president then made a stop in Trinidad and inspected American military forces stationed there.

Secret Service Agent Anthony Lobb, who had left the White House detail in 1942 and now was in the army's Counter-Intelligence Corps (CIC), was stationed in Trinidad at the time of Roosevelt's visit. Lobb was permitted to join Roosevelt for some refreshments at the navy club. Lobb remembers "a little friction" between Dwight Eisenhower and the Secret Service during the visit. "Eisenhower wanted his driver, Kay Summersby, to drive the jeep carrying the president," Lobb recalled. The Secret Service would not permit it, insisting that the president would be driven by one of their agents. That was the last time Lobb saw Roosevelt.[10]

After the Trinidad inspection was complete, Roosevelt again boarded his plane. Now the president could relax from the grueling trip—but not before one more "event." Roosevelt was pleasantly surprised with a cake, champagne, and presents for his sixty-first birthday, celebrated eight thousand feet above the blue waters of the Caribbean.

Landing in Miami, FDR soon boarded his presidential special, bound for a cold and snowy Washington. His seventeen-thousand-mile, twenty-two-day journey was concluded. The president was tired but satisfied with the results of his early version of "shuttle diplomacy."

Shortly after arriving in the capital, he received news of the Russian victory at Stalingrad, which marked the turning point in Germany's war against Russia. Approximately 330,000 Germans had been killed or captured during the lengthy battle.[11] Within a few days, U.S. forces would retake Guadalcanal, providing even better news for Roosevelt and a tremendous psychological lift for the nation. Roosevelt called it "the turning point" in the war, while Churchill proclaimed it "the end of the beginning."[12]

Meanwhile, the president took additional actions on the home front. By executive order, he froze all prices, wages, and salaries in an attempt to control inflation. He expanded the list of products subject to rationing. Rationing covered a variety of items including meat, fruits, vegetables, and sugar. The previous year, Roosevelt had initiated the rationing program. It was designed to conserve supplies and materials that were needed for the war effort. Gasoline rationing was instituted to preserve dwindling U.S. petroleum reserves. Ration books were distributed annually to every adult and child in the nation. When a rationed product was purchased, a certain number of ration coupons, along with cash, were required to buy the item.

Even the White House was not immune to rationing. Henrietta Nesbitt, housekeeper for the Roosevelts, had to stay within her allotments; she hoarded ration books in her White House basement office. When she discovered supplies were missing from the pantry, kitchen, and storage closets, she had the navy padlock the refrigerators and closets. Finally, she turned over control of the supplies to the Secret Service, and the pilfering stopped.[13]

Mrs. Nesbitt simplified White House menus by reducing the number of courses to three—soup, entree, and dessert. Roosevelt insisted the White House adhere to the same restrictions that other Americans were enduring. When a wealthy Texas oilman sent magnificent beefsteaks to Roosevelt during the height of the war, they were declined because the White House did not have sufficient ration stamps to accept them.[14]

The freezing of wages and prices was met with stiff opposition from John L. Lewis, the United Mine Workers' union president. He called for a strike that would cut off coal supplies for the U.S. war effort. President Roosevelt responded immediately. He ordered the federal government to take control of the mines. In the face of a steadfast and determined president, and an angry public upset with the workers for jeopardizing supplies for the war, Lewis backed down and called off the strike.

The snows of winter receded. The cherry blossoms began blooming along Potomac Drive. The cherry trees, a gift to President and Mrs. William Howard Taft in 1911 from the mayor of Tokyo, symbolized the "national friendship between the U.S. and Japan" in a very different time.[15] The spring and summer months of 1943 proved to be a very busy time for the president. He made inspection tours of defense plants, attended wartime conferences, and, for the first time since the attack on Pearl Harbor, took a full-scale fishing vacation.

Just before he left Washington in mid-April, Roosevelt dedicated the new memorial to Thomas Jefferson. In a brief ceremony that, including Roosevelt's remarks, lasted only fifteen minutes, the president said, "Today, in the midst of a great war for freedom, we dedicate a shrine to freedom." In an obvious reference to the current state of national affairs, Roosevelt said that Jefferson was aware that "men who will not fight for liberty can lose it," adding that "men are capable of their own government, and that no king, no tyrant, no dictator can govern for them as well as they can govern for themselves."[16]

With his remarks concluded, Roosevelt boarded the Ferdinand Magellan once again, to begin his second wartime trip to thank the American people for their many sacrifices. He toured military posts, naval stations, and war factories, all working at full tilt on behalf of the war effort. He also would make a stop in Mexico to meet with President Manuel Avila Camacho, marking the first meeting in thirty-four years between leaders of the two countries.

First Dog Fala accompanied the president, along with Adm. Ross McIntire, Grace Tully, Daisy Suckley, and Laura Delano (another Roosevelt cousin). A large group of White House aides, as well as a contingent of twenty-six Secret Service agents, also took the cross-country journey. According to a log prepared following the 13–29 April 1943 trip, all details were arranged under strict wartime secrecy. All arrangements with the various railroad companies, over whose tracks the presidential train would pass, were made "verbally and in a person-to-person manner." Nothing was put in writing.[17]

Roosevelt spent most of the 7,668-mile trip aboard the presidential special; only about 425 miles was conducted by automobile. Both this train tour, and the one taken the previous year, involved extensive security. More than 150,000 soldiers checked every mile of the track over which the president's train would travel, and the U.S. Army was responsible for locking switches to prevent collisions or derailments.[18]

Meanwhile, *Queen Mary* was steaming toward North America with Winston Churchill on board. He would meet with Roosevelt in Washington to discuss plans for the 1944 cross-channel invasion of France. They also needed to iron out last minutes details of the Allied invasion of Sicily scheduled for later in 1943. The invasion of France, code named "Overlord," would begin on 1 May 1944, and Allied forces would proceed against Sicily within two months. After their meeting, Roosevelt and Churchill parted company, promising to meet again later in the summer, probably in Quebec. On the heels of this Washington conference came the welcome news that Mussolini had resigned.

Despite security concerns, a tired and travel-worn Roosevelt decided he was going to return to his first love—the water. He scheduled a real fishing vacation, something that he had been unable to do since the Japanese attack on Pearl Harbor. Security would have to be very tight so enemy agents would not learn of his travel plans.

Before departing, Roosevelt personally addressed a concern that some might view as trivial given the other weighty issues confronting the chief executive. Throughout his life, however, Roosevelt had an extraordinary ability to focus both on the major issues before him while still taking time to address smaller, seemingly inconsequential matters that could easily be delegated to an assistant.

This July he attended to the business of a stopped-up floor drain in the basement of his mother's Campobello cottage. Roosevelt received a letter from a repairman who had inspected the basement to see why ice formed in the basement during the winter months. The repairman advised Roosevelt that a new floor drain should be installed to rid the cellar of water and prevent ice formation. "If you wish," the repairman wrote the president, "I will put a level on the ground and find how much earth has to be removed and stone filled in, also how much earthen pipe it will require." President Roosevelt, always a frugal fellow, replied that he believed the assessment was correct. "Please take a look at it and let me know what it would cost to make the cellar dry again," Roosevelt wrote. "I hope it will cost as little as possible!"[19]

After his personal and presidential business was complete, Roosevelt quietly left Washington aboard his train on the night of 31 July 1943. White House press correspondents were kept in the dark about the president's travel plans.[20] The Secret Service observed the strictest of wartime security, second only to the arrangements leading up to the clandestine 1941 Atlantic Charter conference between Roosevelt and Churchill. Only, this time, Roosevelt really was going fishing.

Secret Service agents were dispatched to the Whitefish Bay area of upper Lake Huron in Ontario, Canada, to scout out the area before the president's arrival. Roosevelt understood from some of his old friends that the lakes in this area of Canada were teeming with black bass, walleye pike, and pickerel, and he intended to try his luck at catching a few of them.

Agents discovered that the Birch Island railroad siding would not be long enough to accommodate the president's train, so the Canadian Pacific Railroad Company agreed to lengthen it at its own expense. Agents also told railroad officials that Roosevelt had hoped "not to use his painful leg braces" on this vacation trip, thus prompting the railroad to build a two-hundred-foot wooden ramp through grass and brush to connect the railroad siding to the dock. The president could simply use his wheelchair when he wanted to travel from train to dock. A special telephone line was installed so the president could be in constant touch with developments back in Washington and around the world.[21]

Called the "The Whitefish Bay U.S. Navy Exploration Expedition" by President Roosevelt, he thoroughly enjoyed the peace and quiet, along with the good fishing spots in this Canadian province. Every morning, according to Assistant Naval Aide William Rigdon, the president would roll his wheelchair down the ramp around 11 A.M. and embark a small launch from the U.S. patrol boat *Wilmette,* for several hours of fishing.[22]

The fishing party accompanying Roosevelt in the launch usually included Adm. William D. Leahy; Rear Adm. Wilson Brown, the president's naval aide; Dr. Ross McIntire; and Gen. Pa Watson. Rigdon; Dewey Long, the president's transportation expert; Lt. George Fox, FDR's therapist; and James F. Byrne, director of war mobilization often fished in a second boat.[23] Harry Hopkins, Grace Tully, and her assistant Dorothy Brady were also along on the trip, but did not fish.

There were the usually daily pools, standard fare on FDR's fishing vacations, for the most fish, largest fish, and smallest fish. At the end of a day's fishing, the president made a ceremony of exhibiting his catch and providing a running commentary about each fish, according to Rigdon. Back on the train, the president's Filipino mess boys would prepare the evening meal.[24]

Presidential mail and newspapers were ferried via navy plane to Roosevelt daily. Rigdon also recalled that the early part of each evening was "lively and informal," with cocktails being served on the Ferdinand Magellan before everyone would partake of the evening meal.

Despite rumors to the contrary, the ten-day trip was not another secret wartime conference with Winston Churchill, although the president did keep in touch with him daily by telephone from his railroad car. This was simply a relaxing fishing vacation with congenial friends—the last such vacation Franklin Roosevelt would take.

On the eve of Allied successes in Sicily and New Guinea, Roosevelt was again traveling aboard the presidential special, heading north to Canada. On the evening of 16 August, FDR boarded the Ferdinand Magellan in Washington for his sixth wartime meeting with Winston Churchill. Once again, Roosevelt had been unsuccessful in his attempts to have Stalin join the conference. The presidential special traveled north from Washington to Claremont, New Jersey, and then passed through Albany, New York, en route to Montreal.

Security was extremely tight along the route, including Royal Canadian Mounted Police at each Canadian station. When the train stopped at the Park Avenue station in Montreal so that Fala could be walked on the station platform for a "limbering up," curious crowds immediately knew President Roosevelt was on board, according to the log of the trip.[25] The train arrived in Quebec around dinner time on 17 August.

The conference, code named "Quadrant," took place at the historic Citadel, a massive nineteenth-century fort-like building overlooking the St. Lawrence River in Quebec. Topics of discussion included the upcoming Normandy invasion and the establishment of a post-war international organization "based on the sovereign equality of all nations," whose goal would be to maintain peace and security among nations.[26]

One Friday morning during the conference, the president and prime minister decided to skip the talks and go fishing. They traveled by automobile to Lac de E'Paule, a nearby lake in the Quebec park system. They fished and enjoyed a picnic. The trout caught were "small" and were caught on wet flys from small rowboats; about fifty trout were taken according to the official log maintained by Assistant Naval Aide Rigdon. Rigdon had a slightly different recollection in his book published about two decades later, however. He remembers Churchill catching one small fish, and FDR catching none. He said the president nicknamed the lake "One Fish Lake" after going home empty-handed.[27]

A "general air of optimism" prevailed at the conference, buoyed by the imminent fall of Italy, the Allies' control of the Atlantic, and the "superhuman" production of naval escort and merchant vessels by American workers.[28] Roosevelt conveyed this feeling during remarks in Washington before heading north for the conference. "Today," the president stated, "on the second anniversary of the signing of the Atlantic Charter, I would cite particularly two of its purposes and principles on which we base our 'hopes for a better future for the world.'" The president cited the "right of all peoples to choose the form of government under which they will live," and "world-wide collaboration with the object of security, for all; of improved labor standards, economic adjustment, and social security."

> We are now fighting a great war. We fight on the side of the United Nations, each and every one of whom has subscribed to the purposes and principles of the Atlantic Charter. Today, we stand upon the threshold of major developments in this war. We are determined that we shall gain total victory over our enemies, and we recognize the fact that our enemies are not only Germany, Italy

and Japan: they are all the forces of oppression, intolerance, inse-
curity, and injustice which have impeded the forward march of
civilization.[29]

At the conclusion of the Quebec conference, Roosevelt traveled by
train to Ottawa. He was met on Parliament Hill by some thirty thousand
citizens, supposedly the largest crowd ever to welcome a distinguished
visitor to Ottawa, even exceeding the welcome accorded King George VI
and Queen Elizabeth.

"There is a longing in the air," Roosevelt told the crowd. "It is not a
longing to go back to what they call 'the good old days.' I have distinct
reservations as to how good 'the good old days' were. I would rather
believe that we can achieve new and better days."[30]

And those days soon would be here.

CHAPTER 15

Fire Horse Refusing
to Go to Pasture

President Roosevelt was sitting in his wheelchair one afternoon on deck just outside the mess on the battleship USS *Iowa* as it was steaming through the Atlantic, east of Bermuda. He and a group of his top wartime advisers were observing an antiaircraft drill on the second day of their voyage. The newest U.S. battleship had departed Hampton Roads, Virginia, on 13 November 1943. During the exercises, weather balloons were launched and then shot down by antiaircraft fire from the accompanying convoy of destroyers.

Suddenly, "This is not a drill!" was shouted from the bridge. "It's the real thing! It's the real thing!" an officer yelled to the president sitting two decks below. A live torpedo, fired at *Iowa,* was racing at full speed toward a direct collision with the battleship's hull, right beneath the president's cabin.

After some initial confusion aboard the ships, one of the destroyers broke strict wartime radio silence and warned the battleship to take immediate evasive action. Capt. John L. McCrea, one of Roosevelt's former naval aides, rapidly maneuvered the fifty-two-thousand-ton battleship, heeling it over in a ninety-degree turn at thirty-one knots, to get out of the way of the deadly fish. The torpedo exploded in a barrage of naval fire from six hundred to three thousand feet astern of the president's ship, according to various accounts of the incident.[1]

The torpedo, first thought to have been an enemy weapon, came from USS *William D. Porter,* an American destroyer that was escorting the battleship and also participating in the military exercises. Some immediately thought an assassination attempt, carried out by secret enemy agents aboard the destroyer, was being made. Later it was determined that the destroyer crew had failed to remove the primer to the torpedo, thus allowing it to ignite when it became wet from the heavy seas.

Harry Hopkins, who was standing next to the president during the harrowing incident, asked Roosevelt whether he wanted to be moved inside the ship. "No—where is it?" the president replied, in his customary fearless manner. Roosevelt called to Arthur Prettyman, his valet, "Arthur! Arthur! Take me over to the starboard rail. I want to watch the torpedo." Prettyman, who was "shaking all over," complied with the president's wishes and wheeled him over to the rail.[2]

If the torpedo had hit its mark, a tragedy of untold proportions could have been the result. In addition to the president of the United States, most top military and civilian brass were aboard *Iowa,* including Gen. George Marshall, Gen. Henry "Hap" Arnold, Gen. Brehon Somervell, Gen. Pa Watson, Adm. William Leahy, Adm. Ernest King, and Dr. Ross McIntire. An investigation was conducted; the responsible crew members would be severely punished. Roosevelt stepped in, however, and decided to absolve all sailors involved in what he judged was an accident.

Four days later, Roosevelt penned a letter to Eleanor and, not wishing to alarm her, never mentioned the incident. Instead, his letter dealt with lighter matters: "All goes well and a very comfortable trip so far," Roosevelt wrote. "Weather good and warm enough to sit with only a sweater as an extra over an old pair of trousers and a fishing shirt."[3]

Roosevelt, traveling through U-boat–infested waters, was now about two days away from reaching Africa, where he would then fly to another wartime conference with Winston Churchill. This time, Roosevelt finally —after two years of trying—was successful at convincing Russia's Marshal Joseph Stalin to attend. The meeting would take place in Teheran and was code-named "Eureka," an obvious acknowledgment of FDR's success in bringing Stalin to the table.

Roosevelt enjoyed his trip on the new battleship and spent a great deal of time relaxing and reading on the large flat bridge deck. William M. Rigdon, Roosevelt's assistant naval aide, said the president was particularly pleased to find that, like all others on the ship, he had been assigned a battle station and an abandon ship station, in the event of an emergency.[4] Because this was one of the most dangerous trips FDR would ever take, security measures were intense. Security was so tight, Rigdon remembers, that even Fala, the president's Scottish terrier, was left at home.

Iowa had weighed anchor on Friday, 12 November, from Hampton Roads but, after fueling was complete, FDR ordered her departure delayed, following the old sailor's superstition of not beginning a voyage on a Friday. So, precisely at six minutes past midnight, the battleship had finally set sail.[5]

This was the first time Rigdon had seen the special "cruise gear" that was installed on ships carrying President Roosevelt. An elevator and ramps facilitated his movement "in president's country" as the area assigned to him aboard ship was known. A bed twelve inches longer than standard had been added, the toilet bowl was raised to the level of his wheelchair, and railings were installed around his bath tub.[6]

"He had a real love affair with the sea," recalled Secret Service Agent James Griffith, who accompanied the president on this and several other cruises. "He really enjoyed the salt air and sitting on deck." Griffith said Roosevelt "didn't stay inside any longer than he had to"; he much preferred to be on deck, smelling the salt air.[7]

Secret Service Agent Michael Reilly had traveled ahead of the president to Cairo in order to make sure security precautions were in place. Reilly received word that the Germans were using the glide torpedo, a new weapon that traveled through the water and was magnetically attracted to Allied vessels. They were being used extensively at the entrance to the Straits of Gibraltar, through which Roosevelt's ship would pass on its way to Oran, Algeria.

Reilly sent word to *Iowa* to change course to avoid the glide torpedoes. Then he received additional intelligence stating that U-boat "wolf packs" were heavily concentrated in the Dakar area, where he had diverted FDR's ship. He wondered whether enemy agents had become aware that the president was on his way. So, it was back to the original plan. U.S. forces led a barrage to knock out the enemy at Gibraltar, successfully clearing the way for Roosevelt's arrival.[8]

At dawn on 20 November, *Iowa* was docked near Oran, after navigating the straits without incident. Rigdon recalled that they used a new procedure to get the president ashore. "He was lifted into a lifeboat at main deck level, the boat was then lowered into the water, tending lines were cast off and it proceeded to shore."[9]

After the president landed, Reilly lifted him into an armored automobile for a fifty-mile trip over steep roads to the La Senia airport, where he boarded a four engine C-54 transport plane for the 653-mile flight to Tunis. The president touched down three and a half hours later at Tunis, where he was met by Gen. Dwight Eisenhower and FDR's sons Elliott and Franklin Jr., along with Harry Hopkins' son Robert, on hand to photograph the event. Eisenhower provided a tour of the war zone to the president, who took the opportunity to appraise the general for a prospective new job—Supreme Allied Commander. In fact, Roosevelt confided as much to McIntire when he told him the main purpose of the Tunis stop was to help determine Eisenhower's ability to do the job.[10]

"Restored to full vigor by the sea voyage and in fine spirits, the president spent Sunday on a tour of the battlefields," McIntire recalled. Later that night, they boarded the plane again for the 1,851-mile trek to Cairo, where the president instructed the pilot to circle so he could view the Nile River and the pyramids, some 150 feet below.[11]

Admiral McIntire, the president's physician, recalled that no American fighter planes were present to escort the president's plane. There was constant danger from German aircraft, especially during the daytime hours, which is when Roosevelt traveled by plane. Apparently, the commander of the squadron had confused local time with Greenwich mean time, a difference of two hours. Luckily, no enemy planes appeared to greet the lone plane carrying the U.S. commander in chief.[12]

McIntire was also worried about a prevalent disease known locally as "jyppy tummy," a dysentery-type malady. The presidential party, however, carried its own water, milk, and cream, and thus escaped the ailment. Winston Churchill wasn't quite as fortunate, according to McIntire, who said the prime minister had a "bad time" with jyppy tummy.

The first part of the Cairo Conference was code-named "Sextant." Roosevelt met with Churchill and China's Chiang Kai-shek in the U.S. ambassador's villa, where Roosevelt stayed. The big news from the conference that convened 23 November was that the three powers agreed upon a future strategy for Japan. When defeated, Japan would be stripped of all territories it had acquired since World War I. The first part of the Cairo Conference concluded with a Thanksgiving dinner, hosted by Roosevelt, who brought two fully dressed frozen turkeys and all the trimmings from home for the occasion. "Light meat or dark?" the president, who was propped up high in his chair, asked his guests as he carved the birds.[13]

Toward the end of the dinner, the president raised his glass of wine to propose a toast, recalled Elliott Roosevelt. "Large families are usually more closely united than small ones," the president said, "and so, this year, with the peoples of the United Kingdom in our family, we are a large family, and more united than ever before. I propose a toast to this unity, and may it long continue."[14]

Churchill, who was already on his feet before Roosevelt finished speaking, lifted his glass, offering a toast. "He started slowly," Robert Hopkins recalled. "His sentences used a very unusual construction. He stopped. He seemed lost. There was a long pause. He can't get out of this, I thought. He's an old man, his faculties are failing. Then suddenly he picked out a word so perfect, so brilliant, that everyone broke into spontaneous applause. It was a tour de force."[15]

Elliott Roosevelt praised the prime minister's toast as "a remarkable thing," marveling at Churchill's ability for "impromptu oratory."[16] An American GI dance band played popular songs. When they played the "Marine Hymn" Roosevelt burst into song, according to Rigdon, who also said Churchill "jumped to his feet and made his V sign for victory."

As the night wore on, dancing began. The prime minister's daughter Sarah was the only woman present—and in great demand as a dance partner. Churchill turned to Pa Watson for a dance. President Roosevelt, sitting on a couch, roared in laughter as he watched the two men waltz around the room.[17]

The following morning was full of meetings and a ceremony at which FDR presented the Legion of Merit medal to General Eisenhower. Elliott Roosevelt recalled the general's eyes filling with tears as he leaned down so that Roosevelt could pin the medal on his tunic.[18]

Heavy fog on Saturday morning briefly delayed takeoff, but soon the fog lifted and Roosevelt and his party were airborne, flying over the Holy Land and the Tigris and Euphrates Rivers, en route to Teheran, Iran, for his first meeting with Stalin. Arriving mid-afternoon, Roosevelt was whisked to the American Legation on the outskirts of Teheran. Stalin sent word that his secret police had unearthed a plot to assassinate either Roosevelt, Churchill, or Stalin himself. Stalin suggested the president move to the Russian Legation, which was in the city and close to the British compound. In fact, Secret Service Agent Reilly had received reports that Nazi parachutists, perhaps as many as thirty-eight, had been dropped into the area only days before. Roosevelt moved to the Russian compound the next day.[19]

Col. Richard Park Jr., a military aide to Roosevelt, expressing his cautiousness about the Russians, issued a list of "suggestions" for Roosevelt and his party during their stay in Teheran:

1. Drink nothing but boiled water, as Teheran Tummy sets in within 24 hours after drinking inflicted water.
2. Assume that *all* rooms and places of tete-a-tete are wired for recording. This applies to Malta as well.
3. Talk in platitudes except in bi or tripartite official conferences.
4. It is best to say nothing in our "map room" on receipt of messages or on request by others for information. Better point it out in writing or produce the necessary document. This can be over-done—so be clever about it.[20]

The summit between Roosevelt, Churchill, and Stalin convened on 28 November and continued until 1 December. Stalin agreed that Russia would join the fight against Japan when Germany was defeated. To Stalin's delight, Roosevelt and Churchill, somewhat reluctantly, announced that the Normandy invasion would take place in May the following year, which would ease some of the pressure on Russia in its battle against the Nazis.[21] Churchill preferred to defer the cross-channel invasion until other military actions were complete, but neither Roosevelt nor Stalin agreed.

With business concluded, Roosevelt returned by air to Cairo, where he had additional meetings with Churchill, in Cairo Conference II. They settled on General Eisenhower as the Supreme Allied Commander.

Before heading home, Roosevelt wanted to visit Malta and Sicily. Roosevelt flew from Cairo to Tunis, where on 8 December, he took off, bound for Malta. As the island came into view, the pilot called Secret Service Agent Reilly to the cockpit to tell him the plane's flaps were malfunctioning. He advised Reilly to tell the president to tighten his seatbelt, and to sit next to him until they were on the ground.

Reilly recalled thinking that he, having full use of his legs, could "crawl out of a wreck. I had a chance. Somebody would have to drag him [Roosevelt] out." Fortunately, the plane landed safely, despite the flap problem. "The Boss just shook his head as he unfastened his seatbelt," Reilly recalled. Reilly said that although FDR loved to travel, and was a "tireless landscape watcher," he was not fond of traveling by air. He could not move around like other passengers, and was unable to brace himself against bumps and jolts with his legs, as others could do.[22]

After Roosevelt inspected the troops at Malta, he was once again airborne, bound for Tunis, and then Dakar, where he boarded the French destroyer *La Gazelle,* which transferred him to the waiting USS *Iowa* for the trip home. Reilly remembered that everyone watching was having "heart failure" as the president was hoisted aboard the battleship in a bo's'n's chair that had been rigged between the two ships.[23]

The return trip was uneventful except for a near collision near the end of the voyage with a merchant ship during a stormy night with zero visibility. Fortunately, *Iowa's* radar saved the day.[24] The president was safely back in the White House on 17 December 1943 after traveling 17,442 miles.

Roosevelt did not return to a quiet and peaceful home front, however. A nationwide railroad strike, which would cripple the U.S. war effort, had been called for 30 December. The president summoned union and management to the White House in an effort to settle the dispute. Unfortunately, FDR was not successful, so he ordered the government to temporarily take control of the nation's railroads until a settlement could be reached.

As Christmas approached, Roosevelt traveled to Hyde Park to spend the holidays with his family. The long Teheran trip, unsettled home front, and the continuing war had taken its toll on the president. He contracted a particularly debilitating flu-like illness, followed by a bronchitis from which he failed to recover. "Coughing spells racked him by day and broke his rest at night," McIntire recalled.[25]

Concerned about the effect of the continual coughing on Roosevelt's heart, McIntire ordered him to lose weight to ease the load.[26] In addition, a vacation in a warm climate was advised. After Guantánamo Bay naval station in Cuba was ruled out because "Cuba is absolutely lousy with anarchists, murderers, et. Cetera and a lot of prevaricators,"[27] the president accepted an invitation from Bernard M. Baruch, a wealthy longtime friend with a twenty-three-thousand-acre estate, Hobcaw Barony, near Georgetown, a South Carolina coastal town.

During his stay at the estate, Roosevelt rested and fished a small pond from the dock. Feeling better, he began trolling in the coastal waters for bluefish and bonita. The U.S. Coast Guard and U.S. Navy patrolled the area, looking for Nazi submarines, and blimps watched the president from above.[28] After a month's rest, sun, and leisurely fishing, Roosevelt returned to Washington in May 1944, refreshed and ready to return to work.

Over the next two months, the Allies scored significant victories in Rome, the Philippine Sea, and, of course, in Normandy with Operation Overlord, the 6 June D-Day invasion that FDR and Churchill had been planning for more than a year.

Roosevelt now was facing another major decision. Should he run for an unprecedented fourth term in what would be the first wartime election since the Civil War? Dr. McIntire spoke privately to the president, advising him that he must consider his age and the "twelve years of grueling strain such as no other chief executive had even been called on to bear."

"With proper care and strict adherence to rules, I gave it my best judgment that his chances of winning through to 1948 were good," McIntire said. He cautioned Roosevelt that, unless the president "slowed down" his pace of traveling, meetings, and work, the doctor "would not be answerable for the consequences."[29]

McIntire bluntly told Roosevelt that he may "feel fine" but he doesn't "look it. Your neck is scrawny and your face is gullied by a lot of lines that have added ten years to your age." The doctor continued, "And while we're on the subject, for heaven's sake, get some new clothes. That old shirt is sizes too large, and the coat hangs on your shoulders like a bag." Roosevelt was amused but, not being a man of fashion, did very little to effect any suggested changes.[30]

Roosevelt had mixed feelings on whether he should attempt to stay in office. Although the war was going well for the Allies, it still was not won. In addition, Roosevelt wanted to advance his goals of establishing a United Nations in an effort to prevent future wars. "All that is within me cries out to go back to my home on the Hudson River," Roosevelt said, adding that "after many years of public service . . . my personal thoughts have turned to the day when I could return to civil life."[31]

Merriman Smith, the White House correspondent for United Press International, doubted that FDR really wanted to retire. "He was like a fire horse refusing to go to pasture," Smith wrote. "His love of political warfare, his vanity and his firm belief that the country needed him got the best of his judgment."[32] In a conversation with Adm. William Leahy, chief of the Joint Chiefs of Staff, however, Roosevelt said, "Bill, I just hate to run for election. Perhaps, the war will by that time have progressed to a point where it will be unnecessary for me to be a candidate."[33]

That was not to be. So Roosevelt concluded, "[R]eluctantly, but as a good soldier" he would accept the nomination of the Democratic party and make the run for a fourth term in the White House. On the eve of the Democratic convention in Chicago, Roosevelt secretly boarded the Ferdinand Magellan for the first leg of a month-long cross-country trip to San Diego, California.

After stopping in Hyde Park to pick up Eleanor, the presidential special headed west. Roosevelt broke with his tradition of accepting the party nomination in person, instead opting to give a radio address from the observation car of his train. "The war waits for no elections," Roosevelt told his listeners, explaining his absence from the convention hall. He added that he was traveling the country "in performance of my duties under the Constitution."[34] Roosevelt was preparing to board the heavy cruiser USS *Baltimore* for a Pacific inspection trip and a round of wartime meetings with his military commanders in Honolulu.

Eleanor Roosevelt had accompanied the president on the continental non-secret portion of this trip. Of course, Fala also went along. Roosevelt's cover was blown several times during the five-day train trip when Informer Fala was spotted being walked on the train platform, sometimes even by the first lady, who usually traveled without any security. Eleanor flew back to Washington before Roosevelt left his train. On 21 July 1944 he ceremonially was piped aboard the fourteen-thousand-ton USS *Baltimore*, moored at San Diego's Broadway Pier. *Baltimore* had actively served in as many as fifteen Pacific battles, emerging unscathed. Prior to the president's arrival, the scuttlebutt was that he might be coming aboard, especially because the ship's carpenters began building wooden ramps that would accommodate a wheelchair-bound passenger. On Friday evening, off-duty swabs saw a Scottie trotting back and forth on the deck plates. "The word was passed. . . . Fala is aboard."[35]

As was his usual practice, however, Roosevelt refused to begin a cruise on a Friday, so departure was delayed until after midnight. With six destroyers providing escort duty and navy airplanes securing the skies above, the ship pulled out of San Diego Harbor, en route to Pearl Harbor.

During the day, the ships followed a pre-arranged zigzag pattern and, from sunset to sunrise, all ships were darkened to avoid being targets for enemy aircraft. The trip was uneventful until the early morning hours of 23 July. The ship went on high alert after intercepting a radio message: "Possible enemy task force located 200 miles north of Oahu. Alert all activities." The message was from the commander of the Hawaiian Sea

Frontier; it warned that the Japanese might be within striking distance of *Baltimore,* a distance certainly much too close to a ship carrying the president of the United States.

The report, originating from an U.S. pilot, was later believed to have been an "optical illusion," although the pilot continued to believe that he had spotted the enemy. The incident served as a startling reminder of the powerful enemy force still on the prowl in the Pacific.[36]

The only casualty reported on the trip was the dignity of Roosevelt's little terrier. Sailors aboard the ship, anxious for a souvenir from the famous First Dog, lured Fala into the mess nightly. They would feed him tidbits of food, while they clipped hair from his back. The president noticed that Fala disappeared each night around the same time and, upon returning, appeared to have less and less hair. When the reason was discovered, Roosevelt had the ship's captain issue an order that Fala would not be fed or clipped.[37] "While Fala's hair grew back by the time he returned to the states," Roosevelt advisor Sam Rosenman recalled, "he was for a short time a strange-looking dog."[38]

The cruiser made its way into Pearl Harbor on the morning of 26 July. Eighteen navy planes roared overhead, awakening Roosevelt who still was asleep in his cabin. The secret trip was apparently not much of a secret anymore; the harbor was full of sailors and a tremendous crowd of island residents yearning to get a glimpse of the president. With the identity of the ship's VIP now an open secret, Roosevelt ordered the presidential flag hoisted, and he was wheeled to the starboard side so he could see the crowds. Flashing a broad smile, the president waved to the white-suited seamen manning the rails of U.S. warships and the thousands of onlookers cheering the commander in chief's arrival at Pearl Harbor, his first trip there since the Japanese attack thirty-one months earlier.[39]

CHAPTER 16

No Earthly Power
Can Keep Him Here

USS *Baltimore,* moored at Pier 22B just astern of USS *Enterprise,* basked in the warm afternoon sun of Pearl Harbor as it lowered its gangplank so Adm. Chester Nimitz and thirty-five U.S. military officers could come aboard. President Roosevelt was waiting on the ship's quarterdeck. Gen. Douglas MacArthur, who had touched down on the island earlier, was not on hand to greet his commander in chief upon his arrival in Hawaii on 26 July 1944.

Just as the president and his party were ready to disembark the cruiser, a loud siren sounded. A motorcycle escort raced to the dock ahead of a long chauffeur-driven limousine. The rear door opened and out came MacArthur, clad in a leather bomber jacket. The general strode up the gangplank, amid applause from onlookers, to greet Roosevelt. "Hello, Doug," the president said. "What are you doing with that leather jacket on—it's darn hot today." MacArthur replied: "Well, I've just landed from Australia. It's pretty cold up there."[1]

MacArthur never was one of Roosevelt's favorites. Some of Roosevelt's dislike possibly stemmed from MacArthur's role in the so-called Battle of Anacostia Flats in the summer of 1930. At that time, MacArthur, serving as President Hoover's chief of staff, led troops in an assault on fifteen thousand World War I veterans and family members camped out on the marshy flats near the Anacostia River. They had come to Washington to convince Congress that they needed their bonuses now, instead of waiting until 1945 as promised. Ignoring orders from Hoover, MacArthur used tear gas and weapons to drive the veterans and their families from the makeshift camp. A fire started and the camp was destroyed.

Years later, Roosevelt's animus for MacArthur was never far from the surface. Secret Service Agent Anthony Lobb recalled a conversation he overheard between Roosevelt and his cousin Laura Delano at Hyde Park. "I was posted right under the porch where he [the president] was sitting with Laura Delano," Lobb recalled. "Franklin," Laura began, "would you ever make General MacArthur chief of staff of the whole army?" Without hesitation, the president firmly replied, "No, I would never do that. I don't want to make him chief of staff."[2]

During the conference in Hawaii, President Roosevelt was housed in a plush villa at 2709 Kalaukan Avenue. It had an outside elevator and fronted Waikiki Beach. In addition to participating in lengthy conferences on the conduct of the war with MacArthur, Nimitz, and Adm. William Leahy, Roosevelt also made several trips around the island of Oahu. He inspected shipyards, training camps, and hospitals. Whenever possible, Roosevelt insisted on visiting injured American soldiers and sailors.

One hospital was filled with soldiers who had lost legs and arms in battle. Roosevelt decided to have a Secret Service agent push him in his wheelchair through each of the wards. As Roosevelt's aides followed on foot, the president—sitting in his chair—greeted each veteran with a cheery smile. His presence provided encouragement and inspiration to these men, who would be facing the same kinds of obstacles Roosevelt had endured for the last twenty-three years.

Samuel Rosenman, with the president on that hospital visit, said the commander in chief "wanted to display himself and his useless legs to those boys who would have to face the same bitterness."[3] Adm. Ross McIntire, also along on the hospital tour, said Roosevelt's words were so inspiring that he still got "a lump in my throat" when he remembered the way the men tried to lift their heads to thank and cheer their president.[4]

A major goal of the Hawaiian military conferences was to settle differences between MacArthur and Nimitz over the future conduct of the war. Nimitz wanted to move forward against Formosa and the Chinese coast. MacArthur first wanted to liberate the Philippines. He warned Roosevelt that if he bypassed the Philippines, "I dare to say that the American people would be so aroused that they would register most complete resentment against you in the polls." Roosevelt sided with MacArthur.[5]

With the primary business concluded, Roosevelt boarded *Baltimore* for a trip to Adak, one of the Aleutian Islands. He inspected the military facilities at the American base and visited the twenty-two thousand troops stationed there. The weather was the worst that Roosevelt had seen since his early days of sailing along New England's stormy coastline. The semitropical Hawaiian weather was just a memory. Dense fog reduced visibility to two hundred yards; torrential rains and high seas persisted during most of Roosevelt's stay. Temperatures were in the low forties with force seven southeast winds whipping up white caps that battered the hull of the ship.

"FDR was not to be completely outdone by the weather," Assistant Naval Aide Rigdon recalled. "To the surprise of us all, he put on a rain slicker and boots and was wheeled out on deck, carrying a campstool. He found a spot on the cruiser's fo'c's'le and dropped his fishing line over the side." After dinner, Roosevelt fished in the pouring rain for about an hour, catching several Dolly Varden trout, which were served as his breakfast the next day.[6]

Dr. Howard Bruenn, who had accompanied the president on this voyage, recalled that fishing and being on the water was "a very pleasant" way for Roosevelt to relax and pass the time. Bruenn remembered the president enjoying the trout he caught that rainy night in Adak Harbor, Alaska. "The president's days aboard ship were restful," Dr. Bruenn recalled. "He continued to sleep well and spent most of his afternoons on the flag bridge enjoying the sun and cool breezes."[7]

The winds abated the following day. Roosevelt inspected the troops, telling them, "I like your food. I like your climate," and adding, in jest, "you don't realize the thousands upon thousands of people who would give anything in the world to swap places with you."[8] The cruiser then shoved off from Adak.

Roosevelt sailed into the Bering Sea, bound for Kodiak Island. He boarded a small open motor boat for some fly fishing on Buskin Lake, where he caught only one small trout. Next, plans called for a visit to Puget Sound via the scenic Inside Passage, which was too narrow for *Baltimore*. FDR transferred to the smaller destroyer USS *Cummings*, a veteran of Pearl Harbor that had suffered some minor damage. At Puget

Sound, Roosevelt inspected various military installations, including the submarine base, naval air station, and Fort Greely.

Many close aides to Roosevelt later wished the president had skipped the Puget Sound visit, because he delivered what most regard as the worst speech of his political career there. The podium was set up on the fo'c's'le of the destroyer for his speech. The fo'c's'le was slanted, which made standing a chore, even for one with full use of both legs. Roosevelt insisted on using the heavy steel braces he had not worn for almost a year. He had lost considerable weight over that time, however, and the braces did not fit properly. The president was in a great deal of pain as he stood.

A stiff wind was blowing that day, and Roosevelt struggled to keep the pages of his speech in order while, all the while, he was gripping the podium for support and suffering great pain from the ill-fitting braces. The result was a disaster—a rambling speech with Roosevelt's delivery described as "hesitant, halting and ineffective."[9]

The president also suffered an acute angina attack during the speech, resulting in "one hell of a pain" in his chest. Remarkably, Roosevelt stood the entire time and finished his speech. He was then taken to a cabin to rest, and he canceled plans to take an automobile tour of the navy yard.[10] Dr. Bruenn, who attended the president in his cabin and administered an electrocardiogram, said this was the "first time [FDR] experienced substernal oppression with radiation to both shoulders." Bruenn said the discomfort lasted about fifteen minutes but resulted in no abnormalities in either the electrocardiogram or his blood count.[11]

Reaction to the speech was swift and universally negative, even among many Roosevelt supporters. Some privately started to think that FDR's days were over. The Roosevelt haters—and there were many—gleefully began whispering that "the old man is through, finished." Even his trusted friend and advisor Sam Rosenman, who had not accompanied FDR when he departed Hawaii, heard the speech on the radio and had a "sinking sensation."[12]

The speech came on the heels of a widely distributed photograph that had been taken of Roosevelt in San Diego during his Democratic Convention address delivered by radio from his train. Because of a bout of cholecystitis, Dr. Bruenn had placed the president on a low fat diet, and Roosevelt had lost fifteen pounds. Bruenn said that the president had lost "flesh from his face," which made him appear in the photograph to be "somewhat haggard, instead of his normal robust appearance."[13]

Rosenman said the photo showed "a tragic-looking figure; the face appeared to be very emaciated because of the downward angle and open mouth; it looked weary, sick, discouraged and exhausted. The picture was completely distorted, bearing no resemblance to the man I watched deliver that speech that night."[14] It appeared to many that New York's young and vigorous Governor Thomas E. Dewey would have an easy time defeating Roosevelt in November.

On 1 September, Roosevelt again boarded his train in Washington and headed to Hyde Park so he could rest over the upcoming Labor Day weekend. Secret Service Agent James Griffith traveled aboard the train with the president and remembered that Roosevelt ordered a brief detour before proceeding to Hyde Park. After traveling through the night, the train came to a stop at Allamuchy, New Jersey, early the next morning. Roosevelt transferred to an automobile along with his cousin, Daisy Suckley, and was driven away. Agent Griffith was among several agents who stood on the car's running boards as it traveled through the rural countryside. They arrived at a large estate that had been owned by the recently deceased Winthrop Rutherfurd. The estate now was the home of his widow, Lucy Mercer Rutherfurd, with whom Roosevelt had been romantically involved in 1916–1917, midway through his term as assistant secretary of the navy.

The president went inside and Agent Griffith was stationed in the backyard to guard the rear entrance of the mansion. Griffith sat in a wicker chair near the swimming pool while Fala trotted around the expansive grounds. Meanwhile, inside, the president, Suckley, and a number of other guests enjoyed a lunch of jelly soup, squabs, vegetables, salad, and ice cream.

After several hours, Mrs. Rutherfurd emerged from the back door and spotted Griffith in the chair. He identified himself and Mrs. Rutherfurd told him the president had left an hour earlier. They jumped into Mrs. Rutherfurd's car and quickly arrived at the train station just in time to see the presidential special disappearing in the distance.

Mrs. Rutherfurd and Agent Griffith met with the railroad president. When he heard the story, he and Griffith got into his car and they sped down the road, crisscrossing train tracks until they finally were ahead of the president's train. "Has that special train passed here yet?" yelled the railroad president to an employee stationed at one of the crossings, the standard practice when the president's train was traveling. "Who are you?"

barked the employee. "I am the president of this railroad!" The worker
quickly flagged down the train as it passed. Agent Griffith boarded but was
a little taken aback: "They hadn't even missed me," he recalled.[15]

Rumors about Roosevelt's failing health continued to spread. Then,
another rumor surfaced about the president's dog, Fala, that provided
grist for the mill of the growing number of Roosevelt detractors. They
wanted Americans to believe their president had lost touch with reality. It
appeared to many that a Republican would finally occupy the White
House in January.

According to the story widely circulated throughout Republican circles, Fala had been inadvertently left behind on the Aleutian Islands during FDR's recent cruise. When the president discovered Fala was missing, according to the story, he diverted a destroyer from its war duty to
retrieve the terrier at a great cost to the American taxpayers.

Unexpectedly, this was exactly what Roosevelt's campaign needed.
The president turned the tables on his opponents by delivering what
Samuel Rosenman called "the greatest political speech of his career."[16]
Addressing the International Brotherhood of Teamsters on 23 September
1944, an energized Roosevelt displayed his legendary skill and vigor once
again as he spoke about his "little dog, Fala."

> These Republican leaders have not been content with attacks on
> me, or my wife, or my sons. No, not content with that, they now
> include my little dog, Fala. Well, of course, I don't resent attacks,
> and my family doesn't resent attacks, but Fala *does* resent them.
> You know, Fala is Scotch, and being a Scottie, as soon as he learned
> that the Republican fiction writers in Congress and out had con-
> cocted a story that I had left him behind on the Aleutian Islands
> and had sent a destroyer back to find him—at a cost to taxpayers of
> two or three, or eight or twenty million dollars—his Scotch soul
> was furious. He has not been the same dog since. I am accustomed
> to hearing malicious falsehoods about myself—such as the old,
> worm-eaten chestnut that I have represented myself as indispensa-
> ble. But I think I have a right to resent, to object to libelous state-
> ments about my dog.[17]

The public went wild. They loved the speech and were thrilled that
the "old" master appeared to be himself again. Although the election was

still about six weeks away, Roosevelt's prospects of winning a fourth term suddenly appeared brighter. The tired president still would have to campaign hard to beat his Republican challenger.

Dr. Bruenn, concerned about the effect of campaigning on the president's health, was surprised to see how well he fared as he traveled the country battling for a fourth term in the White House. A spark in the old campaigner obviously had reignited. "As a result of the campaign," Dr. Bruenn noted, "there was a complete disregard [by the president] of the rest regimen, together with prolonged activity." As a concession to Bruenn, FDR did agree to deliver speeches while seated instead of standing with his painful braces.

"It may be noted that during this period of stress he was very animated," Dr. Bruenn said. "He really enjoyed going to the 'hustings' and, despite this, his blood pressure levels, if anything, were lower than before." The physician said Roosevelt was eating better and "despite prolonged periods of exposure, he did not contract any upper respiratory infections," a malady that plagued him frequently over the years.[18]

In November, Roosevelt handily defeated Dewey, winning thirty-six states to the Republican's twelve, even though the popular vote was a little closer. Roosevelt garnered 25,602,505 votes; Dewey had 22,006,278. Roosevelt's wish to return to his beloved Hudson River would never be fulfilled, but he would achieve his goal of continuing to lead the United States and its allies in the war—at least for the next five months.

On 20 January 1945, with his hand resting on the family's old Dutch Bible, Roosevelt took the oath of office for the fourth consecutive time in a very brief ceremony on the South Portico of the White House. A gusty wind blew as Roosevelt looked out at the snow-covered ground. The coatless and hatless president stood at the podium, wearing his ill-fitting braces, and accepted the will of the American people that he continue to reside at 1600 Pennsylvania Avenue. As Roosevelt proceeded with his brief Inaugural Address, which lasted less than five minutes, his body started to shake and he suffered intense pain in his chest, presumably the same as he had suffered when he gave his speech on the deck of a ship in Bremerton in August of the previous year. Yet, once again, a determined president finished his speech and retired to the White House to rest.[19]

Jimmy Roosevelt wheeled his father into the Green Room. His son reported that FDR "was thoroughly chilled" and had a stabbing chest pain. "He gripped my arm hard and said: 'Jimmy, I can't take this unless you get me a stiff drink,'" Jimmy Roosevelt recalled. "I said I would and as I started out he called to me: 'You'd better make it straight.'"

"I brought him a tumbler half full of whiskey, which he drank as if it were medicine. In all my life, I never had seen Father take a drink in that manner," Jimmy said. Dr. Bruenn remarked that Roosevelt appeared to be in "excellent spirits" at the reception later in the evening.[20]

Roosevelt wanted a very simple inaugural ceremony this time around. He felt there was no need for an elaborate grandstand for spectators, a fancy post-inaugural dinner, or other festivities. As Samuel Rosenman observed: "In this way, the president saved money on gasoline, lumber, train transportation, food, labor," which would have been required for a traditional inauguration; the savings achieved could better be used to support the war effort. An abbreviated ceremony helped conserve the president's limited energy as well.[21] Roosevelt, perhaps with a premonition of what was to come, insisted that all thirteen of his grandchildren attend the inaugural so a family photograph could be snapped, the last such family photograph taken.

Two days later, Roosevelt and a group of his top advisers secretly left Washington during the night, traveling by train to Newport News, Virginia. Under cover of darkness, the president and his party boarded the heavy cruiser USS *Quincy*. FDR's last sea voyage, he was bound for his last wartime conference with Churchill and Stalin.

With a German U-boat reportedly lurking off the east coast, Roosevelt's ship carefully plied through the submarine net gate and sailed into the North Atlantic, with a stiff wind blowing from the west. *Quincy* was accompanied by the light cruiser USS *Springfield* and three destroyers, all traveling ahead to screen for U-boats. The destination was the Mediterranean Sea, some four thousand miles away.

In anticipation of the trip, the navy had taken *Quincy* out of service so that modifications could be made for its distinguished passenger. At the Boston Navy Yard a kitchen was added to the captain's quarters, two elevators were installed on the port side, and a wooden ramp was added on the starboard side so the president could move from the main deck to the superstructure deck with ease. Even new silverware was added to the mess.[22]

In addition to his top civilian and military advisors, Roosevelt—for the first time—broke his strict rule on not allowing women to accompany him on his sea voyages. Although Eleanor was disappointed that the president would not allow her to go along this time, he did permit his daughter, Anna, to sail with him; she provided important personal assistance to a tired president.

At sunset, the ship was darkened to prevent being spotted by enemy aircraft. On his first night at sea, Roosevelt retired to the flag cabin and watched the movie "Our Hearts Were Young and Gay." Nightly movies became the routine during the cruise; the president enjoyed a number during the crossing. "The Princess and the Pirate" was one that would not be shown in American theaters until some months later. Other movies included "Here Come the Waves," "The Fighting Lady," "The Lady in the Window," "Laura," and "The Unknown Guest."[23]

The thought of going to sea always excited Franklin Roosevelt. Although Jimmy Roosevelt remained troubled about what he had observed on Inauguration Day, he said the president seemed invigorated when he spoke about his upcoming meeting with Churchill and Stalin. "As he talked about it [the Yalta trip], one almost could see him throw off his fatigue as he became stimulated with the thought of the challenging task that faced him," Jimmy Roosevelt recalled.[24]

During the crossing, Roosevelt worked on his mail and other paperwork, sorted his stamp collection, or simply relaxed on deck, even in inclement weather. Roosevelt enjoyed watching the crew take part in three-legged races, a battle royal, and tug-of-war on the ship's fantail. Because of strict wartime radio silence, outgoing presidential mail was transferred to one of the accompanying destroyers; it was placed in a sealed powder can, with a line attached, and tossed overboard from *Quincy*'s stern. A trailing destroyer would recover the can, with its precious contents, and transport it to a nearby naval station where it would be flown to Washington.[25]

Roosevelt was the guest of honor at a party for his sixty-third birthday, celebrated 30 January on board *Quincy*. Five rival groups of bakers each baked a cake. The crew presented the president with a handsomely inscribed brass ashtray made from a piece of a shell fired from *Quincy* during the invasion of Normandy.[26]

On 31 January, as the moonlight faded to daylight, *Quincy* safely passed through the Straits of Gibraltar. The ship moored in Grand Harbor, Valetta, at Malta on 2 February. Churchill and his daughter, Sarah, came aboard and lunched with the president. Later that evening, they met for their first formal conference before beginning the next leg of their journey. Again, in the cover of darkness, Roosevelt boarded the "Sacred Cow," a C-54 transport plane converted for use by the president, the first official presidential aircraft. With an escort of five fighter planes, he flew for six hours and forty minutes to the snow-covered airfield at Saki, about eighty miles from the Crimean conference site of Yalta on the Black Sea.

After the president's airplane flight to Casablanca in 1943, Secret Service Agent Mike Reilly had decided Roosevelt needed his own secure airplane. Built under tight security by the Douglas Aircraft Company, the plane had special modifications to accommodate FDR's disability, including a battery-powered elevator to allow him to enter the plane in his wheelchair and a set of removable steel rails so that he could wheel himself about the plane. Other modifications allowed FDR access to the cockpit, where he could sit between the pilot and copilot and observe the flight firsthand.[27]

Winston Churchill watched as Roosevelt descended from the plane's elevator and was lifted to a waiting automobile. The prime minister thought the president looked "frail and ill."[28] An eight-hour automobile ride proceeded past war-torn, gutted buildings, burned tanks and railroad cars, and over mountain roads lined with Russian soldiers. Roosevelt finally arrived at Livadia Palace in Yalta, where the conference code-named "Argonaut" with FDR, Winston Churchill, and Joseph Stalin would occur. The president was housed in a suite once used as a summer home for Czar Nicholas II.

The eight-day conference focused on the final battle plans for the war and the shape of the postwar world, including what would become of Poland. Despite criticism by some that Roosevelt was too ill and frail to lead the conference, and that Stalin took advantage of that frailty, most top advisers accompanying the president disagreed. Adm. William D. Leahy, Roosevelt's chief of staff, remembered: "It was my feeling that Roosevelt had conducted the Crimean Conference with great skill and that his personality had dominated the discussions."[29] The lengthy and emotionally draining meetings, all chaired by the president, did take their toll on Roosevelt who, on 8 February, suffered a condition that Dr. Bruenn described as "pulsus alternans," an irregularity in the pulse that usually indicates serious myocardial disease.[30]

Bruenn ordered Roosevelt to reduce his hours of activity. After two days, the president started feeling better. "His mood was excellent. His appetite was excellent and he appeared to enjoy the Russian food and cooking. There was no cough and the pulsus alternans had disappeared."[31]

Award-winning American historian Robert Dallek believes that some of Roosevelt's foreign policy efforts remain misunderstood:

> No part of Roosevelt's foreign policy has been less clearly under-stood than his wartime diplomacy. The portrait of him as utterly naive or unrealistic about the Russians, for example, has been much overdrawn. Recognizing that postwar stability would require a Soviet-American accord, and that Soviet power would then ex-tend into East-Central Europe and parts of East Asia, Roosevelt openly accepted these emerging realities in his dealings with Stalin. The suggestion that Roosevelt could have restrained this Soviet expansion through greater realism or a tougher approach to Stalin is unpersuasive.[32]

To bolster his view that Roosevelt was in control during the Yalta Con-ference, Dallek notes that the president acted "to limit the expansion of Russian power in 1945 by refusing to share the secret of the atomic bomb, agreeing to station American troops in southern Germany, endorsing Churchill's arrangements for the Balkans, working for the acquisition of American air and naval bases in the Pacific and the Atlantic, and encour-aging the illusion of China as a Great Power with an eye to using her as a political counterweight to the USSR."[33] This hardly describes the work of a tired old man who had lost touch with reality.

Rather, Roosevelt continued his lifelong consistent technique of not revealing everything during discussions and negotiations, thus giving him-self greater flexibility to arrive at a settlement. Although Roosevelt's body was failing him, his mind remained clear. He continued to be the same shrewd and careful politician he always had been, until the end finally came. In describing his manner of operation, Roosevelt once said, "You know, I am a juggler, and I never let my right hand know what my left hand does."[34]

Late in the afternoon on Sunday, 11 February, the president departed Yalta by car for Sevastopol. He traveled over high and winding roads along the Black Sea to reach his destination some eighty miles away. He passed a century-old battlefield, the site of the historic charge of the Light

Brigade during the Crimean War of 1854–1856. Roosevelt reached Sevastopol near dusk and boarded the amphibious ship USS *Catoctin*.

Roosevelt and his party enjoyed a steak dinner aboard *Catoctin*, where they slept overnight. FDR then proceeded by car the next morning to the airfield at Saki. Roosevelt was lifted by elevator to the Sacred Cow. The plane flew him to Egypt's Great Bitter Lake and a rendezvous with USS *Quincy*.[35] This would be the last time Roosevelt would use his new presidential airplane.

Roosevelt spent two days at Great Bitter Lake. King Farouk I of Egypt, Haile Selassie, Emperor of Ethiopia, and King Ibn Saud of Saudi Arabia visited him. The most colorful and unusual of these visitors was King Ibn Saud, who arrived on the destroyer USS *Murphy*, dispatched by Roosevelt to pick up the monarch at the port of Jiddah, Saudi Arabia. "King Ibn Saud set up a tent on deck and brought live sheep on board," recalled Secret Service Agent James Griffith. Although a cabin was available for the king, he preferred to sleep outdoors in his tent, which was heated by charcoal bucket fires.[36] William Rigdon, Roosevelt's assistant naval aide, said that in addition to the eighty-six live sheep, the king also brought along a large contingent that included members of his family, guards, a fortuneteller, cooks, religious attendants, and a ceremonial coffee server.[37]

On Valentine's Day *Murphy* arrived at Great Bitter Lake, and moored port side to the president's cruiser. As the destroyer came into view, the president, Rigdon and *Quincy*'s crew were treated to an extraordinary sight. The king was seated in a large gilt chair on top of the ship's superstructure, with a large number of guards, family, and aides, all in colorful ceremonial garb, standing on beautiful oriental rugs that had been placed around the destroyer's deck. Live sheep were grazing on food scattered around the deck, and an animal slaughter scaffold was rigged to the ship's flagstaff. The king insisted on freshly slaughtered lamb daily.[38]

The rotund king, who had difficulty walking and impaired vision, traveled more than eight hundred miles to meet President Roosevelt; it was the first time he ever had left his country's soil. In addition to an extraordinary sight, his visit was a distinct honor for Roosevelt. The two heads of state exchanged gifts. The president even gave the king one of his wheelchairs after Ibn Saud expressed an interest in having one.[39]

After the king departed from *Quincy*, the cruiser got under way. It was bound for Alexandria, Egypt, for a final round of meetings. Roosevelt and his aides went to the movies that night, viewing "Irish Eyes Are Smiling" in the flag cabin.

At Alexandria, Roosevelt met with Secretary of State Edward Stettinius Jr. and other aides. Winston Churchill stopped by the seaport for one last session with FDR. The prime minister's son, Major Randolph Churchill, came aboard and joined his father and the president for lunch. As they bid farewell, Churchill had no way of knowing that he never again would see Roosevelt, although, years later, he would admit that he suspected Roosevelt had a "slender contact with life."[40]

Quincy departed, bound for Algiers. During the cruise, Roosevelt enjoyed movies almost every night, including "The Climax," "None but the Lonely Heart," and "Meet Me in St. Louis." White House correspondents came aboard in Algiers, and the cruiser set sail for Newport News. It would not be a happy voyage for Roosevelt.

On Tuesday, 20 February, Roosevelt received some very sad news. Gen. Pa Watson, his military aide and close adviser for seventeen years, had died in his cabin from a cerebral hemorrhage. He had been ill since Great Bitter Lake.

Watson's death hit Roosevelt especially hard. He was taking it very personally, just as he had the deaths of Louis Howe, Gus Gennerich, Missy LeHand. and, of course, his beloved mother, Sara. The president was "deeply depressed" by this latest loss, according to Sam Rosenman. He said Roosevelt was reluctant to work on his report to Congress on the Yalta Conference, which was scheduled to be delivered soon after his return to Washington.[41]

Despite his depression over the death of his friend, the president's general health remained "good," according to Dr. Bruenn. The president was bothered by some nasal stuffiness, but no other health problems arose.[42] The rest of the trip back to Washington was uneventful.

Back home from his fourteen-thousand-mile trip, Roosevelt worked late into the evening. Dr. Bruenn was concerned because the president again was ignoring his rest regimen and had lost his appetite.[43] During his report to the Congress on the Yalta Conference, Roosevelt delivered the address while sitting, the first time in twelve years he had not stood while addressing the lawmakers. Samuel Rosenman was upset by what he heard as he listened to the president's speech: "I was dismayed at the halting, ineffective manner of delivery."[44]

By the end of March, Bruenn said Roosevelt "began to look badly. His color was poor and he appeared to be very tired, although he continued to sleep well." The doctor advised a period of total rest.[45] On 29 March, Roosevelt departed for Warm Springs, Georgia. His special place there previously had rejuvenated him, filling him with new life; maybe it could happen again. At least, that's what everyone hoped.

Just after lunch on Good Friday, Roosevelt's train arrived at the Warm Springs station. Ruth Stevens, an old friend from the Pine Mountain town, was on hand to greet the president, as she had done so many times before. This time something was different. "When the president left the train he was wheeled on the observation platform and lowered to the ground on a tiny elevator," Ruth Stevens recalled. "He was dressed in a navy blue suit—but no smile or bob of his head this time. We all remarked how tired and worn he looked."[46]

Secret Service Agent Michael Reilly noticed something else as he lifted Roosevelt to the waiting car. "He was absolutely dead weight," Reilly said. "So the job of lifting him, which was complicated by my complete surprise at his condition, was quite a task." He passed the word to the rest of the security detail that "the Boss is heavy."[47]

William D. Hassett, FDR's confidential secretary during 1942–1945, was also troubled by the president's appearance. He pulled Dr. Bruenn aside and told him his concerns the night they arrived at the Little White House. "He is slipping away from us and no earthly power can keep him here," Hassett said. Bruenn replied that his obligation was to save life, not admit defeat.[48]

On Easter Sunday, a service was held in the Warm Springs Foundation chapel. Ruth Stevens remembered that the chapel was filled that Sunday with patients, staff, and guests as the Secret Service wheeled President Roosevelt to the front pew. During the service, when it was time to kneel, Stevens remembered Roosevelt leaning forward in his wheelchair "as a gesture of kneeling." Everyone immediately bowed their heads, obviously moved by the president's symbolic gesture.

"He was wearing a gray suit which seemed to accentuate his pallor," Stevens said. Although he participated in the entire service, she said Roosevelt seemed "unusually nervous throughout the service and dropped a hymn book and his glasses at different times." The Secret Service agents retrieved them. "He stared straight ahead the entire time and did not smile or speak to anyone on entering or leaving the chapel, which was most unusual."[49] Stevens hoped he would be well enough to attend a barbecue she was hosting in his honor on 12 April.

After a few days at Warm Springs, Roosevelt did show some improvement, both in his health and in his general spirits, according to Dr. Bruenn. "The weather was ideal, and within a week there was a decided and obvious improvement in his appearance and sense of well-being. He had begun to eat with appetite, rested beautifully and was in excellent spirits. He began to go out every afternoon for short motor trips, which he clearly enjoyed."[50]

Around midnight on 11 April, James Griffith and Neil Shannon, two Secret Service agents standing guard beneath President Roosevelt's bedroom window, suddenly heard the president begin coughing violently. Griffith described the "prolonged hacking cough," as an "unusual spell." Shannon told his colleague to listen carefully to the president's cough. "That's a death rattle," Shannon warned Griffith.

Shortly after midnight, the agents went off duty. When they returned to the Little White House the following afternoon, they immediately knew something was wrong. "The marines had cordoned off the Little White House," Griffith said. Their boss, Supervising Agent James Beary, came out of the house. He placed his fingers to his lips, motioning for the agents to be quiet because the president was ill.[51]

Earlier that morning, Dr. Bruenn examined the president. Roosevelt had complained of a slight headache and some stiffness of the neck, and he believed it was due to a soreness of the muscles, which was relieved by slight massage. "He had a good morning and his guests commented upon the fact as to how well he looked," Dr. Bruenn said.[52]

In fact, Elizabeth Shoumatoff, who was painting the president's portrait, exclaimed upon seeing Roosevelt: "Mr. President, you look so much better than yesterday, I am glad I did not start working before today." Daisy Suckley, who also was present 12 April, recorded in her diary: "He looked so good looking; much as some of his earlier pictures show him— his features, at once strong and refined."[53]

Roosevelt, in a double-breasted gray suit and crimson tie, was sitting at a card table, signing paperwork given to him by William Hassett, his confidential aide. Positioned next to the stone fireplace with a Nantucket whaler model displayed on the mantle, FDR's feet were propped on a small wicker stool. Fala was sleeping on the floor. The artist was painting.

It was almost time for lunch. Daisy Suckley, who was crocheting on the sofa, noticed that Roosevelt's head was forward, as if he were looking for something. "Have you dropped your cigarette?" Suckley asked, looking directly into Roosevelt's face.

"I have a terrific pain in the back of my head," Roosevelt replied. His forehead furrowed in pain as he placed his left hand up to the back of his head. He tried to smile, and then slumped forward in the chair. Arthur Prettyman, Suckley, Laura Delano, and a Filipino aide carried the president into the bedroom. He was dead weight. He was changed into his pajamas.[54]

Dr. Bruenn, who was eating lunch, arrived within fifteen minutes. He said the president was pale, cold, sweating profusely, and unconscious. His breathing was labored. It was clear to Bruenn that the president had suffered a massive cerebral hemorrhage. He immediately called the White House to alert Admiral McIntire, and continued to monitor the president's condition.[55] Later, Roosevelt's pupils became dilated and there were occasional spasms of rigidity. His respiration slowed, and his face turned blue, which is often indicative of a cerebral vascular accident or stroke.

At 3:31 P.M. Roosevelt's breathing stopped; occasionally he gasped for breath. Bruenn could no longer detect a heartbeat, so he began artificial respiration and injected caffeine sodium benzoate. Adrenalin was injected directly into the heart.[56]

Secret Service Agent Michael Reilly was at the swimming pool when Roosevelt slumped in his seat. When he arrived at the Little White House a half hour later, Roosevelt was stretched out on his bed, clad in pajamas, and Bruenn was working on him.

"I knew he was down," Reilly recalled, "but I never for a single solitary second thought he'd die. I'd seen him in many tough spots before, and he'd yet to lose." But, this time was to be different. Despite the heroic efforts of Bruenn and heart specialist Dr. James E. Poullin, who rushed from Atlanta within ninety minutes of being summoned, the president would not recover.

Agent Reilly, Hassett, Grace Tully, and cousins Daisy Suckley and Laura Delano all sat quietly in the living room, praying, staring at the closed bedroom door where the president—their friend—was about to take his last breath. "The room was quiet," Agent Reilly remembered, "only Bruenn's voice, low and indistinct was heard coming in from the hallway."

Suddenly, the silence was broken, Reilly said, by a "terrifying howl." "It was little Fala. Forgotten for hours, the Informer had lain quietly in the corner. Now he was barking madly as we all stared at him," Reilly said. "Still screaming, the little black Scottie took off in full run, crashed head on into a screen door, and smashed it open. Out he went, running and barking hysterically until he reached the top of a near-by hill. He stiffened his legs and stood there howling, until he was exhausted."[57]

The time was 3:35 P.M., Thursday, 12 April 1945. All signs of life disappeared from the president.

Both Fala, and the American people, had lost a friend. Franklin D. Roosevelt was the only president that millions of Americans had ever known. The courage and determination of this wheelchair-bound man had inspired confidence in millions of his fellow citizens during the country's darkest hour. He lifted the spirits of a crippled nation from the depths of the Great Depression, and toward ultimate victory in the greatest war the world had ever seen. Although Roosevelt knew the end of the war was near, fate would deprive him of seeing the victory finally declared by the Allies.

The end of the road in this remarkable sixty-three-year journey had come. With his work complete, Franklin D. Roosevelt could now rest. He closed his eyes one last time on that spring day in Georgia's beautiful Pine Mountains, and was gone.

EPILOGUE

Amyas and Evelyn Ames were sitting on the edge of the big double bed feeling a little lost in the luxurious Lincoln Room, a bedroom much larger than they were accustomed to back in New York. They had arrived at the White House earlier on that balmy spring evening in April 1934, at the invitation of President Franklin D. Roosevelt.

Evelyn, pregnant with Ned, was not feeling well, particularly after the long trip to Washington. The president, however, wanted to assemble his crew from the New England cruise aboard *Amberjack II* the previous year, so Amyas and Evelyn had decided to make the journey. After all, it is not often that one receives an invitation for a private dinner with the president of the United States.

As Amyas was comforting his wife, a knock came at the door. In came Eleanor Roosevelt, carrying a tray of hot chocolate and crackers for the weary travelers. The first lady sat on the edge of the bed and talked with the young couple for quite some time before leaving to see to the arrangements for the president's *Amberjack II* reunion dinner.

Amyas Ames, who sailed with the president from Marion, Massachusetts, to Southwest Harbor, Maine, in 1933, remembered the evening as a "family occasion" with the president and members of his crew recalling the exciting cruise. Ames said the reunion was a "very happy time" with the same "mood and spirit" that they all had enjoyed aboard *Amberjack II* the previous June.

Ames described Roosevelt as a "natural sailor," who was "down to earth, with a likeable personality," adding that "he was a very self-contained man." Despite most of his traveling companions being half the president's age, Ames said there were "very little generational differences" between Roosevelt and his young crew. "If I had a choice of anybody to go on a cruise with, it would be the president," Ames said.

Ames served with the War Shipping Administration during World War II. Following a career as an investment banker, he became chairman of the New York Philharmonic and of Lincoln Center. He said the atmosphere on the four-hundred-mile 1933 cruise was one of "relaxed intimacy" in which Roosevelt always was addressed as "skipper" by the entire crew. "The president was never 'president' on the cruise," Ames recalled.[1]

Days on the sea were most cherished by Franklin Roosevelt. He loved the freedom of being in a boat or ship on the water. Roosevelt spent more time aboard large and small sailing vessels than any U.S. president before or since. He remains our nation's greatest seagoing president. He spent time afloat every year of his presidency except 1942, when security concerns kept him on dry land.

Roosevelt sought out the sea frequently during his presidency as a source of relaxation, as well as a means to clear away "personal cobwebs" accumulated primarily in Washington.[2] "The best escape of all was the sea," noted historian Arthur M. Schlesinger Jr., explaining that being at sea allowed the president to "cast off weariness and irritability under the healing beneficence of sun and spray and salt." Schlesinger said that when Roosevelt was sailing aboard one of the small schooners, he would wear his "oldest sweater and dirtiest flannels and he never shaved."[3]

Roosevelt felt completely at home on the water—whether he was skipper of a tiny yawl or twin-masted schooner, or distinguished guest aboard a forty-five-thousand-ton warship. The water is where he most loved to be. And, in the days before modern navigational devices, Roosevelt skillfully used dead reckoning as his means to navigate through pea-soup thick fogs and ship-swallowing seas. He calculated where he had been, where he currently was, and where he was going, using nothing more than a compass, chart, and his keen know-how gained from years of sailing the foggy New England coastline as well as the Bay of Fundy, which is known for its monumental tides.

An accomplished blue-water sailor, Roosevelt was adept at dealing with the unexpected and adapting quickly to the vagaries of the weather.

On the sea—and throughout his life—he was a master of improvisation, rapidly issuing orders to his crew to alter course and adjust sails as conditions warranted. Franklin Roosevelt was in command, both on the sea and in the White House.

Roosevelt carried his sailor instincts into the White House. The halls of Congress were fraught with hidden dangers and pitfalls, just as were the waters along New England's treacherous coastline. He always was willing to alter his plans or make compromises in order to reach his goal, whether that goal was to reach landfall or to get a piece of important legislation through Congress. Franklin Roosevelt was a consummate sailor-politician.

"Roosevelt reacted, shifted, rethought and recalculated," just as he did when sailing over shoal-ridden seas, noted historian Warren F. Kimball in his book *The Juggler.* "Consistency may be the hobgoblin of small minds," Kimble said, "but it is a hobgoblin rarely associated with Franklin Roosevelt."[4]

He was, however, consistent in his approach to the Axis powers, which he viewed as a threat to the very survival of the United States. Historian Robert Dallek points out: "From day one of his presidency, he determined to have the United States play a part in defending democracy against the competing totalitarian system in Germany, Italy and Japan." To reach these goals, Dallek said that "the president believed it essential to accommodate himself to changing opinion at home and altering circumstances abroad. He saw temporary compromises as inevitable in the pursuit of larger design," much in the same way the expert sailor adapts to changing winds and tides, never losing sight of the ultimate goal of reaching his port. "Living by the assumption that Americans would come to share his concerns about emerging world problems, he bided his time until national sentiment came into closer harmony with what he felt needed to be done," Dallek wrote, explaining Roosevelt's approaches to economic reform, isolationism, and pacifism.[5]

Frances Perkins served as Roosevelt's secretary of labor during his entire presidency. Also a close friend from his days in Albany, he marveled at FDR's vibrant optimism and ability to tackle even the most difficult tasks with determination and confidence. "There's always a way to get through it," Roosevelt would remark when he was advised that a favorite project was being blocked by lawyers, budget constraints, or a rebellious Congress. "It became his policy," Perkins said, "that what has to be done can be done somehow."[6] Whether success involved a compromise, a quid pro quo, or some firm presidential arm twisting, Roosevelt would tackle the challenge with the same gusto and vigor he exhibited in navigating a sloop through rough waters, rife with obstacles and hidden dangers.

He was a man of infinite patience and one who was able to keep life in perspective even when things around him were in turmoil. Asked how he kept from worrying about problems, Roosevelt replied, "If you had spent two years in bed trying to wiggle your big toe, after that anything else would seem easy."[7]

"He was a great believer in alternatives. He rarely got himself sewed tight to a program from which there was no turning back," Perkins noted. This is much the same way a good sailor uses keen skills to prevent getting trapped by wind and weather. "He worked with his instincts. He relied upon his intuitive judgment," Perkins observed.[8]

"This dislike of firm commitments, this belief in alternatives, further reduced the significance of any single decision," Schlesinger wrote. "The very ambiguity of his scheme of organization—the overlapping jurisdictions and duplicated responsibilities—made flexibility easy," Schlesinger said. "If things started to go bad, he could reshuffle people and functions with speed which would have been impossible in a government of clear-cut assignments and rigid chain-of-command. Under the competitive theory, he always retained room for administrative maneuver." Schlesinger notes that "only a man of limitless energy and resource could hold such a system together."[9] Roosevelt was able to successfully accomplish this feat throughout his twelve years in the White House. His frequent sea cruises gave him opportunities to relax, recharge, and think through problems.

Perkins said Roosevelt believed that "nothing in human judgment is final. One may courageously take the step that seems right today because it can be modified tomorrow if it does not work well." Perkins also noted:

> Roosevelt's plans were never thoroughly thought out. They were burgeoning plans; they were next steps; they were something to do next week or next year. One plan grew out of another. Gradually they fitted together and supplemented each another. . . . Whatever happened, he loved the great game of politics, and he played it like a master.[10]

Adm. Emory S. Land, appointed in 1938 by Roosevelt to oversee the world's greatest shipbuilding program, described the commander in chief as a "great trial and error guy." After trying one approach to a problem and failing, he was ready to take a different tack, always maintaining flexibility and adaptability as conditions warranted.[11] Admiral Land credits Roosevelt's deep understanding of the sea with U.S. success in World War II. "Franklin Delano Roosevelt knew more about ships and the men who sailed them . . . than any other man who ever held high office. His understanding and knowledge of ships made possible a building and operations program without which this war would have been lost."[12]

Roosevelt had an extraordinarily keen ability to deal effectively with the unexpected, whether it was at sea, in Washington, or during his sparring with the White House Press Corps. He seemed to relish the give-and-take with reporters covering his presidency. President Roosevelt conducted nearly one thousand press conferences during his twelve years in the White House. They were usually held twice a week when he was in residence—truly a remarkable and unprecedented number of opportunities for the press to have access to the nation's president. Gone were the days of Herbert Hoover, when reporters were required to submit their questions in writing, in advance of the press conference.

Roosevelt also conducted his press conferences while traveling; whether aboard his special railroad car or a U.S. warship, the president made time for the press. "Traveling with Mr. Roosevelt was an experience in leisurely luxury," wrote United Press White House Correspondent Merriman Smith. "He was rarely in a hurry to get anywhere and made his trips—except during campaign years—by easy stages."[13]

Of all the modes of travel available to the president, Roosevelt loved most to be on the water. When he couldn't be afloat, he would relive those times through his extensive collection of nautical memorabilia. Ship models and an impressive collection of maritime prints and paintings were located in every room in the White House.

Franklin Roosevelt was the U.S. Navy's salvation. Beginning in 1933, the newly elected president used a bit of "backdoor financing" to construct twenty-nine new ships and four submarines, the first new navy vessels authorized in more than four years. He loved the navy. Frances Perkins said that President Wilson had offered FDR two other posts back in 1913; both were more important and more financially rewarding than the assistant naval secretary position. Roosevelt declined the offers and said he wanted the navy job, Perkins recalled. He told President Wilson: "I'd rather have that place, than any other in public life."[14]

Adm. William D. Leahy first met Roosevelt when Leahy commanded USS *Dolphin,* used by Roosevelt for frequent cruises while he was assistant secretary of the navy. They became friends. In 1937, President Roosevelt appointed Leahy chief of naval operations; in 1942 he became chief of staff to the president and Roosevelt's personal military adviser.

FDR "knew the history, details of the composition and of the operations of the United States Navy since its original establishment," Leahy would later write about his old boss. "Roosevelt also was a highly-competent small-boat sailor and coast pilot. He had a deep affection for everything that had to do with sailing craft."[15]

Years later, President John F. Kennedy, who also loved the sea, speculated about the source of such love of the sea. During an address in September 1962 at the America's Cup Races in Rhode Island, President Kennedy commented: "It is an interesting biological fact that all of us have in our veins the exact same percentage of salt in our blood that exists in the ocean and, therefore, we have salt in our blood, in our sweat, in our tears. We are tied to the ocean. And when we go back to the sea—whether it is to sail or watch it—we are going back from whence we came."[16]

And the sea is where Franklin Roosevelt felt most at home. In fact, a year before his death, he confided to Grace Tully, his trusted secretary, "If anything should happen to me while I am at sea, I want to be buried at sea. You know, it has always seemed like home to me."[17] His sailing ability was second to none. He garnered rave reviews from both professional navy men and old salts alike. On his 1933 New England cruise, the newly elected president was in full command of his twin-masted schooner. "Logging a good nine knots, the old man's carting canvas," one old timer remarked as he watched *Amberjack II,* with FDR at the helm, speed by Martha's Vineyard off the coast of Massachusetts. Then, the skies turned dark and a fierce squall with drenching rains hit, forcing Roosevelt to reverse course and steer his vessel into the safety of Edgartown.

Onlookers, standing in the pouring rain, were amazed to see the president on deck, clad in dripping oilskins, checking the schooner's gear and rigging, just as a fishing skipper would do after a day on the sea. Roosevelt made sure everything was shipshape on deck, sails properly stopped, and sheets and halyards coiled down before he went below out of the pelting rain. "He was the calmest man in sight," one islander said, watching the president and his crew.[18]

Over the course of the next dozen years, Franklin Roosevelt, who became larger than life for millions of Americans, would see the nation through its most tumultuous days—both at home and abroad. He would continue to keep a firm hand on the tiller, calming the fears of the American people and inspiring people throughout the world to fight against the forces threatening freedom and democracy.

Herb Coffin, who met Roosevelt when the president sailed into Nantucket Harbor to escape a heavy squall back in 1933, summed up his assessment of Roosevelt in a journal written after he rowed out to greet the new president. In a classic New England tradition of brevity and clarity, Coffin wrote of Roosevelt: "He seems a fine man."[19]

And history would judge him so.

Named Vessels
Franklin D. Roosevelt
Was Aboard

Every effort has been made to chronologically identify all named vessels that Franklin D. Roosevelt was aboard. Due to his avid interest in boats and ships of all sizes, however, this listing must be viewed as partial. Also, FDR sailed aboard many unnamed, smaller vessels.

NAME OF VESSEL	TYPE	YEAR(S)
RMS *Germanic*	White Star transatlantic liner	1885, 1890, 1892
Icicle	49-foot ice yacht	1888–on
RMS *Adriatic*	White Star transatlantic liner	1889
Yampa	yacht	1890
Merry Chanter	scow	1890
RMS *Teutonic*	White Star transatlantic liner	1891, 1895, 1901
Half Moon	51-foot sailing yacht	1891–1898
RMS *Majestic*	White Star transatlantic liner	1892
Augusta Victoria	Hamburg-American transatlantic liner	1893
Fürst Bismarck	Hamburg-American transatlantic liner	1896
Intrepid	yacht	1897
New Moon	21-foot knockabout	1898–on
Pelican	sailboat	1898
Sailing Canoe	canoe	1900s–1921
Vermont	paddlewheel steamer	childhood
Reindeer	paddlewheel steamer	childhood

NAME OF VESSEL	TYPE	YEAR(S)
Chateaugay	paddlewheel steamer	childhood
Half Moon II	60-foot auxiliary schooner	1900–1917
Deutschland	Hamburg-American transatlantic liner	1901
Prinzessin Victoria Luisa	Cruising yacht	1901, 1904
Hohenzollern	German emperor's yacht	1901
Barracoutta	sailboat	1903
RMS *Celtic*	White Star transatlantic liner	1903
Kaiser Wilhelm II	Norddeutscher-Lloyd transatlantic liner	1903
Hawk	28-foot ice yacht	1904–on
Birch Bark Canoe	canoe	1905–on
Kronprinz Wilhelm	Norddeutscher-Lloyd transatlantic liner	1905
RMS *Oceanic*	White Star transatlantic liner	1905
RMS *Mauretania*	Cunard transatlantic liner	1906–1913
SS *Bruce*	Newfoundland ferryboat	1908
Manhattan	U.S. Coast Guard cutter	1910
Androscoggin	U.S. Coast Guard cutter	1910
SS *Carrillo*	British steamship	1912
SS *Abangarez*	British steamship	1912
USS *Sylph* (PY-5)	123-foot navy yacht	1913–1920
USS *Dolphin* (later PG-24)	240-foot dispatch boat	1913–1920
USS *Mayflower* (PY-1)	presidential yacht	1913–1920
USS *North Dakota* (BB-29)	battleship	1913
USS *McDougal* (DD-54)	destroyer	1914
K-7 (SS-38)	submarine	1915
USS *John Paul* (DD-10)	destroyer	1915
USS *Flusser* (DD-20)	destroyer	1916
USS *Cherokee* (PY-1104)	patrol boat	1917, 1918
USS *Wainwright* (DD-62)	destroyer	1917
USS *Vermont* (BB-20)	battleship	1917
USS *Hancock* (AP-3)	troop transport ship	1917
USS *Macdonough* (DD-9)	destroyer	1917
USS *Pennsylvania* (BB-38)	battleship	1917
USS *Neptune* (AG-8)	collier	1917
USS *Texas* (BB-35)	battleship	1918
HMS *Obedient*	British destroyer	1918

USS *Dyer* (DD-84)	destroyer	1918
NAME OF VESSEL	TYPE	YEAR(S)
USS *Kimberly* (DD-80)	destroyer	1918
HMS *Velox*	British destroyer	1918
USS *Leviathan*	U.S. troopship; former Hamburg-American transatlantic liner	1918
USS *George Washington*	U.S. troopship; former Hamburg-Norddeutscher-Lloyd liner	1919
USS *Aztec* (SP-590)	steam yacht	1919
USS *Yarnall* (DD-143)	destroyer	1919
USS *Palmer* (DD-161)	destroyer	1918
USS *New York* (BB-34)	battleship	1920
Vireo	24-foot knockabout	1920–1921
USS *Hatfield* (DD-231)	destroyer	1920, 1921
Sabalo	140-foot power yacht	1921
Weona II	60-foot houseboat	1923
Squaw	40-foot sailboat	1923 or 1924
Larooca	70-foot houseboat	1924–1926
Inspector I	New York State yacht	1928–1932
Inspector II	New York State yacht	1930–1932
USS *Fairfax* (DD-93)	destroyer	1930
RMS *Aquitania*	Cunard transatlantic liner	1931
SS *Bremen*	Norddeutscher-Lloyd transatlantic liner	1931
Myth II	37-foot yawl	1932
Orca	Vincent Astor fishing sloop	1933
Malolo	fishing tug	1933
Amberjack II	45-foot schooner	1933
USS *Ellis* (DD-154)	destroyer	1933
Nourmahal	263-foot diesel yacht	1933–1935
USS *Indianapolis* (CA-35)	heavy cruiser	1933, 1936
USS *Sequoia* (AG-23)	presidential yacht	1933–1936
Itasca (CGC-50)	U.S. Coast Guard cutter	1934
USS *New Orleans* (CA-32)	heavy cruiser	1934
USS *Houston* (CA-30)	heavy cruiser	1934, 1935, 1938, 1939
USS *Portland* (CA-33)	heavy cruiser	1935
USS *Farragut III* (DD-348)	destroyer	1935
Sewanna	56-foot schooner	1936
Judge the II	fishing boat	1936

NAME OF VESSEL	TYPE	YEAR(S)
USS *Potomac* (AG-25)	presidential yacht	1936–1945
USS *Clark* (DD-361)	destroyer	1936
USS *Monaghan* (DD-354)	destroyer	1936
USS *Phelps* (DD-360)	destroyer	1937
USS *Selfridge* (DD-357)	destroyer	1937
USS *Philadelphia* (CL-41)	light cruiser	1938
USS *Tuscaloosa* (CA-37)	heavy cruiser	1939, 1940, 1941
USS *Moffett* (DD-362)	destroyer	1941
USS *Augusta* (CL-31)	light cruiser	1941
HMS *Prince of Wales*	British battleship	1941
USS *Mayrant* (DD-402)	destroyer	1941
USS *McDougal II* (DD-358)	destroyer	1941
La Gazelle	French destroyer	1943
USS *Black Hawk* (AD-9)	support tender	1943
HMS *Aimwell*	British navy tug	1943
USS *Memphis* (CL-13)	light cruiser	1943
USS *Humboldt* (AVP-21)	seaplane tender	1943
USS *Iowa* (BB-61)	battleship	1943
USS *Wilmette* (IX-29)	gunboat	1943
USS *Cummings* (DD-365)	destroyer	1944
USS *Baltimore* (CA-68)	heavy cruiser	1944
USS *Murphy* (DD-603)	destroyer	1945
USS *Catoctin* (AGC-5)	amphibious ship	1945
USS *Quincy* (CA-71)	heavy cruiser	1945

Note: In many cases, Roosevelt was aboard a vessel more than a single time, often several times in the same year. In other cases, the exact date is unknown; therefore, a range of dates is listed.

GLOSSARY OF NAUTICAL TERMS

The following definitions were compiled using a number of sources, including *The Oxford Companion to Ships and the Sea*, edited by Peter Kemp; *Nautical Dictionary* by Joseph P. O'Flynn; *An A–Z of Sailing Terms* by Ian Dear and Peter Kemp; and the U.S. Navy's *Bluejackets' Manual, 1944.*

aft	located near the rear of the vessel
astern	behind the vessel
batten	wooden slat used to stiffen a mainsail
beam	the greatest width of a vessel
berth	place where vessel moors or rests at anchor, usually in a harbor
bilge	lowest point of the interior of a vessel where the sides meet the vessel's flat bottom
bluejacket	a seaman in the U.S. Navy
boatswain (bos'n)	a ship's officer; in charge of workers on deck, and calls the crew to duty
boatswain's chair	a swing-type chair, suspended from a rope, used to lift a crew member aloft to work on masts
boom	horizontal spar along lower edge of sail
bow	front end of a boat
brow	temporary gangway between vessels or between a vessel and the wharf
bulkhead	wall
catboat	small boat with single sail

centerboard	a device, often a thin board, that can be lowered through the keel to counteract a sailboat's tendency to move sideways
coaming	raised ledge around hatch to prevent water from entering vessel
companion way	ladder-like passageway into a boat's cabin
crossing the line	crossing the equator, at which time there usually is a ceremony during which the pollywog (landlubber) becomes a shellback
dinghy	a small rowboat often carried aboard larger vessels
dory	small, flat-bottomed rowboat used for line fishing
draft	depth of water required for a vessel to float
ebb tide	outgoing tide
fantail	the after section of the main deck on destroyers and cruisers
fathom	a unit of depth measure equal to six feet
flood tide	incoming tide
foghorn	a horn aboard vessels or shore facilities that is used to warn others during foggy conditions
fore	located in the front of the vessel
forecastle (fo'c's'le)	the forward deck forward of the foremast
foredeck	forward part of the main deck
foremast	a vessel's forward mast
gaff	the spar to which the head of a fore-and-aft sail is secured
halyard	a line used for raising a flag or sail
hard alee	an order to put the helm of a vessel away from the wind
hatchway	an opening in the deck providing access to space below
headstay	the foremost stay
heave to	to bring a ship's head into the wind or sea and hold it there by use of engines or rudder
helm	the tiller or steering mechanism of the vessel
hook	slang for anchor
hull	the body of a vessel
jib	a triangular sail on the headstay
keel	the backbone of a vessel, running from stem to stern at the bottom
ketch	a twin-masted sailboat with a shorter aftermast
knot	a nautical measure of speed; one knot equals one nautical mile per hour
leeward	away from the direction of the wind
log	a book containing the official record of a vessel's activities
luff	the leading edge of a sail
mainmast	a sailing vessel's principal mast
mainsail	the principal sail on a vessel
mainsheet	the line, usually a rope, used to control the mainsail
mast	vertical spars that support sails, booms, and gaffs

nautical mile	6,080 feet
oilskins	garments made waterproof by coats of linseed oil
port	the left side of a vessel facing forward
schooner	a vessel rigged with two or sometimes more masts; foremast is shorter than main mast
scow	barge-like vessel with flat bottom
screw	propeller
signal flags	early communication between ships using flags of different colors and designs
skiff	a small boat propelled by sails, oars, or a motor
sloop	boat with a single mast, mainsail, and jib
spar	a pole
spinnaker	three-cornered sail normally set forward of a yacht's mast
starboard	the right side of a vessel facing forward
stay	rigging used to support mast
staysail	triangular fore and aft sail
stern	rear end of a boat
swell	a long, large wave
tack	a sailing maneuver that changes the direction of the vessel
tender	a vessel that supplies and repairs ships and aircraft
tiller	helm or steering mechanism of a small sailboat
transom	flat area across the stern of a vessel
U-boat	German submarine (*unterseeboot*)
windward	direction from which the wind is blowing
yardarm	a spar crossing the mast horizontally
yawl	small, twin-masted sailing boat, used largely for pleasure

NOTES

Chapter 1. *He Always Had His Eyes on the Sails*

1. Ms. Linnea Calder, personal correspondence with the author, 1 April 1993.
2. James Roosevelt and Paul Rust Jr., "President Goes Cruising," *Yachting*, August 1938.
3. "The President's Visit," *Inquirer and Mirror*, 24 June 1933.
4. Charles W. Hurd, "Roosevelt Greeted Royally by Canada at Campobello Isle," *New York Times*, 30 June 1933.
5. Mr. A. J. Drexel Paul, telephone interviews by the author, 1 and 22 November 1992; "Hero's Daughter, 1, at Ship Launching," *New York Times*, 29 November 1943; *Dictionary of American Naval Fighting Ships*, 8 vols. (Washington, D.C.: U.S. Navy, 1959–1981), 3:576.
6. Edmund W. Starling and Thomas Sugrue, *Starling of the White House* (New York: Simon and Schuster, 1946), 308–11.
7. Franklin D. Roosevelt, letter to George Briggs, 30 December 1932, President's Personal File, Manuscript Collection, Franklin D. Roosevelt Library, Hyde Park, N.Y. (hereafter cited as FDRL).
8. Mr. Paul D. Rust III, telephone interviews by the author, 3 and 31 July 1993.
9. Ibid.; Ms. Eleanor P. Fischer, personal correspondence with the author, 13 April 1992; "Amberjack Tossed a Week in Storm," *New York Times*, 20 August 1931. Paul D. Rust II commissioned the construction of *Amberjack II* in 1931, after the wreck of his first schooner, *Amberjack I*, near Gloucester, Massachusetts. Rust sold *Amberjack II* in 1934 to a Long Island man, who resold it the same year to another New Yorker. In 1939, it was sold to an individual in

Philadelphia, who kept the schooner for seven years before selling it to a Providence, Rhode Island, man in 1946. It was purchased in 1951 by Lawson R. Corbitt, who operated a photography studio in Bridgeport, Connecticut. Corbitt was commodore of the Milford (Connecticut) Yacht Club, where *Amberjack II* was homeported, and the schooner served as the club's flagship. In 1960, it was sold to a man in Florida, who re-sold it to a Texan nine years later. After a year, the yacht was sold to a pair of Texans. On 9 June 1972, while being hauled on a marine railway in Seabrook, Texas, it suffered severe damage to the hull. The following year, it was broken up and sold for scrap. Although yacht names frequently change with a change of ownership, the *Amberjack II*, remarkably, retained its name through nine successive owners over a period of forty-two years.

10. Franklin D. Roosevelt, letter to George Briggs, 11 May 1933, President's Personal File, FDRL.
11. Dr. William McDonald, letter to Franklin Roosevelt, 8 June 1933, President's Personal File, FDRL.
12. Edmund Tripp, personal correspondence to the author, 14 March 1993.
13. Charles Hurd, *When the New Deal Was Young and Gay* (New York: Hawthorn Books, 1965), 155.
14. Ms. Helen Baxter, telephone interview by the author, 3 July 1993.
15. "The President's Visit," *Inquirer and Mirror*, 24 June 1933.
16. Ibid.
17. Hurd, *New Deal*, 153.
18. Mr. Charles Sayle, personal and telephone interviews by the author, 12 September 1992 and 31 January 1993.
19. Alden Hatch, *Franklin D. Roosevelt: An Informal Biography* (New York: Henry Holt and Company, 1947), 211–12.
20. Francis M. Stephenson, "Pres. Roosevelt at Gloucester after Daring Run at Night," *Salem Evening News*, 21 June 1933.
21. "Roosevelt at Little Harbor, N.H.; Visited by House and Douglas," *New York Times*, 22 June 1933.
22. Mr. Amyas Ames, telephone interviews by the author, 28 February and 28 March 1993.
23. Lt. H. C. Pound memorandum, 28 June 1933, President's Official File, FDRL.
24. James Roosevelt, "Admiral Grayson's Ham Served Amberjack Crew," *Boston Daily Globe*, 24 June 1933.

Chapter 2. Flames Licking out of the Bilge

1. Roosevelt and Rust, "President Goes Cruising."
2. James Roosevelt, "Destroyer Less Gullible Now, Says James," *Boston Globe*, 23 June 1933.
3. *Blue Jackets' Manual*, 1922, 348.

4. James Roosevelt and Sidney Shalett, *Affectionately, FDR* (New York: Harcourt, Brace and Company, 1959), 155–56.
5. Ames, interviews, 28 February and 28 March 1993.
6. "Defective Motor Delays President," *New York Times*, 25 June 1933.
7. F. B. Sibley, "Roosevelt Yacht Sails from North Haven, ME," *Boston Globe*, 23 June 1933.
8. Hazel McCrum, "Pulpit Rock," summer 1933, 24, Oral History of Hazel McCrum on Pulpit Rock, Accession Number 257, Northeast Archives of Folklore and Oral History, University of Maine, Orono, Maine.
9. Seward Beacom, *Pulpit Harbor—200 Years: A History of Pulpit Harbor, North Haven, Maine, 1784–1984* (North Haven, Maine: North Haven Historical Society, 1985), appendix 8.
10. Ms. Eleanor S. Beverage, personal correspondence with the author, 20 March 1993.
11. Ames, interviews, 28 February and 28 March 1993.
12. Hurd, *New Deal*, 158.
13. Robert McKenna, "Bubbly Baptisms: The Fine Art of Christening," *Nautical Collector*, April 1994, 8–11.
14. Ames, interviews, 28 February and 28 March 1993.
15. Hurd, *New Deal*, 160.
16. James Roosevelt, "James Finds Crew Happy Despite Long Wait in Fog," *Boston Daily Globe*, 29 June 1933.
17. Franklin D. Roosevelt, letter to George O. Beal, 26 June 1933, President's Official File, FDRL; Franklin D. Roosevelt, letter to F. W. Harford, 10 August 1933, President's Official File, FDRL.
18. Sara Roosevelt, *My Boy Franklin* (New York: Ray Long and Richard R. Smith, 1933), 47.
19. Paul, interviews, 1 and 22 November 1992.

Chapter 3. He Must Have His Relatives with Him

1. "Roosevelt Sails to Pulpit Harbor," *New York Times*, 24 June 1933.
2. Eleanor Seagraves, *Delano's Voyage of Commerce and Discovery* (Stockbridge, Mass.: Berkshire House Publishing, 1994), xvii–xxiv; Ms. Eleanor Roosevelt Seagraves, telephone interview by the author, 20 November 1994; Daniel W. Delano Jr., *Franklin Roosevelt and the Delano Influence* (Pittsburgh, Pa.: James S. Nudi Publications, 1946), 69.
3. Allen Churchill, *The Roosevelts* (London: Frederick Muller Limited, 1966), 149–52; Karl Schriftgiesser, *The Amazing Roosevelt Family, 1613–1942* (New York: Wilfred Funk, 1942), 196–98.
4. Kenneth S. Davis, *A Beckoning of Destiny* (New York: G. P. Putnam's Sons, 1972), 23.
5. Sara Roosevelt, *My Boy Franklin*, 7.
6. Sara Delano Roosevelt Diaries, FDRL, 47.

7. Ibid., 49.

8. Gordon Newell, *Ocean Liners of the 20th Century* (Seattle: Superior Publishing Company, 1963), 20.

9. Ibid., 25.

10. Ibid., 27.

11. Elliott Roosevelt, *FDR: His Personal Letters, Early Years* (New York: Duell, Sloan and Pearce, 1947), 6.

12. Don Wharton, *Roosevelt Omnibus* (New York: Alfred A. Knopf, 1934), 39.

13. Geoffrey Ward, *Before the Trumpet: Young Franklin Roosevelt, 1882–1905* (New York: Harper and Row, 1985), 159.

14. Clifford W. Ashley, *Whaleships of New Bedford* (Boston: Houghton Mifflin Company, 1929), v–vi.

15. James Roosevelt, *My Parents: A Differing View* (Chicago: Playboy Press, 1976), 51–54.

16. Ibid., 51–54.

17. Blanche Wiesen Cook, *Eleanor Roosevelt*, Vol. 1, *1884–1933* (New York: Viking, 1992), 182.

18. Sara Delano Roosevelt Diaries, FDRL, 7.

19. Sara Roosevelt, *My Boy Franklin*, 49–50.

20. Ibid., 53–54.

21. Hall Roosevelt with Samuel Duff McCoy, *Odyssey of an American Family* (New York: Harper and Brothers, 1939), 317–27.

22. Raymond A. Ruge, "Iceboating on the Hudson River," *NAHO*, New York State Museum and Science Service (fall 1974): 3–5.

23. Raymond A. Ruge, "The History and Development of the Ice Boat. Part I, 1600–1930." *Wooden Boat* (January–February 1981): 64–70.

24. Mr. Curtis Roosevelt, telephone interview by the author, 15 October 1994. Today, FDR's *Hawk* resides at the FDRL. *Icicle,* which had been installed in the FDRL basement in 1940 under FDR's personal supervision, currently is on long-term loan to the Hudson River Maritime Museum in Kingston, New York.

25. Mr. J. Winthrop Aldrich, personal interview by the author, 16 July 1993. The U.S. Coast Guard, in letters to Albany officials over the period of 1932 to 1935, repeatedly declined to send vessels to maintain an ice-free channel, stating that no such vessels, adapted for ice breaking, were available for assignment on the Hudson River. In the fall 1932, when the owner of an ice-breaking tug boat offered to charter his vessel to the U.S. Coast Guard to keep the Hudson ice-free, his offer was politely declined for lack of funds. Letters are located in the U.S. Coast Guard files for the New York Division, Washington, D.C.

26. Mr. Curtis Roosevelt, interview, 15 October 1994.

27. Elliott Roosevelt, *FDR: His Personal Letters, 1905–1928,* 199.

28. James MacGregor Burns, *The Lion and the Fox* (New York: Harcourt, Brace and Company, 1956), 50.

29. E. David Cronon, *The Cabinet Diaries of Josephus Daniels 1913–1921* (Lincoln: University of Nebraska Press, 1995), 4.

30. Frank Freidel, *Franklin D. Roosevelt: The Apprenticeship* (Boston: Little, Brown and Company, 1952), 249; "Assistant Secretary of Navy Who Went Down for Half an Hour in Submarine," *Washington Times,* 29 March 1915.

31. Livingston Davis, Log of Trip to Haiti and Santo Domingo, 1917, Log of Assistant Navy Secretary Cruise, Assistant Secretary of the Navy Papers, FDRL, 1.

32. Ibid., 2.

33. Franklin D. Roosevelt, "Trip to Haiti and Santo Domingo," undated memorandum, Assistant Secretary of the Navy Papers, FDRL, 5.

34. Ibid., 8.

35. Ibid., 17.

36. Elliott Roosevelt, *FDR: His Personal Letters, 1905–1928,* 377.

37. Ibid., 378.

38. Ibid., 382–83.

39. Ibid., 440; Davis, *Beckoning of Destiny,* 529.

40. Paul S. Boyer, ed., *Oxford Companion to United States History* (New York: Oxford University Press, 2001), 189; William N. Still, "Everybody Sick with the Flu," *Naval History* (April 2002): 36–40.

41. Elliott Roosevelt, *FDR: His Personal Letters, 1905–1928,* 439–40.

42. Ibid., 445.

43. Freidel, *Roosevelt: Apprenticeship,* 165.

44. Mr. Curtis Roosevelt, interview, 15 October 1994.

45. Otis Graham and Meghan Robinson Warder, *FDR: His Life and Times* (New York: DaCapo Press, 1985), 10.

46. Davis, *Beckoning of Destiny,* 627.

47. Ibid.; "Summer Home, Summer Boat," *Maine Boats and Harbors* (June–July 1993): 15, 32–33. FDR purchased *Vireo* for $700 in 1920. The destroyer USS *Hatfield* delivered the boat to Campobello in July. Roosevelt wanted a safe boat for his children: "I am particularly anxious that she be made as unsinkable as possible because the waters around Campobello and Eastport, Maine, are so cold that it is impossible to keep afloat for more than a minute or two." Today, *Vireo* is owned and displayed at the Mystic Seaport Museum in Mystic, Connecticut.

48. Hugh Gregory Gallagher, *FDR's Splendid Deception* (New York: Dodd, Mead and Company, 1985), 18.

49. Eleanor Roosevelt, *The Autobiography of Eleanor Roosevelt* (New York: Harper and Brothers, 1958), 116–17.

Chapter 4. The Water Has to Bring Me Back

1. Eleanor Roosevelt, *Autobiography,* 142.

2. Arthur M. Schlesinger Jr., *Crisis of the Old Order* (Boston: Houghton Mifflin Company, 1957), 406.

3. Frances Perkins, *The Roosevelt I Knew* (New York: Viking Press, 1946), 45.
4. Ibid., 29.
5. Brooke Astor, *Footprints* (Garden City, N.Y.: Doubleday and Company, 1980), 265.
6. Roosevelt and Shalett, *Affectionately, FDR,* 162.
7. Tripp, correspondence, 14 March 1993.
8. Elliott Roosevelt, *FDR: His Personal Letters, 1905–1928,* 588, 591.
9. Alfred B. Rollins, *Roosevelt and Howe* (New York: Alfred A. Knopf, 1962), 189.
10. James Roosevelt, *My Parents,* 163.
11. Franklin D. Roosevelt, "Log of *Weona II,*" 1923, Papers Pertaining to Family, Business and Personal Affairs, FDRL.
12. Franklin D. Roosevelt, letter to Miami Grocery Company, 19 February 1925, Papers Pertaining to Family, Business and Personal Affairs, FDRL.
13. Elliott Roosevelt, *FDR: His Personal Letters, 1905–1928,* 609.
14. *The Story of Franklin D. Roosevelt, Warm Springs and the Little White House.* (Atlanta: Georgia Department of Natural Resources, n.d.), 2.
15. Eleanor Roosevelt, *Autobiography,* 154.
16. Elliott Roosevelt, *FDR: His Personal Letters, 1928–1945,* 1:42–43.
17. Kenneth S. Davis, *FDR: The New York Years* (New York: Random House, 1985), 125.
18. Ms. Ann Easter, telephone interview by the author, 23 October 1994.
19. Samuel I. Rosenman, *Public Papers and Addresses of Franklin D. Roosevelt, 1943* (New York: Harper and Brothers, 1950), 89.
20. Mr. James H. Griffith, telephone interview by the author, 28 January 1995.
21. Mr. Robert Hopkins, telephone interview by the author, 4 February 1995.
22. Davis, *FDR: New York Years,* 30.
23. Gallagher, *FDR's Splendid Deception,* 73.
24. Frank Freidel, *Franklin D. Roosevelt: The Triumph* (Boston: Little, Brown and Company, 1956), 210.

Chapter 5. Get out of My Wind

1. "Roosevelt Plans Cruise; Wins More Republicans; Smith Drafts Statement," *New York Times,* 6 July 1932.
2. Ibid.
3. Mrs. Sarah Powell Huntington, telephone interview by the author, 3 and 17 July 1993. *Myth II* was built in 1928. Mrs. Huntington said she and her husband sold the yawl around 1936–1937. In 1939, the *Myth II's* owner of record was A. B. Taylor, and it was homeported in New York.
4. Roosevelt and Shalett, *Affectionately, FDR,* 229.
5. Huntington, interview, 3 July and 17 July 1993.
6. "Roosevelt Starts New England Cruise," *New York Times,* 12 July 1932.
7. George Briggs, "Log of *Myth II,*" 11–16 July 1932, Cruise Log, Papers Pertaining to Family, Business and Personal Affairs, FDRL.
8. "Roosevelt Starts New England Cruise."

9. Briggs, "Log of *Myth II*."

10. "Roosevelt Cruise on Political Track," *New York Times*, 13 July 1932.

11. Briggs, "Log of *Myth II*."

12. Michael Beschloss, *Kennedy and Roosevelt* (New York: W. W. Norton and Company, 1980), 73–75.

13. Davis, *FDR: New York Years*, 100–101.

14. Briggs, "Log of *Myth II*."

15. "Move by Roosevelt to Support Lehman for Governor Likely," *New York Times*, 15 July 1932.

16. Mr. Curtis Roosevelt, interview, 15 October 1994.

17. Gaddis Smith, "Sailor in the White House: A Key to Understanding FDR," lecture at FDRL, Hyde Park, N.Y., 12 August 1993.

18. Briggs, "Log of *Myth II*."

19. Davis, *FDR: New York Years*, 343–44.

20. Mr. Curtis Roosevelt, interview,15 October 1994.

21. "Roosevelt Greeted by 50,000 Admirers in New Hampshire," *New York Times*, 18 July 1932.

Chapter 6. Ready to Be Shanghaied

1. Elliott Roosevelt, *FDR: His Personal Letters, 1928–1945*, 1:290–91.

2. Ibid., 299.

3. Wharton, *Roosevelt Omnibus*, 85, A-2.

4. William Seale, *The President's House*, 2 vols. (Washington, D.C.: White House Historical Association with cooperation of the National Geographic Society, 1986), 2:922–25.

5. "The Roosevelt Era: Selections from the Private Collections of Franklin and Eleanor Roosevelt and Family," *Christies Auction Catalog* (14–15 February 2001); John G. Waite, ed., *The President as Architect: Franklin D. Roosevelt's Top Cottage* (Albany, N.Y.: Mount Ida Press, 2001), 61.

6. Wharton, *Roosevelt Omnibus*, 85, A-2.

7. William J. Steward and Charyl C. Pollard, "Franklin D. Roosevelt, Collector," *Prologue*, Journal of the National Archives (winter 1969): 13–28; Eugene Kinkead, "The Great Philatelist," *New Yorker*, March 1946, 48–54; Lena Shawen, *A President's Hobby: The Story of FDR's Stamps* (New York: H. L. Linquist Publications, 1952), 5–49; Ross T. McIntire, *White House Physician* (New York: G. P. Putnam's Sons, 1946), 79.

8. Graham and Warder, *FDR: His Life and Times*, 280.

9. Newman McGirr, Oral History, 12 November 1950, FDRL.

10. Ibid.

11. John F. Kennedy, "The Strength and Style of our Navy Tradition," *Life*, 10 August 1962, 79–83.

12. Ibid.

13. McGirr, Oral History.

14. Ms. Brooke Astor, personal correspondence with the author, 22 January 1998.

15. Wharton, *Roosevelt Omnibus,* 78.

16. Elliott Roosevelt, *FDR: His Personal Letters, 1928–1945,* 1:327.

17. Roosevelt and Shalett, *Affectionately, FDR,* 278.

18. Ibid., 275–77.

19. James A. Hagerty, "Assassin Fires into Roosevelt Party at Miami; President-Elect Uninjured; Mayor Cermak and 4 Others Wounded," *New York Times,* 16 February 1933.

20. Davis, *FDR: New York Years,* 432.

21. McIntire, *White House Physician,* 85.

22. Elliott Roosevelt, *FDR: His Personal Letters, 1928–1945,* 1:394.

23. Jeffrey M. Dorwart, "The Roosevelt-Astor Espionage Ring," *New York History* (July 1981): 307–22.

24. Franklin D. Roosevelt, letter to Vincent Astor, 4 August 1933, Vincent Astor Copies of Correspondence with Franklin D. Roosevelt, FDRL.

25. "Roosevelt Fishes All Day off Long Island, Hauling in Biggest Share of Party's Catch," *New York Times,* 3 September 1933.

26. Ibid.

27. "Roosevelt Quits Yacht at Capital," *New York Times,* 6 September 1933.

28. Dorwart, "The Roosevelt-Astor Espionage Ring."

29. Vincent Astor, letter to Franklin D. Roosevelt, 30 April 1936, Vincent Astor Copies of Correspondence with Franklin D. Roosevelt, FDRL.

30. A. J. Kirk Order on Vincent Astor, 28 March 1941, Vincent Astor Copies of Correspondence with Franklin D. Roosevelt, FDRL.

31. Roosevelt and Shalett, *Affectionately, FDR,* 280–81.

32. "Roosevelt Leads Easter Service on Yacht; Acting as the Navy's Commander-in-Chief," *New York Times,* 2 April 1934.

33. Franklin D. Roosevelt, letter to Vincent Astor, 22 August 1934, Vincent Astor Copies of Correspondence with Franklin D. Roosevelt, FDRL.

34. *Dictionary of American Naval Fighting Ships,* 5:117.

35. Capt. Wilson Brown, USN, Log of the President's Cruise–Bahama Waters, 26 March 1935, Trips of the President, Cruises and Logs, FDRL.

Chapter 7. Floating White House

1. Harold L. Ickes, *The Secret Diaries of Harold L. Ickes,* 3 vols. (New York: Simon and Schuster, 1953–1954), 1:173.

2. Kenneth S. Davis, *FDR: The New Deal Years, 1933–37* (New York: Random House, 1986), 372.

3. Capt. Walter B. Woodson, USN, Trip of the President, summer 1934, Trips of the President, Cruises and Logs, FDRL, 1–11.

4. "Roosevelt Fishing Boat Is Converted Gig; Used 30-Footer Being Reconditioned Here," *New York Times,* 9 June 1934.

5. "President's Ship Cozily Outfitted," *New York Times,* 21 June 1934.

6. "Roosevelt to Find Rare Sea Comforts," *New York Times,* 1 July 1934.

7. Ickes, *Secret Diaries,* 1:174–84.

8. Roosevelt and Shalett, *Affectionately, FDR*, 282–83.

9. Elliott Roosevelt, *FDR, His Personal Letters, 1928–1945*, 1:404–5.

10. Frank Freidel, *Franklin D. Roosevelt: Rendezvous with Destiny* (Boston: Little, Brown and Company, 1990), 191; Cruise of the President on Board USS *Houston*, 2–23 October 1935, Trips of the President, Cruises and Logs, FDRL, 1–17.

11. Hopkins, interview, 4 February 1995.

12. Robert E. Sherwood, *Roosevelt and Hopkins* (New York: Harper and Brothers, 1948), 78; Cruise of the President on Board USS *Houston*.

13. William M. Rigdon, *White House Sailor* (Garden City, N.Y.: Doubleday and Company, 1962), 60.

14. Ibid., 60.

15. Ibid., 61.

16. Davis, *FDR: New Deal Years*, 583.

17. Memorandum, Chief of Naval Operations, "Equipping Naval Vessels to Carry the President," 26 December 1943, Trips of the President, Cruises and Logs, FDRL.

18. J. F. Curriran, letter to Franklin D. Roosevelt, 11 November 1944, Secret Service File, FDRL.

19. Elliott Roosevelt, *FDR: His Personal Letters, 1928–1945*, 1:512; Cruise of the President on Board USS *Houston*.

20. Ickes, *Secret Diaries*, 1:449.

21. Paul, interviews, 1 and 22 November 1992.

22. Ickes, *Secret Diaries*, 1:449–50.

23. McIntire, *White House Physician*, 126.

24. Fred. E. Crockett, *Special Fleet: The History of Presidential Yachts* (Camden, Maine: Down East Books, 1985), 68. Both *Sequoia* and *Potomac* survive to this day. President Truman used *Sequoia* in the closing days of the war. It was later returned to presidential duty in John F. Kennedy's administration, and was used as the presidential yacht by Presidents Lyndon Johnson, Richard Nixon, and Gerald Ford. President Jimmy Carter sold the vessel in 1977. Eventually *Sequoia* was purchased by the Presidential Yacht Trust and restored to its original condition. *Potomac* was decommissioned in November 1945. The following year it was sold to the Maryland Tidewater Fisheries Commission. It then passed to several successive owners, including Elvis Presley and St. Jude Hospital in Memphis, Tennessee. Today, *Potomac* has been restored as an FDR-era museum and is moored at Pier 26 in San Francisco. The Association for the Restoration of the Presidential Yacht *Potomac*, led by FDR's son, Jimmy, conducted a successful fund drive to restore President Roosevelt's "floating White House."

25. Virginia Livingston Hunt, 28 April 1935, Collections of the Manuscript Division, Virginia Livingston Hunt Papers, Library of Congress, Washington, D.C.

26. Walter W. Jaffee, *The Presidential Yacht Potomac* (Palo Alto, Calif.: Glencannon Press, 1998), 63.

27. Frank L. Kluckhohn, "Sea-Going White House," *New York Times Magazine,* 18 May 1941.

28. White House Memorandum, "List of Movies for *Potomac,*" undated memorandum, President's Personal File, FDRL.

29. Crockett, *Special Fleet,* 68.

30. Henry Morgenthau memorandum to Franklin D. Roosevelt, 24 September 1937, President's Official File, FDRL; Franklin D. Roosevelt note to James Roosevelt, 27 September 1937, President's Official File, FDRL; W. B. Woodson memorandum to James Roosevelt, 9 October 1937, President's Official File, FDRL.

Chapter 8. Praying for Fog

1. Geoffrey Ward, *Closest Companion* (Boston: Houghton Mifflin Company, 1995), 72.

2. Ibid., 76.

3. Ibid., 72.

4. Samuel I. Rosenman, *Public Papers and Addresses of Franklin D. Roosevelt, 1936* (New York: Random House, 1938), 159.

5. Ibid., 236.

6. Ibid., 260.

7. Franklin Roosevelt, letter to Joseph M. Price, 1 July 1936, President's Personal File, FDRL.

8. Charles W. Hurd, "President Pledges Flood-Control Aid," *New York Times,* 14 July 1936.

9. Charles W. Hurd, "Roosevelt Starts Cruise as Skipper," *New York Times,* 15 July 1936.

10. "Harrison Tweed, Lawyer and Civic Leader, Dead," *New York Times,* 17 July 1969.

11. Log of the Cruise of President Franklin D. Roosevelt Aboard the Schooner Yacht *Sewanna,* 14–28 July 1936, Trips of the President, Cruises and Logs, FDRL, 1–19. Within four years after FDR's 1936 cruise, *Sewanna* was sold. According to the New York Yacht Club, from 1940 to 1950, it was owned by T. H. A. Tiedman, and its name had been changed to *Altura III.* The yacht was sold in 1951 to Roscoe S. Miller, and the name was changed to *White Wing.* Four years later, George Breed purchased the yacht and the name was changed to *Ballymena.* Finally, the New York Yacht Club notes that the yacht was sold to Henry N. Whitney in 1957. After 1961, the vessel no longer appears in Lloyd's Register.

12. "Roosevelt Sons Sail On," *New York Times,* 8 July 1936.

13. Log of *Sewanna.*

14. Charles W. Hurd, "Roosevelt Sails Up Coast Swiftly," *New York Times,* 16 July 1936.

15. Charles W. Hurd, "Roosevelt Sails Through Fog Bank," *New York Times,* 19 July 1936.

16. Log of *Sewanna*.

17. Mr. Abe Barron, telephone interview by the author, 16 October 1994. Abe Barron managed Franklin and Lasoff in the 1940s, a Boston custom hat-making company. He said Roosevelt's floppy white sailing hat was Style Number 639, and was handmade of Cramerton cloth, a fine twill. Franklin and Lasoff sold their hats to a number of retail stores, which is where Barron believes FDR purchased them. Barron said the style became known in the trade as the "Campobello hat" because it became so closely identified with FDR.

18. Log of *Sewanna*.

19. Ibid.

20. Bernard Asbell, *Mother and Daughter: Letters of Eleanor and Anna Roosevelt* (New York: Fromm International Publishing Company, 1988), 70.

21. Charles W. Hurd, "Roosevelt Sails Dangerous Seas," *New York Times*, 25 July 1936.

22. Roosevelt and Shalett, *Affectionately, FDR*, 283–84.

23. Ibid., 284.

24. Charles W. Hurd, "Roosevelt Nears Campobello Goal," *New York Times*, 26 July 1936.

25. Elliott Roosevelt, *FDR: His Personal Letters, 1928–1945*, 1:604.

26. Graham J. White, *FDR and the Press* (Chicago: University of Chicago Press, 1979), 5.

27. Steve Early, memorandum to Col. Starling, 7 July 1936, President's Official File, FDRL.

Chapter 9. Davy Jones, Peg Leg, and Senior Pollywog Roosevelt

1. Elliott Roosevelt, *FDR: His Personal Letters, 1928–1945*, 1:626.

2. Freidel, *Roosevelt: Rendezvous*, 195.

3. Randall Bennett Woods, *The Roosevelt Foreign Policy Establishment and the Good Neighbor* (Lawrence: Regents Press of Kansas, 1979), 12.

4. Grace Tully, *FDR, My Boss* (New York: Charles Scribner's Sons, 1949), 217.

5. Elliott Roosevelt, *FDR: His Personal Letters, 1928–1945*, 1:631.

6. Ward, *Closest Companion*, 88–89.

7. Elliott Roosevelt, *FDR: His Personal Letters, 1928–1945*, 1:632–33.

8. Ward, *Closest Companion*, 90–91.

9. Ibid., 91.

10. Frederick W. Marks, *Wind over Sand* (Athens: University of Georgia Press, 1988), 217.

11. Freidel, *Roosevelt: Rendezvous*, 218.

12. Elliott Roosevelt, *FDR: His Personal Letters, 1928–1945*, 1:635.

13. Samuel I. Rosenman, *Public Papers and Addresses of Franklin D. Roosevelt, 1937* (New York: Macmillan Company, 1941), 1–6.

14. McIntire, *White House Physician*, 85.

15. Arthur M. Schlesinger Jr., *The Almanac of American History* (New York: Barnes and Noble Books, 1993), 472–73.

16. Elliott Roosevelt and James Brough, *A Rendezvous with Destiny* (New York: G. P. Putnam's Sons, 1975), 166.

17. Mr. Anthony W. Lobb, telephone interview by the author, 17 and 24 April, and 8 August 1993. Ian Sayer and Douglas Botting, *America's Secret Army: The Untold Story of the Counter Intelligence Corps* (London: Grafton Books, 1989), 1–21, 45–46. Sayer and Botting explore the elite CIC in exquisite detail in their book. The CIC's mission was to work with the army on detection of treason, sedition, and subversive activity, and neutralize enemy espionage and sabotage plans in approximately sixty countries during the war. The CIC's postwar duties included dismantling Japanese intelligence and hunting down Nazi war criminals in Germany. According to the authors, former CIC agents—known as "G-men in khaki"—included Henry Kissinger and J. D. Salinger.

18. L. P. Johnson, U.S. Navy memorandum, 1933, President's Personal Files, FDRL.

Chapter 10. Clearing Away Personal Cobwebs

1. Rosenman, *Public Papers and Addresses, 1943,* 88–89.
2. Rosenman, *Public Papers and Addresses, 1938,* 463.
3. Seagraves, interview, 20 November 1994.
4. Mr. Curtis Roosevelt, interview, 15 October 1994.
5. Elliott Roosevelt, *FDR: His Personal Letters, 1928–1945,* 2:781.
6. Jaffee, *Presidential Yacht Potomac,* 13.
7. Elliott Roosevelt, *FDR: His Personal Letters, 1928–1945,* 1:677–78.
8. Staff Correspondent, "Roosevelt Rests for Day of Fishing," *New York Times,* 3 May 1937.
9. Staff Correspondent, "President to Spur Start on Housing," *New York Times,* 9 May 1937.
10. "Roosevelt Busy at Desk," *New York Times,* 7 May 1937.
11. Rosenman, *Public Papers and Addresses, 1937,* 196–97.
12. Ibid., 201–2.
13. Randall Brink, *Lost Star* (New York: W. W. Norton and Company, 1994), 92–99.
14. Rosenman, *Public Papers and Addresses, 1937,* 354.
15. Ibid., 411.
16. Ibid., 412–13.
17. Russell D. Buhite and David W. Levy, *FDR's Fireside Chats* (New York: Penguin Books, 1992), 96–105.
18. "President Plans Florida Fishing Trip; Pens Jest on the Tooth to News Questions," *New York Times,* 24 November 1937.
19. Felix Blair Jr., "Roosevelt Sails South on Cruiser," *New York Times,* 1 May 1938.
20. *Dictionary of American Naval Fighting Ships,* 3:261–63.

21. Staff Correspondent, "'SOS' Call Turns Roosevelt's Ship," *New York Times*, 8 May 1938.

22. "Says Roosevelt's Ship Sprang Leak on Cruise," *New York Times*, 19 May 1938; Capt. James, memorandum, 4 May 1938, President's Official File, FDRL.

23. Kenneth S. Davis, *FDR: Into the Storm* (New York: Random House, 1993), 275.

24. Elliott Roosevelt, *FDR: His Personal Letters, 1928–1945*, 2:800; Inspection Cruise and Fishing Expedition of President Franklin D. Roosevelt on Board USS *Houston*, 16 July–9 August 1938, Trips of the President, Cruises and Logs, FDRL, 1–22.

25. "Roosevelt Sets Davy Jones Watch," *New York Times*, 24 July 1938.

26. Waldo L. Schmitt and Leonard P. Schultz, *List of Fishes Taken on Presidential Cruise of 1938* (Washington, D.C.: Smithsonian Institution, 1940), 1.

27. Freidel, *Roosevelt: Rendezvous*, 298; Inspection Cruise and Fishing Expedition of President Franklin D. Roosevelt on Board USS *Houston*, 16 July–9 August 1938, 1–22.

28. Michael F. Reilly, *Reilly of the White House* (New York: Simon and Schuster, 1947), 111–12.

29. Ibid., 113–14.

30. Elliott Roosevelt, *FDR: His Personal Letters, 1928–1945*, 2:801.

Chapter 11. Storm Signals from across the Seas

1. Rosenman, *Public Papers and Addresses, 1939*, 2.

2. Ibid., 1.

3. Ibid., 143–44.

4. "Midnight Starts Navy's Warfare," *New York Times*, 13 February 1939.

5. Felix Blair Jr., "Roosevelt Warns Dictators to Stay Out of Americas," *New York Times*, 19 February 1939.

6. "Big Fleet Attack Starts War Games," *New York Times*, 20 February 1939.

7. Elliott Roosevelt, *FDR: His Personal Letters, 1928–1945*, 2:851–54.

8. Ibid., 912.

9. Felix Blair Jr., "President Silent on Kelly's Speech," *New York Times*, 15 August 1939.

10. "Aide of Roosevelt Nets Humber Salmon," *New York Times*, 19 August 1939.

11. Hatch, *Franklin D. Roosevelt: Informal Biography*, 250.

12. Buhite and Levy, *FDR's Fireside Chats*, 150–51.

13. Rosenman, *Public Papers and Addresses, 1939*, 526–27.

14. Felix Blair Jr., "President Moves," *New York Times*, 25 August 1939.

15. Rosenman, *Public Papers and Addresses, 1939*, 552–53.

16. "President Decides on Vacation at Sea in Air of Mystery," *New York Times*, 13 February 1940.

17. McIntire, *White House Physician*, 19, 82.

18. Bruenn, interview, 21 January 1995.

19. Felix Blair Jr., "Roosevelt Sails on 'Mystery' Cruise," *New York Times*, 16 February 1940.

20. Elliott Roosevelt, *FDR: His Personal Letters, 1928–1945*, 2:1002–3.

21. "President Studies Canal Approaches," *New York Times*, 20 February 1940.

22. Elliott Roosevelt, *FDR: His Personal Letters, 1928–1945*, 2:1003.

Chapter 12. Rattlesnakes of the Atlantic

1. Eileen Shields-West, *Almanac of Presidential Campaigns* (New York: World Almanac, 1992), 179.

2. "Roosevelt on Cruise for Week-end Rest," *New York Times*, 2 June 1940.

3. Rosenman, *Public Papers and Addresses, 1940*, 312.

4. Ibid., 376–77, 391.

5. Ibid., 481; Shields-West, *Almanac of Presidential Campaigns*, 179.

6. Rosenman, *Public Papers and Addresses, 1940*, 499–510.

7. Ibid., 502.

8. Samuel Eliot Morison, *History of the United States Naval Operations in World War II*, 15 vols. (Edison, N.J.: Castle Books, 2001), 3:31(n); Rosenman, *Public Papers and Addresses, 1940*, 515.

9. Francis L. Loewenheim, Harold Langley, and Manfred Jonas, *Roosevelt and Churchill: Their Secret Wartime Correspondence* (New York: E. P. Dutton and Company, 1975), 122–25; Nathan Miller, *FDR: An Intimate History* (Garden City, N.Y.: Doubleday and Company, 1983), 460.

10. Rosenman, *Public Papers and Addresses, 1940*, 633–44; E. R. Stettinius Jr., *Lend-Lease: Weapon for Victory* (New York: Macmillan Company, 1944), 6.

11. Peter Kemp, ed., *Oxford Companion to Ships and the Sea* (New York: Oxford University Press, 1994), 479; Rosenman, *Public Papers and Addresses, 1940*, 647.

12. Col. Starling Memorandum to Wilson, 18 March 1941, Secret Service Files, FDRL.

13. Freidel, *Roosevelt: Rendezvous*, 371; Ickes, *Secret Diaries*, 3:466.

14. "President's Yacht Sunk," *New York Times*, 28 March 1941.

15. Freidel, *Roosevelt: Rendezvous*, 371.

16. Ickes, *Secret Diaries*, 3:457.

17. Freidel, *Roosevelt: Rendezvous*, 371.

18. Elliott Roosevelt, *FDR: His Personal Letters, 1928–1945*, 2:1196–97.

19. Douglas Brinkley and David R. Facey-Crowther, eds., *The Atlantic Charter* (New York: St. Martin's Press, 1994), 177.

20. Ward, *Closest Companion*, 140–43.

21. Brinkley and Facey-Crowther, *Atlantic Charter*, 178.

22. Ibid., 180.

23. Ward, *Closest Companion*, 140–43.

24. Capt. J. R. Beardall, memorandum, 9 August 1941, Secret Service Files, FDRL.

25. H. V. Morton, *The Atlantic Meeting* (London: Methuen and Company Ltd., 1944), 91–92.
26. Ward, *Closest Companion*, 143.
27. Lobb, interview, 17 and 24 April, and 8 August 1993.
28. Tully, *FDR, My Boss*, 246.
29. Miller, *FDR: Intimate History*, 466–67.
30. Buhite and Levy, *FDR's Fireside Chats*, 188–96.
31. Rosenman, *Public Papers and Addresses, 1941*, 438.
32. John Terraine, *The U-Boat Wars* (New York: Henry Holt and Company, 1989), 393.
33. Lobb, interview, 17 and 24 April, and 8 August 1993.

Chapter 13. New Secret Base at Shangri-La

1. Rosenman, *Public Papers and Addresses, 1942*, 212–16.
2. Nathan Miller, *War at Sea* (New York: Scribner, 1995), 233–34.
3. Morison, *History of Naval Operations*, 3:391.
4. McIntire, *White House Physician*, 148.
5. Hugh D. McClendon, *A History of Camp David* (Thurmont, Md.: Department of the Navy, 1985), A-3–A-7.
6. Ibid., A-2.
7. Ibid., 12.
8. Rigdon, *White House Sailor*, 218–19.
9. McClendon, *History of Camp David*, 2.
10. W. Dale Nelson, *The President Is at Camp David* (Syracuse, N.Y.: Syracuse University Press, 1995), 6–7, 22.
11. McClendon, *History of Camp David*, 7.
12. Ibid., 4.
13. Nelson, *President Is at Camp David*, 10.
14. Edwin P. Hoyt, *U-Boats Off-Shore* (Chelsea, Mich.: Scarborough House, 1990), 150–57.
15. Rosenman, *Public Papers and Addresses, 1942*, 298.
16. Nelson, *President Is at Camp David*, 10, 12.
17. Tully, *FDR: My Boss*, 115; Roosevelt and Brough, *Rendezvous with Destiny*, 321; Nelson, *President Is at Camp David*, 16; Arthur M. Schlesinger Jr., *The Coming of the New Deal* (Boston: Houghton Mifflin Company, 1959), 578; Lobb, interview, 17 and 24 April, and 8 August 1993.
18. Tully, *FDR, My Boss*, 20–21.
19. Rosenman, *Public Papers and Addresses, 1942*, 246–47.
20. Edward J. Marolda, *FDR and the U.S. Navy* (Bloomsburg, Pa.: Macmillan, 1998), 96–99.
21. Morison, *History of Naval Operations*, 5:31–35.
22. Rosenman, *Public Papers and Addresses, 1944–1945*, 71.
23. Martin Davis, ed., *Destroyer Escorts of World War II* (Albany, N.Y.: Destroyer Escort Historical Foundation, 2000), inside front cover.

24. Rosenman, *Public Papers and Addresses, 1942,* 322–23.

25. Ibid., 377–78.

26. Ibid., 416–26.

Chapter 14. Greatest Man I Have Ever Known

1. Ward, *Closest Companion,* 195.

2. Gold Coast Railroad Museum, "Ferdinand Magellan: Presidential Rail Car, U.S. Number 1," <http://www.goldcoast-railroad.org/>; William D. Siuru Jr. and Andrea Steward, eds., *Presidential Cars and Transportation* (Iola, Wis.: Krause Publications, 1995), 16–19; Rigdon, *White House Sailor,* 19.

3. Rigdon, *White House Sailor,* 20.

4. Reilly, *Reilly of the White House,* 136–47.

5. Ibid., 137.

6. Sherwood, *Roosevelt and Hopkins,* 672.

7. Reilly, *Reilly of the White House,* 152.

8. Sherwood, *Roosevelt and Hopkins,* 685; Log of the Trip of the President to the Casablanca Conference, 9–31 January 1943, Trips of the President, Cruises and Logs, FDRL.

9. Eric Larrabee, *Commander in Chief* (New York: Harper and Row, 1987), 39.

10. Lobb, interview, 17 and 24 April, and 8 August 1993.

11. Schlesinger, *Almanac of American History,* 491.

12. Morison, *History of Naval Operations,* 4:287.

13. Seale, *The President's House,* 2:12.

14. Henrietta Nesbitt, *White House Diary* (Garden City, N.Y.: Doubleday and Company, 1948), 233.

15. Seale, *The President's House,* 2:750.

16. Rosenman, *Public Papers and Addresses, 1943,* 162–64.

17. Log of the President's Inspection Tour, 13–29 April 1943, Trips of the President, Cruises and Logs, FDRL.

18. Merriman Smith, *Thank You, Mr. President* (New York: Harper and Brothers, 1946), 90.

19. Harvey Johnston, letter to Franklin D. Roosevelt, 5 July 1943, President's Personal File, FDRL; Franklin D. Roosevelt, letter to Harvey Johnson, 9 July 1943, President's Personal File, FDRL.

20. Rigdon, *White House Sailor,* 27.

21. Ibid., 31.

22. Ibid., 32.

23. Ibid., 32.

24. Ibid., 33.

25. "The Log of the President's Visit to Canada," 16–26 August 1943, Trips of the President, Cruises and Logs, FDRL.

26. Rosenman, *Public Papers and Addresses, 1943,* 354.

27. "Log of the President's Visit to Canada," 16–26 August 1943, 9; Rigdon, *White House Sailor,* 44.

28. Rosenman, *Public Papers and Addresses, 1943,* 354.
29. Ibid., 351–52.
30. "Log of the President's Visit to Canada," 16–26 August 1943, 15–18.

Chapter 15. Fire Horse Refusing to Go to Pasture

1. Sherwood, *Roosevelt and Hopkins,* 768; Roosevelt and Brough, *Rendezvous with Destiny,* 346.
2. Sherwood, *Roosevelt and Hopkins,* 768; Rigdon, *White House Sailor,* 64.
3. Elliott Roosevelt, *FDR: His Personal Letters, 1928–1945,* 2:1469.
4. Rigdon, *White House Sailor,* 57.
5. Ibid., 54.
6. Ibid., 60.
7. Griffith, interview, 28 January 1995.
8. Reilly, *Reilly of the White House,* 165–66.
9. Rigdon, *White House Sailor,* 67.
10. McIntire, *White House Physician,* 164.
11. Ibid., 165.
12. Ibid., 165–66.
13. Rigdon, *White House Sailor,* 74.
14. Elliott Roosevelt, *As He Saw It* (New York: Duell, Sloan and Pearce, 1946), 160.
15. Doris Kearns Goodwin, *No Ordinary Time* (New York: Simon and Schuster, 1994), 474.
16. Elliott Roosevelt, *As He Saw It,* 160.
17. Rigdon, *White House Sailor,* 74–75.
18. Elliott Roosevelt, *As He Saw It,* 166.
19. Reilly, *Reilly of the White House,* 175.
20. Col. Richard Park Jr., undated memorandum, President's Personal File, FDRL.
21. I. C. B. Dear, *The Oxford Companion to World War II* (New York: Oxford University Press, 1995), 341–42.
22. Reilly, *Reilly of the White House,* 185–86.
23. Ibid., 188.
24. Sherwood, *Roosevelt and Hopkins,* 768; Roosevelt and Brough, *Rendezvous with Destiny,* 346.
25. McIntire, *White House Physician,* 182.
26. Ibid., 183.
27. Rigdon, *White House Sailor,* 97.
28. Smith, *Thank You, Mr. President,* 139.
29. McIntire, *White House Physician,* 194.
30. Ibid.
31. Rosenman, *Public Papers and Addresses, 1944–1945,* 198.
32. Smith, *Thank You, Mr. President,* 145.
33. William D. Leahy, *I Was There* (New York: Whittlesey House, 1950), 239.

34. Rosenman, *Public Papers and Addresses, 1944–1945,* 204.

35. Jim Bishop, *FDR's Last Year* (New York: William Morrow and Company, 1980), 113.

36. Rigdon, *White House Sailor,* 115–16; Log of the President's Inspection Trip to the Pacific, July–August 1944, Trips of the President, Cruises and Logs, FDRL, 11.

37. Bishop, *FDR's Last Year,* 114.

38. Samuel I. Rosenman, *Working with Roosevelt* (New York: Harper and Brothers, 1952), 456.

39. Log of the President's Inspection Trip to the Pacific, July–August 1944, 15.

Chapter 16. No Earthly Power Can Keep Him Here

1. Rosenman, *Working with Roosevelt,* 456–57.

2. Larrabee, *Commander in Chief,* 305–8; Lobb, interview, 17 and 24 April, and 8 August 1993.

3. Rosenman, *Working with Roosevelt,* 458–59.

4. McIntire, *White House Physician,* 200.

5. Goodwin, *No Ordinary Time,* 532.

6. Rigdon, *White House Sailor,* 127; Log of President's Inspection Trip to the Pacific, July–August 1944.

7. Bruenn, interview, 21 January 1995; Howard Bruenn, "Clinical Notes on the Illness and Death of President Franklin D. Roosevelt," *Annals of Internal Medicine* 72 (1970): 16.

8. Rosenman, *Public Papers and Addresses, 1944–1945,* 213.

9. Ibid., 227.

10. Ward, *Closest Companion,* 321.

11. Bruenn, "Clinical Notes," 18.

12. Rosenman, *Working with Roosevelt,* 462.

13. Bruenn, "Clinical Notes," 18.

14. Rosenman, *Working with Roosevelt,* 453.

15. Griffith, interview, 28 January 1995; Ward, *Closet Companion,* 322–25.

16. Rosenman, *Working with Roosevelt,* 462.

17. Rosenman, *Public Papers and Addresses, 1944–1945,* 284–92.

18. Bruenn, "Clinical Notes," 19–20.

19. Bishop, *FDR's Last Year,* 266–67; Bruenn, "Clinical Notes," 21.

20. Roosevelt and Shalett, *Affectionately, FDR,* 354–55.

21. Rosenman, *Public Papers and Addresses, 1944–1945,* 525.

22. Bishop, *FDR's Last Year,* 242; Log of the President's Trip to the Crimea Conference and Great Bitter Lake Egypt, 22 January–28 February 1945, Trips of the President, Cruises and Logs, FDRL, 2.

23. Smith, *Thank You, Mr. President,* 164–65.

24. Roosevelt and Shalett, *Affectionately, FDR,* 355–56.

25. Log of the President's Trip to the Crimea Conference and Great Bitter Lake Egypt, 22 January–28 February 1945, 5, 8.

26. Ibid., 10.
27. Rigdon, *White House Sailor,* 139; Siuru and Steward, *Presidential Cars and Transportation,* 140.
28. Winston Churchill, *Memoirs of the Second World War* (Boston: Houghton Mifflin Company, 1987), 913.
29. Leahy, *I Was There,* 320–21.
30. Bruenn, "Clinical Notes," 24; *Stedman's Medical Dictionary,* 23d ed. (Baltimore: Williams and Wilkins Company, 1978), 1171.
31. Bruenn, "Clinical Notes," 24.
32. Robert Dallek, *Franklin D. Roosevelt and Foreign Policy* (New York: Oxford University Press, 1995), 533.
33. Ibid., 534.
34. Warren F. Kimball, *The Juggler* (Princeton, N.J.: Princeton University Press, 1991), 7.
35. Rigdon, *White House Sailor,* 154.
36. Griffith, interview, 28 January 1995.
37. Rigdon, *White House Sailor,* 163–64; Log, 45.
38. Rigdon, *White House Sailor,* 167; Log, 44.
39. Log of the President's Trip to the Crimea Conference and Great Bitter Lake Egypt, 22 January–28 February 1945, 46.
40. Churchill, *Memoirs,* 928.
41. Rosenman, *Working With Roosevelt,* 522–24.
42. Bruenn, "Clinical Notes," 25.
43. Ibid., 26.
44. Rosenman, *Working with Roosevelt,* 527.
45. Bruenn, "Clinical Notes," 26.
46. Ruth Stevens, *Hi Ya Neighbor* (New York: Tupper and Love, 1947), 81.
47. Reilly, *Reilly of the White House,* 226–27.
48. William D. Hassett, *Off the Record with FDR* (New Brunswick, N.J.: Rutgers University Press, 1958), 327.
49. Stevens, *Hi Ya Neighbor,* 83–84.
50. Bruenn, "Clinical Notes," 26.
51. Griffith, interview, 28 January 1995.
52. Bruenn, "Clinical Notes," 27.
53. Ward, *Closest Companion,* 417.
54. Ibid., 418; Bruenn, "Clinical Notes," 27.
55. Ward, *Closest Companion,* 419.
56. Bruenn, "Clinical Notes," 28.
57. Reilly, *Reilly of the White House,* 232–34.

Epilogue

1. Ames, interviews, 28 February and 28 March 1993.
2. Elliott Roosevelt, *FDR: His Personal Letters, 1928–1945,* 2:781.
3. Schlesinger, *Coming of the New Deal,* 582.

4. Kimball, *Juggler*, 8.
5. Dallek, *Roosevelt and American Foreign Policy*, 550.
6. Perkins, *The Roosevelt I Knew*, 20–21.
7. Schlesinger, *The Crisis of the Old Order*, 406.
8. Perkins, *The Roosevelt I Knew*, 137.
9. Schlesinger, *Coming of the New Deal*, 531–32.
10. Perkins, *The Roosevelt I Knew*, 137, 163, 164.
11. Burns, *The Lion and the Fox*, 63.
12. Delano, *Roosevelt and the Delano Influence*, 262.
13. Smith, *Thank You, Mr. President*, 31.
14. Perkins, *The Roosevelt I Knew*, 18–19.
15. Leahy, *I Was There*, 3.
16. John F. Kennedy, Speech at America's Cup Races, September 1962, John F. Kennedy Library, Newport, Rhode Island.
17. Tully, *FDR, My Boss*, 367.
18. "Seagoing President Spends Night Here," *Vineyard Gazette*, 23 June 1933.
19. Nantucket Wharf Rat Club Journal, 1933, Nantucket Wharf Rat Club, Old North Wharf, Nantucket, Mass.

BIBLIOGRAPHY

Books

Abbazia, Patrick. *Mr. Roosevelt's Navy: The Private War of the U.S. Atlantic Fleet, 1939–1942.* Annapolis: Naval Institute Press, 1975.

Albion, Robert Greenhalgh, and Rowena Reed, eds. *Makers of Naval Policy 1798–1947.* Annapolis: Naval Institute Press, 1980.

Alden, John D. *Flush Decks and Four Pipes.* Annapolis: Naval Institute Press, 1989.

Asbell, Bernard. *The FDR Memoirs: A Speculation on History.* Garden City, N.Y.: Doubleday and Company, 1973.

———. *Mother and Daughter: Letters of Eleanor and Anna Roosevelt.* New York: Fromm International Publishing Company, 1988.

———. *When F.D.R. Died.* New York: Holt, Rinehart and Winston, 1961.

Ashley, Clifford W. *Whaleships of New Bedford.* Boston: Houghton Mifflin Company, 1929.

Astor, Brooke. *Footprints.* Garden City, N.Y.: Doubleday and Company, 1980.

Baer, George W. *One Hundred Years of Sea Power.* Stanford, Calif.: Stanford University Press, 1999.

Bailey, Thomas A., and Paul B. Ryan. *Hitler vs. Roosevelt: The Undeclared Naval War.* New York: Free Press, 1979.

Beacom, Seward. *Pulpit Harbor—200 Years: A History of Pulpit Harbor, North Haven, Maine, 1784–1984.* North Haven, Maine: North Haven Historical Society, 1985.

Bellush, Bernard. *Franklin D. Roosevelt as Governor of New York.* New York: Columbia University Press, 1955.

Beschloss, Michael. *Kennedy and Roosevelt.* New York: W. W. Norton and Company, 1980.

Bishop, Jim. *FDR's Last Year.* New York: William Morrow and Company, 1980.

Boyer, Paul S., ed. *Oxford Companion to United States History.* New York: Oxford University Press, 2001.

Brink, Randall. *Lost Star.* New York: W. W. Norton and Company, 1994.

Brinkley, Douglas, and David R. Facey-Crowther, eds. *The Atlantic Charter.* New York: St. Martin's Press, 1994.

Brinnin, John Malcolm. *The Sway of the Grand Saloon: A Social History of the North Atlantic.* New York: Delacorte Press, 1971.

Brogan, Denis W. *The Era of Franklin D. Roosevelt.* New Haven, Conn.: Yale University Press, 1950.

Buhite, Russell D., and David W. Levy, eds. *FDR's Fireside Chats.* New York: Penguin Books, 1992.

Bullitt, Orville H. *For the President: Personal and Secret.* Boston: Houghton Mifflin Company, 1972.

Burns, James MacGregor. *The Lion and the Fox.* New York: Harcourt, Brace and Company, 1956.

———. *Roosevelt: The Soldier of Freedom.* New York: Harcourt Brace Jovanovich, 1970.

Byrnes, James F. *Speaking Frankly.* New York: Harper and Brothers, 1947.

Churchill, Allen. *The Roosevelts.* London: Frederick Muller Limited, 1966.

Churchill, Winston. *Memoirs of the Second World War.* Boston: Houghton Mifflin Company, 1987.

Collier, Peter, and David Horowitz. *The Roosevelts: An American Saga.* New York: Simon and Schuster, 1994.

Collins, Aileen Sutherland. *Travels in Britain 1794–1795: The Diary of John Aspinwall, Great-grandfather of Franklin Delano Roosevelt: With A Brief History of His Aspinwall Forebears.* Virginia Beach, Va.: Parsons Press, 1994.

Cook, Blanche Wiesen. *Eleanor Roosevelt,* Vol. 1, *1884–1933.* New York: Viking, 1992.

———. *Eleanor Roosevelt,* Vol. 2, *1933–1938.* New York: Viking, 1999.

Crockett, Fred E. *Special Fleet: The History of the Presidential Yachts.* Camden, Maine: Down East Books, 1985.

Cronon, E. David. *The Cabinet Diaries of Josephus Daniels, 1913–1921.* Lincoln: University of Nebraska Press, 1995.

Dallek, Robert. *Franklin D. Roosevelt and Foreign Policy.* New York: Oxford University Press, 1995.

Daniels, Jonathan. *The End of Innocence.* New York: DaCapo Press, 1972.

Davis, Kenneth S. *A Beckoning of Destiny.* New York: G. P. Putnam's Sons, 1972.

———. *FDR: Into the Storm.* New York: Random House, 1993.

———. *FDR: The New Deal Years, 1933–1937.* New York: Random House, 1986.

———. *FDR: The New York Years.* New York: Random House, 1985.

———. *FDR: The War President*. New York: Random House, 2000.

———. *Invincible Summer: An Intimate Portrait of the Roosevelts*. New York: Atheneum, 1974.

Davis, Martin, ed. *Destroyer Escorts of World War II*. Albany, N.Y.: Destroyer Escort Historical Foundation, 2000.

Day, Donald. *Franklin D. Roosevelt's Own Story*. Boston: Little, Brown and Company, 1951.

Dear, I. C. B. *The Oxford Companion to World War II*. New York: Oxford University Press, 1995.

Dear, Ian, and Peter Kemp. *An A–Z of Sailing Terms*. New York: Oxford University Press, 1987.

Delano, Daniel W., Jr. *Franklin Roosevelt and the Delano Influence*. Pittsburgh, Pa.: James S. Nudi Publications, 1946.

Dictionary of American Naval Fighting Ships, 8 vols. Washington, D.C.: U.S. Navy, 1959–1981.

Dows, Olin. *Franklin Roosevelt at Hyde Park*. New York: American Artists Group, 1949.

Ferrell, Robert H. *The Dying President*. Columbia: University of Missouri Press, 1998.

Freidel, Frank. *Franklin D. Roosevelt: The Apprenticeship*. Boston: Little, Brown and Company, 1952.

———. *Franklin D. Roosevelt: Launching the New Deal*. Boston: Little, Brown and Company, 1973.

———. *Franklin D. Roosevelt: Rendezvous with Destiny*. Boston: Little, Brown and Company, 1990.

———. *Franklin D. Roosevelt: The Triumph*. Boston: Little, Brown and Company, 1956.

Gallagher, Hugh Gregory. *FDR's Splendid Deception*. New York: Dodd, Mead and Company, 1985.

Gibbs, C. R. Vernon. *Passenger Liners of the Western Ocean: A Record of the North Atlantic Steam and Motor Passenger Vessels from 1838 to the Present Day*. London and New York: Staples Press, 1952.

Goldberg, Richard Thayer. *The Making of Franklin D. Roosevelt: Triumph over Disability*. Lanham, Md.: University Press of America, 1981.

Goodwin, Doris Kearns. *No Ordinary Time*. New York: Simon and Schuster, 1994.

Grafton, David. *The Sisters*. New York: Villard Books, 1992.

Graham, Otis, and Meghan Robinson Warder. *FDR: His Life and Times*. New York: DaCapo Press, 1985.

Gunther, John. *Roosevelt in Retrospect*. New York: Harper and Brothers, 1950.

Hassett, William D. *Off the Record with FDR*. New Brunswick, N.J.: Rutgers University Press, 1958.

Hatch, Alden. *Franklin D. Roosevelt: An Informal Biography*. New York: Henry Holt and Company, 1947.

Hoyt, Edwin P. *U-Boats Off-Shore.* Chelsea, Mich.: Scarborough House, 1990.

Hurd, Charles. *When the New Deal Was Young and Gay.* New York: Hawthorn Books, 1965.

Ickes, Harold L. *The Secret Diaries of Harold L. Ickes,* 3 vols. New York: Simon and Schuster, 1953–1954.

Jaffee, Walter W. *The Presidential Yacht Potomac.* Palo Alto, Calif.: Glencannon Press, 1998.

Kemp, Peter, ed. *Oxford Companion to Ships and the Sea.* New York: Oxford University Press, 1994.

Kimball, Warren F. *The Juggler.* Princeton, N.J.: Princeton University Press, 1991.

Kleeman, Rita Halle. *Gracious Lady: The Life of Sara Delano Roosevelt.* New York: D. Appleton-Century Company, 1935.

Klein, Jonas. *Beloved Island: Franklin and Eleanor Roosevelt and the Legacy of Campobello.* Forest Dale, Vt.: Paul S. Eriksson, 2000.

Larrabee, Eric. *Commander in Chief.* New York: Harper and Row, 1987.

Lash, Joseph P. *Eleanor and Franklin.* New York: W. W. Norton and Co, 1971.

Leahy, William D. *I Was There.* New York: Whittlesey House, 1950.

Lippman, Theo, Jr. *The Squire of Warm Springs.* Chicago: Playboy Press, 1977.

Loewenheim, Francis L., Harold Langley, and Manfred Jonas. *Roosevelt and Churchill: Their Secret Wartime Correspondence.* New York: E. P. Dutton and Company, 1975.

Maas, Peter. *The Terrible Hours.* New York: HarperCollins Publishers, 1999.

Mackenzie, Compton. *Mr. Roosevelt.* New York: E. P. Dutton and Company, 1944.

Mahan, Alfred Thayer. *The Influence of Sea Power upon History.* Boston: Little, Brown and Company, 1918.

Mares, Bill. *Fishing with the Presidents.* Mechanicsburg, Pa.: Stackpole Books, 1999.

Marks, Frederick W. *Wind over Sand.* Athens: University of Georgia Press, 1988.

Marolda, Edward J. *FDR and the U.S. Navy.* Bloomsburg, Pa.: Macmillan, 1998.

Matone-Graham, John. *The Only Way to Cross.* New York: Macmillan Publishing Company, 1974.

McClendon, Hugh D. *A History of Camp David.* Thurmont, Md.: Department of the Navy, 1985.

McIntire, Ross T. *White House Physician.* New York: G. P. Putnam's Sons, 1946.

Miller, Nathan. *FDR: An Intimate History.* Garden City, N.Y.: Doubleday and Company, 1983.

———. *War at Sea.* New York: Scribner, 1995.

Morison, Samuel Eliot. *History of the United States Naval Operations in World War II,* 15 vols. Edison, N.J.: Castle Books, 2001.

———. *The Two-Ocean War.* Boston: Little, Brown and Company, 1963.

Morton, H. V. *The Atlantic Meeting.* London: Methuen and Company Ltd., 1944.

Muskie, Stephen O. *Campobello: Roosevelt's "Beloved Island."* Lubec, Maine: Roosevelt Campobello International Park Commission, 1994.

Nelson, W. Dale. *The President Is at Camp David.* Syracuse, N.Y.: Syracuse University Press, 1995.

Nesbitt, Henrietta. *White House Diary.* Garden City, N.Y.: Doubleday and Company, 1948.

Newell, Gordon. *Ocean Liners of the 20th Century.* Seattle: Superior Publishing Company, 1963.

Nixon, Edgar B., ed. *Franklin D. Roosevelt and Foreign Affairs, 1933–1937,* 3 vols. Cambridge, Mass.: Belknap Press of Harvard University Press, 1969.

Nowlan, Alden. *Campobello: The Outer Island.* Toronto: Clarke, Irwin and Company, 1975.

O'Flynn, Joseph P. *Nautical Dictionary.* Boyne City, Mich.: Harbor House Publishers, 1992.

Parks, Lillian Rogers, and Frances Spatz Leighton. *The Roosevelts: A Family in Turmoil.* Englewood Cliffs, N.J.: Prentice-Hall, 1981.

Perkins, Frances. *The Roosevelt I Knew.* New York: Viking Press, 1946.

Persico, Joseph E. *Roosevelt's Secret War: FDR and World War II Espionage.* New York: Random House, 2001.

Reilly, Michael F. *Reilly of the White House.* New York: Simon and Schuster, 1947.

Richardson, Eleanor Motley. *North Haven Summers: An Oral History.* Westford, Mass.: Courier Companies, 1992.

Rigdon, William M. *White House Sailor.* Garden City, N.Y.: Doubleday and Company, 1962.

Rollins, Alfred B. *Roosevelt and Howe.* New York: Alfred A. Knopf, 1962.

Roosevelt, Eleanor. *The Autobiography of Eleanor Roosevelt.* New York: Harper and Brothers, 1958.

———. *My Day, 1936–1945.* New York: Pharos Books, 1989.

Roosevelt, Elliott. *As He Saw It.* New York: Duell, Sloan and Pearce, 1946.

———. *FDR: His Personal Letters,* 4 vols. New York: Duell, Sloan and Pearce, 1947–1950.

Roosevelt, Elliott, and James Brough. *A Rendezvous with Destiny.* New York: G. P. Putnam's Sons, 1975.

Roosevelt, Franklin D. *On Our Way.* New York: John Day Company, 1934.

Roosevelt, Hall, with Samuel Duff McCoy. *Odyssey of an American Family.* New York: Harper and Brothers, 1939.

Roosevelt, James. *My Parents: A Differing View.* Chicago: Playboy Press, 1976.

Roosevelt, James, and Sidney Shalett. *Affectionately, FDR.* New York: Harcourt, Brace and Company, 1959.

Roosevelt, Sara. *My Boy Franklin.* New York: Ray Long and Richard R. Smith, 1933.

Rosenman, Samuel I. *Public Papers and Addresses of Franklin D. Roosevelt, 1928–1936,* 5 vols. New York: Random House, 1938.

———. *Public Papers and Addresses of Franklin D. Roosevelt, 1937–1940,* 4 vols. New York: Macmillan Company, 1941.

————. *Public Papers and Addresses of Franklin D. Roosevelt, 1941–1945,* 4 vols. New York: Harper and Brothers, 1950.

————. *Working with Roosevelt.* New York: Harper and Brothers, 1952.

Sayer, Ian, and Douglas Botting. *America's Secret Army: The Untold Story of the Counter Intelligence Corps.* London: Grafton Books, 1989.

Schlesinger, Arthur M., Jr. *The Almanac of American History.* New York: Barnes and Noble Books, 1993.

————. *The Coming of the New Deal.* Boston: Houghton Mifflin Company, 1959.

————. *Crisis of the Old Order.* Boston: Houghton Mifflin Company, 1957.

————. *The Politics of Upheaval.* Boston: Houghton Mifflin Company, 1960.

Schmitt, Waldo L., and Leonard P. Schultz. *List of Fishes Taken on the Presidential Cruise of 1938.* Washington, D.C.: Smithsonian Institution, 1940.

Schriftgiesser, Karl. *The Amazing Roosevelt Family, 1613–1942.* New York: Wilfred Funk, 1942.

Seagraves, Eleanor, ed. *Delano's Voyage of Commerce and Discovery.* Stockbridge, Mass.: Berkshire House Publishing, 1994.

Seale, William. *The President's House,* 2 vols. Washington, D.C.: White House Historical Association with cooperation of the National Geographic Society, 1986.

Shawen, Lena. *A President's Hobby: The Story of FDR's Stamps.* New York: H. L. Linquist Publications, 1952.

Sherwood, Robert E. *Roosevelt and Hopkins.* New York: Harper and Brothers, 1948.

Shields-West, Eileen. *Almanac of Presidential Campaigns.* New York: World Almanac, 1992.

Silverstone, Paul H. *U.S. Warships of World War II.* Annapolis: Naval Institute Press, 1989.

Siuru, William D., Jr., and Andrea Steward, eds. *Presidential Cars and Transportation.* Iola, Wis.: Krause Publications, 1995.

Smith, Merriman. *Thank You, Mr. President.* New York: Harper and Brothers, 1946.

Starling, Edmund W., and Thomas Sugrue. *Starling of the White House.* New York: Simon and Schuster, 1946.

Stedman's Medical Dictionary, 23d ed. Baltimore: Williams and Wilkins Company, 1978.

Steeholm, Clara, and Hardy Steeholm. *The House at Hyde Park.* New York: Viking Press, 1950.

Stettinius, E. R., Jr. *Lend-Lease: Weapon for Victory.* New York: Macmillan Company, 1944.

Stevens, Ruth. *Hi Ya Neighbor.* New York: Tupper and Love, 1947.

The Story of Franklin D. Roosevelt, Warm Springs and the Little White House. Atlanta: Georgia Department of Natural Resources, n.d.

Suckley, Margaret L., and Alice Dalgliesh. *The True Story of Fala.* New York: Charles Scribner's Sons, 1942.

Terraine, John. *The U-Boat Wars*. New York: Henry Holt and Company, 1989.

Tripp, H. Edmund. *Reflections on a Town*. Marion, Mass.: Sippican Historical Society, 1991.

Tully, Grace. *FDR, My Boss*. New York: Charles Scribner's Sons, 1949.

U.S. Navy. *The Bluejackets' Manual 1922*. Washington, D.C.: U.S. Government Printing Office, 1924.

———. *The Bluejackets' Manual 1927*. Washington, D.C.: U.S. Government Printing Office, 1928.

———. *The Bluejackets' Manual 1940*. Annapolis: Naval Institute Press, 1940.

———. *The Bluejackets' Manual 1944*. Annapolis: Naval Institute Press, 1944.

Waite, John G., ed. *The President as Architect: Franklin D. Roosevelt's Top Cottage*. Albany, N.Y.: Mount Ida Press, 2001.

Walker, Turnley. *Roosevelt and the Warm Springs Story*. New York: A. A. Wyn, 1953.

Ward, Geoffrey C. *Before the Trumpet: Young Franklin Roosevelt, 1882–1905*. New York: Harper and Row, 1985.

———. *Closest Companion*. Boston: Houghton Mifflin Company, 1995.

———. *A First Class Temperament: The Emergence of Franklin Roosevelt*. New York: Harper and Row, 1989.

Wharton, Don. *Roosevelt Omnibus*. New York: Alfred A. Knopf, 1934.

White, Graham J. *FDR and the Press*. Chicago: University of Chicago Press, 1979.

Wilson, Frank J. *Special Agent*. New York: Holt, Rinehart and Winston, 1965.

Wimmel, Kenneth. *Theodore Roosevelt and the Great White Fleet*. Washington, D.C.: Brassey's, 1998.

Woods, Randall Bennett. *The Roosevelt Foreign Policy Establishment and the Good Neighbor*. Lawrence: Regents Press of Kansas, 1979.

Periodicals and Journals

Bruenn, Howard. "Clinical Notes on the Illness and Death of President Franklin D. Roosevelt." *Annals of Internal Medicine* 72 (1970): 1–30.

Butow, R. J. C. "A Notable Passage to China: Myth and Memory in FDR's Family History." *Prologue: The Journal of the National Archives* (fall 1999): 159–77.

———. "Thar She Spaouts and Blows." *Naval History* (summer 1989): 22–27.

Cross, Robert F. "The Day the President Came to Nantucket." *Historic Nantucket* (June 1992): 31–34.

———. "No Reserved Seats for the Mighty." *Historic Nantucket* (summer 1993): 24–26.

Dorwart, Jeffrey M. "The Roosevelt-Astor Espionage Ring." *New York History* (July 1981): 307–22.

German, Andrew W. "*Vireo*: A Boat for Franklin D. Roosevelt." *The Log of the Mystic Seaport* (summer 2001): 23–28.

Kennedy, John F. "The Strength and Style of Our Navy Tradition." *Life*, August 1962, 83–84.

Kinkead, Eugene. "The Great Philatelist." *New Yorker,* March 1946, 48–54.

Mackaye, Milton. "The Governor-I." *New Yorker,* 15 August 1931, 8–22.

———. "The Governor-II." *New Yorker,* 22 August 1931, 24–26.

McKenna, Robert. "Bubbly Baptisms: The Fine Art of Christening." *Nautical Collector,* April 1994, 8–11.

Orzell, Bill. "Headwaters of the New Deal." *Bottoming Out,* Canal Society of New York State (1994): 6–26.

"The Roosevelt Era: Selections from the Private Collections of Franklin and Eleanor Roosevelt and Family." *Christies Auction Catalog* (14–15 February 2001).

Roosevelt, James, and Paul Rust Jr. "The President Goes Cruising." *Yachting,* August 1938.

Ruge, Raymond A. "The History and Development of the Ice Boat. Part I, 1600–1930." *Wooden Boat* (January–February 1981): 64–70.

———. "Iceboating on the Hudson River." *NAHO,* New York State Museum and Science Service (fall 1974): 3–5.

Sloan, George B. "The Franklin D. Roosevelt Stamp Collection." *Stamps,* 24 November 1945, 290–300.

Steward, William J., and Charyl C. Pollard. "Franklin D. Roosevelt, Collector." *Prologue,* Journal of the National Archives (winter 1969): 13–28.

Still, William N. "Everybody Sick with the Flu." *Naval History* (April 2002): 36–40.

"Summer Home, Summer Boat." *Maine Boats and Harbors* (June–July 1993): 15, 32–33.

Newspapers

Boston Daily Globe	*New York Post*
Boston Globe	*New York Sun*
Eastport Sentinel (Maine)	*New York Times*
Inquirer and Mirror (Nantucket, Mass.)	*Salem Evening News* (Massachusetts)
Lubec Herald (Maine)	*Vineyard Gazette* (Martha's Vineyard)
New York Daily News	*Washington Times*

Personal Communications

INTERVIEWS

Mr. J. Winthrop Aldrich, 16 July 1993.

Mr. Amyas Ames, 28 February and 28 March 1993.

Mr. Abe Barron, 16 October 1994.

Mrs. Helen Baxter, 3 July 1993.

Dr. Howard Bruenn, 21 January 1995.

Ms. Ann Easter, 23 October 1994.

Mr. James Griffith, 28 January 1995.

Mr. Robert Hopkins, 4 February 1995.

Mrs. Sarah Powell Huntington, 3 and 17 July 1993.

Mr. Anthony W. Lobb, 17 and 24 April, and 8 August 1993.

Mr. A. J. Drexel Paul, 1 and 22 November 1992.

Mr. Curtis Roosevelt, 15 October 1994.

Mr. Paul Drummond Rust III, 3 and 31 July 1993.

Mr. Charles Sayle, 12 September 1992 and 31 January 1993.

Ms. Eleanor Roosevelt Seagraves, 20 November 1994.

CORRESPONDENCE

Ms. Brooke Astor, 22 January 1998.

Mr. Abe Barron, 31 October 1994.

Mr. Seward E. Beacom, 9 April, and 5, 9 May 1993.

Ms. Eleanor S. Beverage, 20 March 1993.

Ms. Linnea Calder, 1 April and 13 July 1993.

Ms. Eleanor P. Fischer, 13 April 1992.

Mr. James Griffith, 8 December 1994.

Mr. Lewis Haskell, 19 October 1996.

Mr. Robert Hopkins, 23 January 1995.

Mr. Joseph A. Jackson, 29 October 1993.

Mr. Woodard P. Openo, 4 March 1993.

Mr. Edmund Tripp, 14 March and 27 May 1993.

Mr. Benjamin Welles, 29 December 1994.

Unpublished Materials

Franklin D. Roosevelt Library, Hyde Park, N.Y. Manuscript Collections:

Astor, Vincent, Copies of Correspondence with Franklin D. Roosevelt, 1932–44.

FDR: Day by Day.

"FDR, My Skipper," 16-mm film.

National Park Service Historian Files.

Plaut, Ed.: Material Relating to 1932 Flight to Chicago by Franklin D. Roosevelt.

Roosevelt, Franklin D.: Papers as Assistant Secretary of the Navy, 1913–20.

Roosevelt, Franklin D.: Papers as Governor of New York, 1929–32.

Roosevelt, Franklin D.: Papers as President, Map Room File, 1941–45.

Roosevelt, Franklin D.: Papers as President, Official File, 1933–45.

Roosevelt, Franklin D.: Papers as President, President's Personal File, 1933–45.

Roosevelt, Franklin D.: Papers as President, President's Secretary's File, 1933–45.

Roosevelt, Franklin D.: Papers Pertaining to Family, Business and Personal Affairs.

Roosevelt, Sara Delano: Diaries.

Secret Service: Records Pertaining to the Safety of the President, 1933–45.

Social Entertainments, Office of the Chief of: Records 1933–45.

Suckley, Margaret L., Archivist: Papers Relating to Roosevelt Library, 1941–62.

Trips of the President, Cruises and Logs.

Vertical File.

White House Police Logs, Logbooks, 1933–45.

White House Ushers' Diaries.

Hunt, Virginia Livingston. 28 April 1935. Collections of the Manuscript Division. Virginia Livingston Hunt Papers, Library of Congress, Washington, D.C.

Kennedy, John F. Speech at America's Cup Races, September 1962. John F. Kennedy Library, Newport, Rhode Island.

McCrum, Hazel. "Pulpit Rock." Summer 1933. Oral History of Hazel McCrum on Pulpit Rock. Accession Number 257. Northeast Archives of Folklore and Oral History. University of Maine, Orono, Maine.

McGirr, Newman. Oral History. 12 November 1950. Franklin D. Roosevelt Library, Hyde Park, N.Y.

Nantucket Wharf Rat Club Journal, 1933. Nantucket Wharf Rat Club, Old North Wharf. Nantucket, Mass.

Smith, Gaddis. "Sailor in the White House: A Key to Understanding FDR." Lecture at Franklin D. Roosevelt Library, Hyde Park, N.Y., 12 August 1993.

Ship Logs

Briggs, George. "Log of *Myth II*," 11–16 July 1932. Cruise Log. Papers Pertaining to Family, Business and Personal Affairs. Franklin D. Roosevelt Library, Hyde Park, N.Y.

Brown, Capt. Wilson, USN. Log of the President's Cruise–Bahama Waters, 26 March–8 April 1935. Cruise Log. Trips of the President, Cruises and Logs. Franklin D. Roosevelt Library, Hyde Park, N.Y.

Cruise of the President on Board USS *Houston*, 2–23 October 1935. Cruise Log. Trips of the President, Cruises and Logs. Franklin D. Roosevelt Library, Hyde Park, N.Y.

Davis, Livingston. Log of the Trip to Haiti and Santo Domingo, 1917. Log of Assistant Navy Secretary Cruise. Assistant Secretary of the Navy Papers. Franklin D. Roosevelt Library, Hyde Park, N.Y.

Inspection Cruise and Fishing Expedition of President Franklin D. Roosevelt on Board USS *Houston*, 16 July–9 August 1938. Cruise Log. Trips of the President, Cruises and Logs. Franklin D. Roosevelt Library, Hyde Park, N.Y.

Log of the Cruise of President Franklin D. Roosevelt Aboard the Schooner Yacht *Sewanna*, 14–28 July 1936. Cruise Log. Trips of the President, Cruises and Logs. Franklin D. Roosevelt Library, Hyde Park, N.Y.

Log of the President's Inspection Tour, 13–29 April 1943. Log of Railroad Trip. Trips of the President, Cruises and Logs. Franklin D. Roosevelt Library, Hyde Park, N.Y.

Log of the President's Inspection Trip to the Pacific, July–August 1944. Cruise Log. Trips of the President, Cruises and Logs. Franklin D. Roosevelt Library, Hyde Park, N.Y.

Log of the President's Trip to Africa and the Middle East, November–December 1943. Cruise Log. Trips of the President, Cruises and Logs. Franklin D. Roosevelt Library, Hyde Park, N.Y.

Log of the President's Trip to the Crimea Conference and Great Bitter Lake, Egypt, 22 January–28 February 1945. Cruise Log. Trips of the President, Cruises and Logs. Franklin D. Roosevelt Library, Hyde Park, N.Y.

"The Log of the President's Visit to Canada," 16–26 August 1943. Log of Railroad Trip. Trips of the President, Cruises and Logs. Franklin D. Roosevelt Library, Hyde Park, N.Y.

Log of the Trip of the President to the Casablanca Conference, 9–31 January 1943. Cruise Log. Trips of the President, Cruises and Logs. Franklin D. Roosevelt Library, Hyde Park, N.Y.

Roosevelt, Franklin D. "Log of *Weona II*," 1923. Cruise Log. Papers Pertaining to Family, Business and Personal Affairs. Franklin D. Roosevelt Library, Hyde Park, N.Y.

USS *Bernadou,* 18 June–4 July 1933. U.S. Navy Deck Log. Record Group 024. Naval Personnel. National Archives, Washington, D.C.

USS *Cuyahoga* (U.S. Coast Guard), 10 June–4 July 1933. U.S. Navy Deck Log. Record Group 024. Naval Personnel. National Archives, Washington, D.C.

USS *Ellis,* 18–30 June 1933 and 1–4 July 1933. U.S. Navy Deck Log. Record Group 024. Naval Personnel. National Archives, Washington, D.C.

USS *Indianapolis,* 1 July–31 July 1933. U.S. Navy Deck Log. Record Group 024. Naval Personnel. National Archives, Washington, D.C.

Woodson, Capt. Walter B., USN. Trip of the President, summer 1934. Cruise Log. Trips of the President, Cruises and Logs. Franklin D. Roosevelt Library, Hyde Park, N.Y.

Internet Sites

Dictionary of American Naval Fighting Ships, DANFS Online.
    <http://www.hazegray.org/danfs>
Franklin D. Roosevelt Presidential Library and Museum.
    <http://www.fdrlibrary.marist.edu>
Gold Coast Railroad Museum. "Ferdinand Magellan: Presidential Rail Car, U.S. Number 1." <http://www.goldcoast-railroad.org>
John F. Kennedy Library and Museum. Selected Speeches.
    <http://www.jfklibrary.org>

INDEX

ABOUT THE AUTHOR

Robert F. Cross, an award-winning newspaper reporter, spent more than a decade exploring FDR's love of the sea. He currently serves as the commissioner of water for the City of Albany, New York, and also oversees operations at the Port of Albany, dedicated in 1932 by Gov. Franklin D. Roosevelt. Cross is a trustee of the museum ship, USS *Slater* (DE-766), the only World War II destroyer escort still afloat in the United States, moored on the Hudson River at Albany. He is a graduate of the State University of New York, where he received bachelor of science and master of arts degrees. Cross's articles have appeared in the *New York Times, Wall Street Journal, Conservationist,* and *Historic Nantucket,* among other publications. He currently is working on a book about destroyer escorts and the men who sailed them. He lives in Albany with his wife, Sheila, and Fala, their West Highland White Terrier.

The Naval Institute Press is the book-publishing arm of the U.S. Naval Institute, a private, nonprofit, membership society for sea service professionals and others who share an interest in naval and maritime affairs. Established in 1873 at the U.S. Naval Academy in Annapolis, Maryland, where its offices remain today, the Naval Institute has members worldwide.

Members of the Naval Institute support the education programs of the society and receive the influential monthly magazine *Proceedings* and discounts on fine nautical prints and on ship and aircraft photos. They also have access to the transcripts of the Institute's Oral History Program and get discounted admission to any of the Institute-sponsored seminars offered around the country.

The Naval Institute also publishes *Naval History* magazine. This colorful bimonthly is filled with entertaining and thought-provoking articles, first-person reminiscences, and dramatic art and photography. Members receive a discount on *Naval History* subscriptions.

The Naval Institute's book-publishing program, begun in 1898 with basic guides to naval practices, has broadened its scope to include books of more general interest. Now the Naval Institute Press publishes about one hundred titles each year, ranging from how-to books on boating and navigation to battle histories, biographies, ship and aircraft guides, and novels. Institute members receive significant discounts on the Press's more than eight hundred books in print.

Full-time students are eligible for special half-price membership rates. Life memberships are also available.

For a free catalog describing Naval Institute Press books currently available, and for further information about subscribing to *Naval History* magazine or about joining the U.S. Naval Institute, please write to:

Membership Department
U.S. Naval Institute
291 Wood Road
Annapolis, MD 21402-5034
Telephone: (800) 233-8764
Fax: (410) 269-7940
Web address: www.navalinstitute.org